Islam and Society in Turkey

Islam and Society in Turkey

David Shankland

THE EOTHEN PRESS

British Library Cataloguing-in-Publication Data
A catalogue record for this book is available from the British
Library

Published 1999

© David Shankland, 1999

Published by The Eothen Press, 10 Manor Road, Hemingford
Grey, Huntingdon, Cambridgeshire, England, PE18 9BX.

ISBN   0 906719 26 7 paperback
       0 906719 27 5 hard covers

To the memory of

ERNEST GELLNER (1925-1995)

and

PAUL STIRLING (1920-1998)

Transliteration and Abbreviations

Turkish is written in the Latin alphabet, with a few special characters.

c	is pronouned like 'j' in jam
ç	is pronounced like 'ch' in chip
i	is pronounced like 'i' in Cyril
ğ	is not pronounced, it lengthens the preceding syllable
j	is pronounced like 'g' in gendarme
ş	is pronounced like 'sh' in ship
ü	as is the 'u' in the French *rue*
ö	is pronounced like '*eu*' in the French *veut*

Throughout, all Turkish words in italics (eg. *Bektaşi*) are spelt according to Turkish usage, but all those in plain text (eg. Bektashi) are written as would be normal in English. English plurals added to Turkish nouns are not italicised.

A list of Turkish political parties, and their acronyms is provided in Appendix 1. In order to avoid confusion, throughout the text I have used only those abbreviations derived from the Turkish, so that, for example, the Republican People's Party, Cumhuriyet Halk Partisi, appears always *as CHP*.

Contents

Appendices

Preface and Acknowledgements

This book is based on five years' residence in Turkey. The first long stay, from 1988-90, was to research my doctorate in Social Anthropology, and the second between 1992-1995 to work as the Assistant and Acting Director of the British Institute of Archaeology at Ankara. About a year and a half of this time has been spent in villages, the remainder in urban areas or travelling around the country. Whilst parts of the work are written from the point of view of ideas prevalent in Social Anthropology, I have attempted to avoid technical terms almost entirely.

I would like to thank the Anthropology Department and the Pantyfedwyn Fund of University of Wales, Lampeter for their generous financial support during the preparation of this book. I would also like to thank Clement Dodd for suggesting that I should undertake it. My thoughts on Turkey have been shaped over a number of years through close discussion with a number of friends. I would like to acknowledge in particular the encouragement and support of David Barchard, Cemil Bezmen, Atilla Çetin, Ernest Gellner, William Hale, Chris and Ildiko Hann, Alan Macfarlane, Andrew Mango, and Paul Stirling.

In Turkey, I have received help from a number of institutions: Hacettepe Anthropology department welcomed me when Turkey was still strange indeed. Later, the Education Faculty at the Middle East Technical University provided me with a generous and stimulating environment in which to work. This project was first envisaged when I was at the British Institute of Archaeology at Ankara. The invariably courteous and efficient assistance of the staff has placed me greatly in their debt. I would like to thank them all, particularly Mrs Gülgün Kazan for her skilful management, and the Librarian, Dr Yaprak Eren, for her very valuable archival assistance. More recently, this manuscript has been read at different stages of preparation by David Barchard, Chris Cook, Clement Dodd, Ayşegül Dorken, Jonathan Liebenau, Andrew Mango, John Norton, Gülberna Özcan, Cihan Saçlıoğlu, Norman Stone, and Christian Troll. I am deeply indebted for their patient and invaluable comments.

Occasionally, and particularly in Chapter 4, I have drawn on text from 'Integrating the rural: Gellner and the study of Anatolia', *Middle Eastern Studies*, 1999, Vol. 35, No. 2, pp 132-49, and from 'The Demise of Republican Turkey's Social Contract?', *Government and Opposition,* 1996, Volume 31, Number 3, pages 304-21. A short passage in Chapter 5 appears also in 'Anthropology and Ethnicity: the place of Ethnography in the new Alevi Movement', in Olsson, T., Özdalga, E. and Raudvere, C. (eds.), 1998, *Alevi Identity*, pages 15-23.

Introduction

Of the Islamic world, Turkey is known as the country that has achieved secularism with democracy. Others may occasionally appear rival candidates: Tunisia, for example, is developing its own version of Maghrebian secularism, but does not have Turkey's democratic credentials. The Muslim countries of the former Soviet Union looked briefly as if they might provide leadership for Turkey rather than the other way round, but they are now dogged by violence and by the heavy heritage of their colonial past. The Fertile Crescent Arab countries likewise have made no more than tentative steps along the democratic road. At least for the present, Pakistan is condemned to corruption and authoritarianism. Only Turkey remains as a potential stable ally with a politically pluralist democracy fashioned on those of the West.

It is for this reason, perhaps, that the steady resurgence of Islam within the country has been so largely overlooked by those very Western countries which would normally be so quick to criticize. According to the liberal tradition, change, particularly if it is imposed on the centre by the populace, is supposed to be a good and natural reflection of the pluralist system, and this holds just as much for religious beliefs as it does for economic or social issues.[1] The problem occurs, of course, if the changes will eventually lead to the demise of the tolerant system that has permitted that pluralism in the first place.[2]

'Tolerance' may seem an unusual way of phrasing the issue. The poor publicity that Turkey has suffered over the years, and the equally appalling conflict in the East, have concealed the fact that there has emerged a fascinating arrangement at the heart of the Republican state: a tacit recognition among secularists and believers alike that the state will be used to serve both their respective aims. The Ministry of Education continues to inculcate Kemalist tenets and to teach Republican history, the Foreign Ministry to hold its dinners and drinks parties with wine, *cin* and *votka* cocktails, the Cultural Ministry to sponsor research into the pre-Islamic heritage of Anatolia and its Folklore Department to hold conferences on folklore illustrating the perennial integrity of the Anatolian peasant.[3]

At the same time, the Ministry of Education oversees compulsory religious lessons in schools and publishes enormous quantities of religiously-inspired as well as secular literature. As part of the existing educational system, it administers *imam-hatip* schools, in which a significant part of the curriculum consists of religious-based subjects such as Islamic jurisprudence, Arabic, and Koranic studies.[4] The Directorate of Religious Affairs, the co-ordinating body for the practice of religion throughout the country, has never had a greater budget than it has today, and employs a total staff that is larger than some ministries. It oversees the pilgrimage to Mecca, employs *imam*s, (prayer leaders) sufficient for almost every mosque in Turkey, pronounces on questions of religious significance and even, more recently, has attempted to take a leading role in the interpretation of the Koran and Islam in the modern world.

To understand in full how the state has come to support so actively both Islam and secularism is perhaps a vain hope. Social change usually becomes more complicated the more it is studied, and Turkey is no exception to this rule. Nevertheless, certain aspects of this transition may be stressed. The Turkish state is often depicted as a confrontational, unyielding force. This might be justified with regard to the catastrophic conflict in the east. However, the most cursory exploration of the changing relationship between the state and religion in Turkey will show that in this respect the model of a monolithic secular state is entirely inadequate. Indeed, it is only through realising that the state can be open, diffuse, and malleable, almost as if it may be drawn in different directions by different groups, that the religious revival can be understood.

The revolution in Iran, the conflict in Algeria and the later victories of the Talibanis in Afghanistan have encouraged a popular conception that Islamists come to power through insurrection.[5] In Turkey, the rise of Islam has taken a different route. The willingness of the state to embrace orthodox Islam means that the religious revival has developed within the Republic's existing social and civil institutions. This is even true of overtly Islamist political parties. These, whilst appealing for revolution, have in fact contributed towards the slow build-up of religious practice. Indeed, we shall see that they should have chosen this route is entirely comprehensible. In Turkey, efforts at revolutionary change are meticulously marked and guarded against. Piecemeal change is more feasible.

The increasingly manifest signs of this political religious revival in Turkey have sometimes caused its practitioners to be identified with the country as a whole. In fact, we are witnessing a gradual, varied upsurge of faith within a society that is simultaneously growing increasingly heterogeneous. Whilst most people are believers, there is an immense variety of positions that they may take up *vis à vis* the place of Islam in the modern world. Many have been pleased to see a partial re-Islamification of Turkish society, but many others are now against its further rise. Others are perhaps not interested in religion at all, or are even actively against it. Still others may be from the unorthodox minority, the Alevis. This means that politically inspired Islam, whilst supremely important, should be considered as only one of a multiplicity of developing lifestyles in Turkey.[6]

Combining these ideas suggests the following: the state is open to conflicting opinions and influence from diverse groups, much more so than is commonly realised. This creates a situation in which the state's power can be diffused between people of different sympathies, creating rival zones of patronage, and making it appear to pursue contradictory policies. Whilst there are many different interpretations of the role of the faith in the Islamic world, groups and movements within Turkish society as a whole are gradually crystallising into Islamist and secularist camps. There is a distinct possibility that their rivalry will cause a sharp internal division both inside and outside the bureaucracy as they seek to increase their zones of influence. The steps that the authorities have taken to restrict Islamist political parties, organisations and patronage, whilst stressing the importance of pious and moderate belief, reflect their desire to prevent this division from becoming an open, running battle. The difficulties they encounter in doing this are linked to the fact that they are attempting to maintain an interpretation of Islam, that though partially acceptable, has not succeeded in gaining universal consent.

The chapters that follow detail this conception of the relationship between faith, power and authority. They are broadly chronological, but do not claim to be an exhaustive historical narrative. It may be helpful to provide at the outset, therefore, an overall vision of religion and its place in modern Turkey.

Islam in Republican Turkey

Within Turkey, about four-fifths of the population are *Sünnis*, or orthodox Muslims. Most of the remaining fifth are *Alevis*, a heterodox group, whose doctrines are looked at in detail in Chapter 6. Conventionally, Sunni Muslims hold that the Koran is the literal word of God, *Allah,* dictated through *Muhammed*, the last of the prophets. Through *Muhammed*, God laid down certain prescriptions on the way that believers should lead their lives, which are partly encapsulated in the five 'pillars', or conditions, of Islam (*İslam'ın beş şartı*). They are: believe in the one God, pray five times a day, pay alms, go on the pilgrimage, and fast during the month of Ramadan (*Ramazan*).[7]

Whilst a person may pray silently, without overt activity, the regular daily worship involves formalised genuflecting known as *namaz*. The *namaz* may be performed anywhere, but it is usual for men to go to a mosque. To go to the mosque once a week, on a Friday, is an obligatory duty, *farz*, and at those mid-day prayers many mosques are full. Women go far less often to mosques, and should they go, they are required to remain to the rear, out of the sight of men. A person may also pray at the tombs of saints (*türbes*), a practice which though frowned upon both by Republican secularists, and by certain orthodox Islamic thinkers, is popular among both sexes.

Religion, as in the West, is often reflected in life-cycle rituals from birth to death: men, whether Alevi or Sunni, are circumcised, and regard this as one of the essential characteristics of being Muslim. The age of circumcision may vary between a few years to near puberty, and is often celebrated by dressing the boy in a mock, brightly-coloured soldier's uniform and inviting relatives and neighbours to a special meal. Weddings may be celebrated in a variety of different ways, but often include a brief ceremony recited by an *imam*. Funerals, whether the deceased is male or female, take place at mosques, though women are not supposed to accompany the procession to the cemetery afterwards or often to visit the graveside afterwards until a certain period has past.

The annual religious cycle is divided into twelve months according to the lunar calendar, which means that it moves about ten days each year. It centres most obviously on the month of *Ramazan*, during which believers are required not to eat or drink during the hours of daylight. During this time religious sensibilities are heightened, mosques hang lights from their minarets, and supplicants can be heard in mosques and on the television reciting from the Koran. The evening meal, held after the sunset, and known as *iftar* is an occasion to invite friends to join in a celebration, and has many foods cooked specially for it. Politicians too, may hold large gatherings and release their guest lists to the press.

The end of *Ramazan* is marked by a public holiday, as is the feast of sacrifice, *Kurban Bayramı*, which takes place two months and ten days later. For this festival, families collect together from far afield. Many sacrifice a sheep, though it is possible also to group together and offer a larger beast. It is widely held to be an auspicious time for reconciliation and for offering alms to those poorer than oneself. At this time also, those who wish, or who can afford it, may make the pilgrimage to Mecca, the *hac*. Both men and women do go from Turkey, though their numbers are restricted by the allocation of visas that may be awarded by the Saudi Arabian authorities. A person may go at any age, though traditionally most tend to leave this visit until they are mature, as it is held widely that the pilgrimage offers an opportunity for personal purification, for the sins, *günah*, accumulated in this world to be forgiven. Men in particular say that the pilgrimage is a chance to leave their bachelor, or youthful days behind them and prepare for a careful old age.[8]

According to both Sunnis and Alevis, God judges all humans

according to their actions on this earth. A person may be admitted to heaven, *cennet*, or if found wanting may be cast into hell, *cehennem*. Exactly what a person must do in order to realise salvation may vary among different groups and thinkers, and may result in complex theological considerations. Simplifying an enormous variety of opinion, active Sunni Islamists may hold that the only way that this can be done is if the body of Holy Law (*şeriat*) given in the Koran and exemplified in the life of the Prophet (*sünnet*) is reflected on this earth. They may regret the passing of the Ottoman Empire, and hold that the re-introduction of the *şeriat* courts into Turkey is a priority.

In contrast, since the early days of the Republic, the dominant official interpretation of Islam has been individualistic, stressing that the annual and daily life-cycle events: the *Ramazan* fast, the daily prayers, reading the Koran, are sufficient for religious fulfilment. It has insisted that the state must be able to administer its citizens through secular, not sacred law, and that all people are equal in the eyes of the state courts. As part of this drive, the Republic disbanded not just the *şeriat* courts, but also made illegal the religiously less orthodox *tarikat*s, or brotherhoods.[9]

Pressure from below

Whilst introducing drastic reforms, the Republicans have always attempted to restrict Islam rather than ban its practice altogether. In 1924 they established the Directorate of Religious Affairs as an immediate replacement for the Ottoman Ministry of Religious Affairs and Charitable Trusts. The Directorate has gone through different phases, but has throughout been expected to authorise and regulate Islamic activity. In 1924, the Republican Government also formed the *Vakıflar Müdürlüğü*, the Directorate of Pious Foundations, in order to maintain charitable estates and monumental religious buildings.[10] Nevertheless, indisputably, the mass of Sunni believers wished that the state would administer Islam and its practice more fully.

As democracy was introduced, governments began to attempt to meet this desire. They were helped enormously by the existing presence of an officially-sanctioned religious bureaucracy, and the Directorate of Religious Affairs has enjoyed steady growth throughout the second half of the Republic. At the same time, the politicians who have sanctioned this expansion have assured those who defend secularism that they are acting in full conformity with the foundations of the Republic, whereby religion is acceptable when it is led, and controlled, by the state.

Civil society and politics

Active believers have been able to encourage and to avail themselves of this expanding state recognition of Islam through creating patronage links within the administration and the political parties. Aided also by organising themselves through charitable and voluntary associations, believers have constructed mosques and requested that the state provide *imam*s to man them; they have paid for *imam-hatip* school buildings and asked that the Ministry of Education provide teachers; they have flown on the pilgrimage and pressured the Foreign Ministry to find visas; they have demanded religious literature for their children and found it through the presses of the Ministry of Education and the Directorate of Religious Affairs. This expanding, dynamic fusion of public sector and private believer has been so successful that by the 1980s, the Motherland Party was to claim that Turkey more than any country in the Middle East was the ideal place to receive an Islamic upbringing.[11]

Reform within the state was throughout the 1990s accompanied by the rise of the Welfare Party, a party explicitly devoted to the furtherance of Islamic belief and practice. Whilst there have long been such parties, they had never before been able to capture more than 10 per cent of the vote. Then, in 1991, the Welfare Party gained 40 seats in the Grand National Assembly. In 1994, they took Istanbul and Ankara in the local elections, then in 1995 became the largest party of all. In 1998, their fortunes changed, and they were closed down by the constitutional court. Their replacement, the *Fazilet Partisi*, Virtue Party, was unable to win the general elections held in April 1999, but still emerged the third largest party in terms of representatives in the Assembly.

The long-term effect that this overt politicisation of Islam will produce on Turkish society is not yet clear, though there can be no doubt that it is now an established and popular mass movement. The situation is further complicated in that the increased resources now available through the private sector offset the state's dominant role in providing services to religion. In particular, a distinctively Islamic business ethos has emerged since the 1980s, one often linked to *tarikat* groups, that funds its own charities, schools, publications, and television channels.[12] The business and media empire run by Fethullah Gülen, who is also the leader of the burgeoning *Nurcu* movement, exemplifies this.

Relaxing the secular
In response to these pressures, there has been a gradual relaxation of strict secularism. The authorities, specifically the courts and the army, appear to have resigned themselves to the return of Islam to life outside the state. Today, though the brotherhoods are theoretically banned, their presence is widespread and their influence in everyday affairs palpable. Islamic notices in shops affirming the absolute sovereignty of God, theoretically actionable, are overlooked. Among ordinary citizens, only the most public calls for the return of the *şeriat*, Islamic Law, are likely to lead to prosecution.

The authorities have been rather more concerned to contest the use of Islamic symbols in the civil service. The headscarf is a good example of this. At the founding of the Republic, it was widely feared that Atatürk might insist on a complete ban on wearing either a veil or using a headscarf to cover the hair. In fact, whilst he clearly favoured the practice of women wearing Western dress, the Republic made it illegal for women to wear the headscarf only within the civil service, or within educational establishments.[13] Increasingly, some women, often but not always from the younger generation, have decided to defy the ban. Their motives appear complex: some are tired of being harassed in public spaces by men, and value the protection that covering may offer. Others may be doing so out of conviction, or influenced directly by their spouses or family. Still others are awarded grants, or a place in lodgings, by Islamic charities in return for wearing their headscarves in public.[14]

However varied the motives, in most small towns, it is now very widespread for women to wear the headscarf in all the public contexts where they are able. In municipal buildings, which are run by political parties, it is common to see women receptionists who cover their hair, and also often decline to shake hands with a male visitor. However, in the government building (*hükümet konağı*), the seat of the governor and sub-province governors (which may include the courts and other official departments such as the field-ownership records office), women functionaries remain bare-headed. In the education sector too, famously, girls have been prevented from attending lectures if they attempt to do so wearing headscarfs. Whilst individual lecturers may turn a blind eye to this, test cases are still passing through the various courts. The debates are likely to continue, with public figures on one side claiming that to wear a headscarf in an official space is a political, not personal, statement, and on the other, that it is a personal right to do so.[15]

This fine line between lobbying for an illegal religious state or legitimate personal religious freedom is perhaps most volatile in the political arena. Here, whilst the authorities have been able to tolerate the rise of Islam within political parties ostensibly secular, they have decided to react more strongly to political groupings whose very purpose is to further Islam. Having banned the Welfare Party, it is quite clear that they are prepared to exercise close control over their successors, the *Fazilet*, Virtue Party. Indeed, in the aftermath of the general elections in April 1999, infuriated by a new Virtue Party deputy, Merve Kavakçi, who insisted on wearing a headscarf in the Assembly itself, the State Prosecutor applied to the constitutional court for the party's closure.

The army
It is widely held in the West that the army is simply, or unambiguously, anti-religious. This is not the case at all. The army abhors fanaticism, and views religion's rise within the political arena with the greatest suspicion. Nevertheless, the army regards its ultimate task to preserve the Republic and its borders. This means that, if necessary, it is fully prepared to use orthodox Islam as a bulwark against communism, or as a means to achieving harmony in the community. There are several occasions when the army has shown this, perhaps most notably when it presided over a substantial increase in funding for Islam after their coup in 1980.

There are sometimes worries that this readiness to use Islam in a functional way has led to the army itself becoming re-Islamicised. This does not appear to be the case. All indications suggest that the army has decided that what is acceptable for civilian life, is, in their midst, simply not even up for discussion. Today, the army monitors extensively, chafes at the level to which Islam and politics appear to be intertwined, makes public its disapproval through press communiqués and speeches by generals at formal occasions, and attempts to stimulate the secular civil process. Whilst outside its ranks, day to day contact and affiliation with conspicuously active Islam is widely tolerated, within its ranks, it is not. Personal piety is permitted, to keep the fast entirely normal. Nevertheless, affiliation to a *tarikat* even if only suspected, is sufficient for both commissioned and non-commissioned officers to be dismissed from their posts. Attempts to proselytize openly for one of the neo-modernist Islamic movements, such as the *Nurcu*s, also results in rapid ejection.

Secularism and authority
Quite definitely, Islam is not imposed from above. The vitality of Sunni belief in Turkey is remarkable. However, it would be equally mistaken to regard Kemalist secularism as a straightforward conflict between authority (or the military) and the mass. In politics, there is a self-avowedly secular, though fractured left, which has long hovered around 30 per cent of the vote. Outside the overtly political, many of the middle classes, particularly the older generation, though believers, regard it as the very characteristic of Turkish Islam that it is not 'fanatical' (*bağnaz*), and maintain that 'fundamentalism' (*kökdendincilik*) is an Arab or Iranian, but not Turkish, characteristic.

There are other, often overlapping, groups in Turkish society as a whole which are firmly in favour of the Republic. Many of the original reforms stressed the emancipation of women, who were exhorted to play a full role in public life. These reforms had a highly significant effect. Even today, it is a surprise to many visitors to Turkey to find that there are women in responsible positions where, even in their own country until very recently, they would have expected to see men. Thus, that Mrs Çiller became the first women Prime Minister of an Islamic country is not an exception, but builds on the successful and influential lives of thousands, even millions, of career women who have gone before her. Many of these women do not wish to wear the headscarf, something that they have never experienced, and regard the prospect of doing so with horror.[16] Among the new generation, in Istanbul and in many larger cities, a large sector of the youth population is simply not interested in religion: they prefer a life based on modern consumerism and mass media attractions, music, dance, clubs and restaurants, pursuing this aim with a dedicated sensuality which can be startling even to those familiar with the country. These people, even if they are not committed to the minutiae of Republican doctrine, resent bitterly any imposition of Islam in their lives.

There are also the Alevis, who have from the outset of the Republic resolutely embraced secularism. Whilst by no means homogenous, there are few signs that they will rescind this commitment. They support the legal constitutional framework of the Republic, and have deeply influenced the distinctive left-wing culture that has emerged since the 1960s.[17] Still today, their most frequently stated desire is to create a social democratic nation along the lines of that envisaged by Ecevit when the Republicans first embraced a left-of-centre policy. I think it no exaggeration to say that, quiescent at present, if threatened, the Alevis are prepared to resist imposition of religious orthodoxy with any means that is in their power.

A balance
Today, then, the situation appears poised. People do change their positions over time, may hold more than one view simultaneously, and one opinion may dominate over another according to the context. Nevertheless, the army, much of the bureaucracy and legislature, the left, many young people, businessmen, the Alevis and a good many women consistently support secularism, or at the very least, the status quo. On the other hand, many Sunni people, usually (though not by any means always) villagers or recent urban migrants, support a large political party explicitly founded on furthering Islam, and a substantial portion of the political right increasingly press for more Islamic involvement in the life and government of Turkish society.

Secularists are diverse: they may be army officers, left-wing students, right-wing free-market economists, and even theologians, and range in perspective from the downright atheist to the pious.

Active Islamists are themselves divided, with the most important division being between those who wish to work through or with, and those wish to reject, the Republican State entirely. Nevertheless, the strength of the structure established by the Welfare Party meant that throughout the 1990s, even if they did not agree with its policies entirely, there was a banner under which Islamic activists could be unified as a political force. The secularists have as yet achieved no such common ground, though there are signs that they may do so in the future.

This study
The different sections of this study reflect this overall picture. The first chapter sets the scene. It describes the reforms, the secularist experiment and the impact of the introduction of democracy after the Second World War on the religious revival. Chapters 2 and 3 concentrate more specifically on the institutions through which Islam has been re-integrated into Turkish public life, describing the place of associations and trusts in the religious revival and the changing fortunes of the *tarikat*s. This section also examines the way that belief may be reformulated through contact with the modern world, and the leading role that the *Nurcu* movement has played in this process.

Chapters 4 and 5 turn to the Welfare Party, headed by Necmettin Erbakan, and its closure by the authorities. They reiterate a key issue. The rhetoric of the Welfare Party called for revolution. In practice it continued with the partial reform that had been established by the previous political parties, emphasising the resources that should be given to the daily practice of religion and to expanding the departments of the state that are dedicated to its administration. The Party's more revolutionary aspirations have been less successful, curtailed by the Party's closure, by the detailed investigations into its activities and by a complex and sharp popular reaction.

The final chapter examines the Alevis. Here, I present a preliminary outline of the processes that I believe are occurring among their communities, one largely based on my own ethnographic fieldwork. I intend to justify its contentions in more detail in a later publication devoted solely to them. I plead allowance for this material's inclusion here in that the description is organised in such a way as to illustrate how a rural, traditional mystical religion can modernise to become a coherent part of urban secular society. Given that this assessment turns out to be correct, the Alevis are likely to become a counter-movement against the rise of political Islam. Any overall perspective on Turkish society must therefore attempt at least to take them into account.

The view from outside

It might be thought that it hardly behoves an outsider to do more than make the most general of remarks on such an intimate topic as religion. However, in spite of the pitfalls, such admirable detachment is not a tenable option. Interaction with other nations has always played an important role in Turkish society. For example, Turkey has been attempting to join the European Union for many years. In 1997, Turkey was not included in the list of possible countries for accession in the foreseeable future. In spite of the claims of the Euro-officials that this was not a rejection, the perceived rebuff was widely reported in Turkey itself, and may play a substantial role in re-orienting Turkey's foreign policy.[18] It is quite possible that perceived and actual relations with the European Union will have a similarly significant impact on the outcome of the struggle between the secular and the overtly religious. Like it or not we in the West are part of the equation.

Further, commentators on Turkey have conspicuously not been neutral. One commonly stated position both among journalists and many Turkish intellectuals, is that Kemalism is a worn-out, authoritarian, ideology that has served any purpose that it might have had. These critics, if pressed, usually take the position that a more fully Islamicised Turkey would not in fact be as significant a transformation as its opponents claim. They maintain, that once in power, however fierce in sentiment, the religious movement is too fractured, too complicated, too intertwined with modern capitalist and consumer society to change Turkey in more than the most superficial way.[19]

Others are less certain. They feel that the gradual separation in Turkey between secular and religious positions has the potential to lead to widespread civil violence. Those outside Turkey who fear this outcome are commonly more sympathetic to Turkey's links with the

European Union in the hope that the more dialogue that can be created, the less chance there is of such a disastrous result.

Whichever position is ultimately held (and whether, indeed, it is believed that the creation of a dialogue can have so significant a role) I believe the discussion should be as wide as possible. This work is offered as contribution to that wider debate.

| 1 |

Religion and the State

The vibrancy of Islam is remarkable in almost all areas of Turkish life. Let us say that a visitor arrives by air to Ankara, the heart of the modern Republic. From the airport, the road into the city cuts through ever-expanding suburbs and shanty towns built on the slopes of bare rock hills. In the midst of almost every settlement, usually in the most conspicuous part of the landscape, lies a mosque, often newly built with dome and minaret. At night these mosques are lit up; during the day they provide a contrast to the apartment buildings and single storey houses painted in bright colours. As the road passes into the heart of the city, the visitor passes the newly completed *Kocatepe* Mosque, a grand mix of Ottoman Imperial styles with four minarets and a dome, towering over the square in which it is built. This structure rivals, if it does not overshadow, the classic monument of modern Ankara, the mausoleum of Atatürk, the founder of modern Turkey, set upon an opposite hill, and acts as a focus for religious belief in Turkey's capital.

This Islam is neither a replacement for, nor an alternative to, the modern world: it is an integral part of life in the city as it grows and develops. Alongside the *Kocatepe* mosque is the headquarters of the Directorate of Religious Affairs. Underneath, in a basement level below the mosque, lies one of the largest and most reasonably priced of all the supermarkets in Ankara, patronized by believers and sceptics alike. Opposite the mosque is an underground station, part of an excellent, clean network opened in 1996. Across the road, and still popular, is the *Kızılırmak* cinema, where generations of Ankara youth have seen the latest European and American films. A few steps further take the visitor to fashionable clothes shops, and the bookshop quarter, the heart of left-wing Ankara. Half a kilometre above the mosque lies the *Karum*, an air-conditioned shopping centre indistinguishable from any in Europe or America, except by being more up-market than most. By a supreme irony, Ankara has therefore come to resemble Istanbul, where modern department stores, offices, bars, theatres, cafés, art galleries, and cinemas exist alongside mosques, Islamic discussion groups, the Islamic brotherhoods and theological book outlets.

In Anatolia too, the same mixture can be seen in a thousand towns and settlements: schools for religious education and Koran courses flourish alongside technical high-schools and small newsagents full of Islamic literature lie next to shops selling the most modern electronic and household appliances. Local brotherhood groups and active religious believers hand out literature, and hold passionate public debates on the role of faith and doctrine in modern life, whilst the rapidly developing free-market in local and national television brings news of the world and of the town. In these town centres previous central mosques are being dismantled to make room for large, sometimes munificent structures with dome, gilt, and minaret. Again after the Ottoman style, these huge structures are built voluntarily at great expense. As development continues apace, and small villages turn into towns and towns turn into sub-province centres, they expand district by district, each outlying area often first building a mosque, then around it, the houses, giving a sense of organic growth in which the nucleus of each settlement is a mosque.

In these villages and growing towns alike the image of the ideal urban life has remained steadfastly Istanbul. Nowhere, indeed, is the combination of a modern infrastructure and the presence of Islam more noticeable than in Istanbul, where the centre of the city, untouched by war, with its banks of minarets leaning over the Golden Horn and the hundreds of mosques of different styles waiting to surprise the walker around the city, often seems curiously remote from the ideals of the

Republic. Istanbul continues to attract the great bulk of rural migrants, despite the appalling lack of amenities which they have to suffer in the outlying areas. Village houses in Anatolia, however remote, often have on their walls a reproduction of an image of Mecca on the one, and on the other, a picture of Istanbul, featuring often a Sinan mosque, or the Bosphorus bridge with its neo-baroque mosque at one end, graceful spans moving into the distance and a ferry boat passing underneath.

The foundation of Republican Turkey

All this might lead the visitor to conclude that Kemalism has failed. In part, they would be right. It is likely that the situation today differs in this, and other ways, from that future envisaged by many of the Republic's founders.[1] On the other hand, conclusions of the demise of Kemalism should not be stated too hastily: the Kemalist system has survived seventy years of economic, political and social transformation with remarkable resilience. The courts, army and large sectors of the government, and indeed the population at large, are becoming increasingly active in response to what they perceive as the threat to secularism. Brotherhoods, particularly a vehement *tarikat* called the *Aczmendi*, are still prosecuted for too open calls for return to Islamic rule.[2] There have been widespread secular popular demonstrations against the Islamification of politics, culminating in mass rallies to Atatürk's tomb. The army has regularly expelled officers accused of opposing the secular basis of the nation. In February 1997, the National Security Council announced a package of measures to protect secularism, and in January 1998, the tempo increased again: the Welfare Party, the largest Islamic party, was closed down by the Constitutional Court.

Outside overt politics, in the areas of culture and administration, many of the Republican structures are still in place. In Ankara, the presidential symphony orchestra still plays Brahms, Beethoven and Mozart to packed houses in a concert hall built in early Republican modernist style whilst in the foyer, amidst exhibitions of abstract art, uniformed army officer recruits mingle self-consciously with students in jeans and bureaucrats in evening gowns and suits. In Anatolia, state-owned industrial complexes built to demonstrate the philosophy with which industrialisation was to take place are still open and running: these include the *Sümerbank* factories, or the water engineering plants established to irrigate whole areas such as the Konya plain, or the sugar-refining plants set up to encourage and process the beet crop in remote parts of the country, each constructed with its own swimming pool, farm, plant nursery, orchard, sports facilities, fire brigade, clinic, crèche, modern administration buildings, primary school, bar, ballroom, theatre, hostel and often palatial guest accommodation. A few have been privatised in their entirety, others have had some of their parcels of land and various of their amenities sold off, but by and large they continue, in state hands, to provide models of Kemalism, and (albeit usually at a great financial loss) to constitute a large proportion of the industrial output of the country.[3]

Thus, if the Kemalist movement has been a failure, it is so only in parts and to parts of the population. To understand exactly where this fascinating and multiple attempt at social reconstruction has been variously successful, and the complex reasons: (resistance, impracticability, over-optimism, inadequate education) that have led it to be so, would be an enormous, perhaps impossible, endeavour. However, it is our task to look only at the place of religion. In order to do so, it is useful to return briefly to the founding period of the Republic.

The reforms

Modern Turkey was founded from the ruins of the Ottoman Empire between the years following the end of the First World War and the death of Atatürk in 1938. Atatürk, then known as Mustafa Kemal, first came to prominence in the First World War, as a successful Ottoman commander. At the conclusion of the war, whilst the British were occupying Istanbul, he was dispatched to Anatolia, in theory to act as an inspector, though in practice he became a focus and leader for opposition to the dismemberment of Anatolia which was being threatened by the allies. In July 1919, he instigated a nationalist congress at Erzurum, then in September 1919, a further congress in Sivas, which declared its opposition to the allied designs. At the time, Anatolia was occupied by the Italians and French in the south, and by a much larger expeditionary force of Greeks who had invaded through the Aegean coast. In this critical situation, Atatürk persuaded the French and the Italians to withdraw from Anatolia, then succeeded in unifying sufficient of Anatolia's population to raise munitions, supplies and money from the countryside and after a bitter campaign, defeated the Greek invading army, finally routing them completely in 1922. In 1923, the Lausanne Treaty granted the great bulk of the Turkish demands. The Turkish Republic was formally established on 29 October 1923, with Mustafa Kemal its president.[4]

Atatürk proceeded to use the immense prestige he had gained from this victory to push through major reforms which were designed to make Turkey a modern, secular nation state based on those of the West at that time. Briefly, the Grand National Assembly abolished the Sultanate in November 1922 and transferred the capital to Ankara from Istanbul in October 1923. In 1924, it voted to abolish the Caliphate, the Ministry of Religious Affairs and Trusts, religious schools (*medrese*), and the şeriat courts. It replaced them with a new educational system, and new laws based on the Swiss civil, German criminal and, later, Italian economic codes. In 1925, it passed Law 677 banning monasteries (*tekkes*), tombs as places of worship (*türbes*), Islamic brotherhoods (*tarikats*), their lodgings (*zaviyes*) and the use of any nomenclature associated with those brotherhoods. In that year, it voted to adopt the western calendar. In 1928, the statement in the constitution, 'The Religion of the Turkish State is Islam', was removed. Also in that year, Atatürk devised a law to replace the Arabic alphabet, which had until then been used to write Turkish, with a modified form of the Latin script. In 1931, he established the Turkish History Society, and in 1932, the Turkish Language Society. In 1937, a further amendment to the constitution declared the state to be secular, *laik*.[5]

Any revolution has to choose the means to implement its vision. Atatürk chose the state, in all its arms: the army, the education system, the bureaucracy, and the provincial administration, to inculcate the laws, symbols, direction and identity he visualized for modern Turkey. He also encouraged the development of a party, the People's Party later the Republican People's Party (*CHP*), which emerged out of the independence movement in 1923. One-party rule continued until 1950, the year of the first genuinely free general elections, twelve years after Atatürk's death. During most of this time, though the only party in power, it served to legitimize Atatürk's rule by participating in the formulation (and sometimes highly disputatious discussion) of the legislation in the Grand National Assembly. It also acted as a country-wide network through which the Kemalist message could be spread, often working very closely with the government provincial apparatus.

So much has been written about the innovatory aspects of the revolution that it is extremely difficult to gain a conception of what was taken over by the Kemalists from the Ottoman way of doing things, and what they actively invented or borrowed from other contemporary single-party republics which were emerging at that time. Certainly, in many ways there was no absolute break with the past, whatever may be implied by the wealth of such comment in contemporary accounts. The Republicans took over what remained of the provincial administration system, which had been founded on the French model in the nineteenth century. Even the secular reforms were remarkable in their thoroughness rather than their inception: the Ottoman Empire had been seeking to modernise for a full two hundred years and had done so largely by permitting sections of the bureaucracy, courts, army and, to a lesser extent, the education system to become secular in parts. Further, and most importantly, the Kemalists, in their authoritative imposition of their reforms, retained the structural relations of ruler and ruled, the unwavering acquiescence to the centre, which was the hallmark of the Ottoman Empire.[6]

The new Turkish nation lacked trained, educated personnel (the speculation as to the whereabouts of a necessary, middle-ranking bourgeoisie within the Republican revolution was later to become the object of study by left-wing intellectuals). Instead, the revolutionary message was conveyed in part by the handful of people who had received higher education, and was sustained in great part by the enthusiasm of the new generation, many of whom were deeply committed to the credo of Westernisation, modernisation and secularism that it extolled. They went out into the countryside to preach their message, sometimes to less than believing villagers. Mahmut Makal became a famous example of these, a school teacher who removed himself to a remote village in Anatolia, full of enthusiasm as to the rational, modernist developmental ethic of the

Kemalist. His description of his troubles with the villagers, and their sceptical reaction to his approach, was a great success when it was published in Turkish, and it appeared also in English in 1954.[7]

Today, what remains of the revolutionary message can be seen still in all parts of the state: school children are exhorted to 'be proud, work and be confident', teachers that the new generation has been entrusted into their hands. Traffic police are told that their work is essential to the running of the country, the air force that its existence is essential to the country's freedom, citizens that their paying taxes is vital, and most famously, the army that it is responsible for the Republican heritage entrusted to it by Atatürk himself. In great part indeed, these Republican exhortations are based on the personality and sayings of Atatürk, a process that took place largely after his death. Today, his portrait is present in relief on many government buildings, hung on the wall in all government offices, printed on the currency, reproduced in the front of all state school text books. Many of the houses in which he lived, or even stayed in for a short time, are preserved as museums. The events of his great journey through Anatolia as he raised support for national resistance are celebrated in national holidays. School children still wear uniforms reminiscent of those of France at the turn of the century, first used in the founding years of the Republic, when schools were opened under his decree.

The new national identity

However awkward and sometimes even clumsy today the outward symbols and slogans of Kemalism might appear, their very longevity is an important indication of just where the revolution has been successful. Atatürk's conception of Turkey as a nation was enthusiastically embraced by the majority of the people, however diverse their background, and (with the exception of the rebellion in the east) that conception is still largely accepted today. The basis of citizenship was simple: anyone living within the political boundaries of modern Turkey was declared *Türk* and expected to accept the tenets of the revolution. Acceptance of this political affiliation was sufficient to qualify for citizenship. This is succinctly summed up in the most famous saying of the new Republic: '*Ne mutlu Türküm diyene*': 'How happy is he or she who says, "I am Turkish"'.

Membership of the new Republic was, therefore, not explicitly predicated on ethnic identity, but rather on allegiance to the newly created political unit, and to a general state-created flexible ideology of 'Turkishness' which emphasised, among other things, the pre-Islamic past of Anatolia, the paramountcy of Turkish over Arabic or other foreign words and the secular, populist basis of the Republic. This lack of a direct connection between ethnic 'Turk' and state-created 'Turkishness' is not always sufficiently appreciated. The Kurdish tribes in the east violently oppose the Turkish state, but there are at least as many Kurds absorbed or partly absorbed into Turkish society as a whole, and the conflict has not yet generalized to include them as well. A multitude of other small ethnic and national groups, such as Azeris, Laz, Circassians, Bulgarians, Arabs, Uygurs, Kazaks, Tatars, Estonians, Kirgiz, Georgians, and Iraqis live successfully and harmoniously within its borders.[8] Of course, ethnicity is a continuously evolving phenomenon, and this harmony may change. There are occasional signs of an emerging ethnic group ethos expressed through organisations devoted to researching or forwarding the interests of a particular people.[9]

Religion and the Republic

A similar device was employed with regard to religion. Though secular, the state did administer religion, but one particular kind: the Sunni, orthodox form of the faith. This means that other religious groups, such as the Christians, Jews, Alevis or the Yezidis find little place in official religious education (though they are permitted access to it), nor indeed, at least officially, do any mystical variants of the Islamic faith. Republican Islam, in down-to-earth fashion, construes the Faith as the practice of the five pillars (Believe in the one God, give alms, fast, go on the pilgrimage, pray five times a day), to correct moral behaviour and an uncomplicated belief in an omniscient but thoroughly transcendent God. The state was careful to argue that this interpretation was not against religion itself, but rather that individuals should now be free to experience piety as they wished, without interference from others, whatever their belief or sect.

This approach is also tinged by the nationalist ethic. Whilst there have been many different currents of Islamic thought within the

Republican interpretation of Islam,[10] the most frequent is that true religion, personal piety, was corrupted in Ottoman days by involvement in politics, and by the use of the clergy as intermediaries to God. The Republicans further claimed that true expression of religion could be found through the use of Turkish prayer, a language that all could understand, through translating the Koran into Turkish, and through only reading the *ezan*, the call to prayer in Turkish, rather than Arabic.[11] They also drew historical parallels, asserting that their revolution mirrors the Protestant battles against Papism in its dislike of intermediaries and direct access to the faith for all. Thus, it was a cleansed religion, without mysticism, without saints, and without independent religious institutions that was aimed at. It was also one closely controlled.

This approach is still taught in schools today, though with varying degrees of sophistication, where compulsory religious lessons were re-introduced into the curriculum in 1982, as 'Lessons in Religion and Morals' *din ve ahlak*. These textbooks are carefully graded. A text for first-year middle school pupils, i.e., children aged twelve or so, by Gündüz, Gülle and Kaya published in about 1992, avoids explicit discussion of secularism. The book covers definitions of certain everyday religious terms and describes various of the practices of the Faith, including the performance of the 'five pillars'. It also gives instructions on how to genuflect correctly during prayer. It is not expansionist or exclusivist in tone, but stresses rather the social use of religion, the importance that Islam gives to good relations with friends, neighbours and elders, and to hard work. Inasmuch as it defines religion at all, it regards it as the pursuit of appropriate moral standards:

RELIGION IS HIGH MORAL BEHAVIOUR

One of the general principles of our religion is the importance given to moral behaviour. High morals are a central point of all the religions of the book. It can be seen that every decree, every law and every advice of our religion, when it is exam-ined carefully, is aimed primarily at encouraging appropriate morals. Faith is the foundation of moral behaviour. Because without faith, it is not possible to talk of morals.[12]

A text given to third-year students, written by Professor Fiğlalı, a highly regarded academic, is more ambitious. It contains sections on religious practices and definitions, just like the earlier books, but further expands *ahlak* to include love for the nation, everyday politeness and good manners, and includes a final section on Islamic art. Most interesting, though, is his detailed justification of the Republican approach to religion, taken here from the tenth printing of the text:

> Secularism is a French word... In the dictionary it is defined as a person who is not of the priestly class, as something without religion... Among Muslims, as distinct from Christianity, there is no priestly class. The Muslim *müftü* [administrator of religion], *vaiz* [preacher], *imam* [prayer leader] and similar men of religion must not be confused with the priests of the Christian world, because their priestly class has various spiritual qualities which makes it superior to other people... In our religion the only superiority we accept is respect for Allah.
>
> In the fifteenth century in the West, the men of the church, that is the priestly class, clashed violently with the people, the laity. In the end, accepting secularism, religion was separated from the affairs of state. The state, though religion no longer mixed with its affairs, itself showed respect to religion... Accordingly, secularism is certainly not unbelieving. In secularism, religion meets the sublime with complete freedom of conscience and belief. As a matter of fact, Atatürk says on this subject:
>
> 'Secularism has never been atheism but has opened the way to struggle against false faith and superstition, and has allowed the development of true religion. Those who want to confuse secularism with atheism are none other than enemies against progress and life, eastern tribal fanatics who have not let the scales fall from their eyes'.

After further discussion, Fiğlalı summarizes his overall argument in the form of five points, as follows.

In a secular country:

* The affairs of religion and state are separate.
* In it, there is freedom of worship, belief and conscience. Fanaticism is never tolerated.
* Extremist movements are avoided.
* No one makes any other person embrace a religion or sect by force.
* Those who wish to use religion for their personal gain are not permitted to do so.

This detailed exposition, expressed in similar terms on many other occasions in schools, on formal religious holidays, in speeches by politicians and on almost any other occasion when the life of Atatürk is mentioned, has not succeeded in convincing the great mass of the people, or at the very most has only partly convinced some of them. Though initially not encouraged in this respect by their Republican leaders, to be Islamic has become as important as to be Turkish. It is an ideological filter through which people mediate and negotiate their citizenship with the Republican state; it is quite inextricably bound up with the way that people create their social and personal identity as members of the nation, and is not confined just to their individual, inner selves. Fiğlalı does show some awareness of this failure in a neat passage of special pleading:

> Let me here note straightaway that the phrase 'The state does not interfere with religion' must not be misunderstood... In fact one of the prime aims of the state is to work for the nation. From this perspective, just as in the case of the people's other needs, the state must consider their religious needs, and take the necessary steps'.[13]

The Bureaucracy
The Turkish State is highly suited to taking the 'steps' noted by Fiğlalı. Administratively, Turkey is divided into provinces, and each province into sub-provinces. Ministries lie in Ankara, with offices in each provincial centre and, in many cases in sub-provinces as well. Civil servants may find themselves transferred between different

provinces partly through stated preference, partly according to a complicated system of points' accumulation, and partly as a result of political influence. This system, pervasive, omnipresent and clearly distinct from normal civilian life, facilitates and accentuates the idea of an abstract, overarching state which is responsible for educating and protecting the people of the country. Indeed, there is an openness and simplicity about this system which strikes starkly at people from Britain, used to a more fuzzy relation between state and citizen. In Turkey, people are either civil servants (*memur*) or they are not.

It is the place of all government departments within this massive world of civil servants to uphold the traditions of the Republic, and today, inasmuch as it is the place of the bureaucracy to administer religion, they do so. The pilgrimage (*hac*) requires the Foreign Ministry to discuss arrangements with Saudi Arabia, and the co-operation of the national carrier, Turkish Airways, in arranging special planes. During *Ramazan*, the state-run Television and Radio Corporation announces the time of the break of fast for each province in turn, and broadcasts soothing music throughout the afternoon as the time to break the fast approaches. Within the university sector, there are a growing number of Theology Faculties, which teach mainly Islam, though they contain also a component of comparative religious study. In addition, there are two enormously important state institutions for the perpetuation and teaching of Islam: the *imam-hatip* schools, and the Directorate of Religious Affairs.[14]

The imam-hatip schools
The Ministry of Education administers the compulsory lessons discussed above in all state schools. It also supervises *imam-hatip* schools. These were founded in 1951 at the *lycée* level with the aim of training mosque prayer leaders and preachers. Their curriculum consists, from about one third to a half, of religious lessons (Arabic, *Hadis* [sayings attributable to the Prophet *Muhammed*], Islamic history and so on), with the remaining lessons being drawn from the core state curriculum. Officially, they are defined as a category of 'vocational' school, and are administered similarly to technical high schools for both girls and boys, also found in most provincial and sub-provincial centres. They are thus firmly part of the Republican

school system: the décor and iconography within them differs little, if at all, from that of other state schools, and teachers at them are drawn from the broader ranks of the profession. Indeed, most will find themselves appointed to one at some stage in their careers.

In spite of their limited intent, the *imam-hatip* schools' rise has been spectacular. According to a brochure published by the Directorate of Religious Education in 1990, their number has risen from the seven that were first opened, passed a hundred in 1975 and reached 383 in 1988. The number of children who attended them in the teaching year 1989-1990 is given as 92,432. In 1971, provision was also made for *imam-hatip* schools to be opened at the middle-school level. These are just as popular as the *lycées*, and that same brochure notes that there were in 1990, 187,160 students at such schools. In the years since 1990, their total number has climbed even further, to 464. (Table 1 below).

Table 1: İmam-hatip Schools by Year of Opening

Teaching Year	Schools opened	Total Schools active
1951-52	7	7
1953-54	8	15
1954-55	1	16
1956-57	1	17
1958-59	2	19
1962-63	7	26
1965-66	4	30
1966-67	10	40
1967-68	18	58
1968-69	11	69
1969-70	2	71
1970-71	1	72
1974-75	29	101
1975-76	70	171
1976-77	77	248
1977-78	86	334

Table 1 cont.

1978-79	1	335
1979-80	5	340
1980-81	34	374
1984-85	1	375
1985-86	1	376
1987-88	7	383
1991-92	6	389
1992-93	1	390
1995-96	3	394
1996-97	70	464

Figures taken largely from *Din Öğretimi* (1990), and *Milli Eğitim İstatistikler* (1994).

The great success of the schools has equally given rise to controversy. The number of pupils trained at the schools far exceeds any possible need that the state's administration of Islam might require. Their supporters have systematically been attempting to gain special concessions for *imam-hatip* graduates arguing, among other things, that they should be permitted to go on to the army officer training schools. The secularists have equally become dismayed at their expansion. They fear that the detailed Islamic training that the schools offer is far more hardline than it might appear on the surface, and they point to the fact that many of them have mosques or small areas for prayer, *mescits*, within the building. They also suggest that frequently the *imam-hatip* schools become dominated by particular religiously-active factions, and that in consequence the state's control over them is weakened. Taking these fears into account, secularist measures introduced in February 1997 proposed that they should be closed by absorbing the 'vocational' category to which they officially belong entirely into the mainstream school system.[15] This has been fiercely resisted. It appears likely, however, that, at least, the *imam-hatip* middle schools will be closed.

The Directorate of Religious Affairs
Since the commencement of the Republic there has also been a distinctive institution, the Directorate of Religious Affairs, *Diyanet*

İşleri Başkanlığı, expressly charged with administering daily religious practice. It was set up in 1923 at the instigation of several members of the Grand National Assembly as a direct replacement for the Ottoman Ministry of Religion. It received a confirmation of its status after the military intervention of 1960, and appears also as a part of the Republic's administration in article 136 of the 1982 constitution. No specific religion is mentioned, the word *diyanet* meaning 'worship' rather than the worship of any one particular group or sect.[16] However, in practice it has always been assumed that the Directorate would look after Islamic affairs, specifically the body of belief represented by the Sunni population.

The Directorate is responsible to the Prime Ministry, and has no direct contact with the cabinet or daily political affairs. It has an extensive organisation; central headquarters in Ankara oversee provincial offices, which in turn look after subordinate offices in each sub-province centre, known as *müftülük*. Its head is not of ministerial rank (a source of grievance for successive holders of that post), and those who work in the Directorate are adjudged civil servants. Accordingly, like all civil servants they are bound by restrictions but benefit from privileges: they are forbidden to take part in political movements or to become members of political parties, but are favoured by social insurance, allowed access to special hospitals, and often (particularly in remote areas) have accommodation provided for them.

In the provinces, the office of the *müftü* acts as a local link between the believer and the state: its officials administer the *imam*s attached to almost every mosque, check that mosques under construction are facing Mecca and distribute sermons and other material that is sent to them from above. The office also has attached to it a professional Koran course teacher who helps to supervise other Koran courses in the area, usually run by the local mosque *imam*. The *imam*s are thus not just part of an administrative structure which runs from the mosque to the centre, they are also subject ideologically to the decisions made by their superiors in the announcements that they make to the congregations and the sermons that they preach. This tight administrative and supervisory structure leaves individual *imam*s with little leeway to create their own interpretation of religion.[17] Indeed, as technology develops, their leeway grows even less: cassettes are often sent out to individual mosques to be played to congregations. There is discussion too, about whether to bring in satellite television, which would allow for identical sermons for Turkish citizens praying at officially sanctioned mosques, whether at home or abroad.

From its headquarters in Ankara, the Directorate oversees the organisation of the pilgrimage, publishes large quantities of literature, distributes and prints the Koran, makes rulings on questions of religious nicety in the form of opinions (*fetvas*), holds conferences on religious issues, oversees the conversion of those who wish to become Muslim, and attends to the physical infrastructure of the modern religious buildings. Thus, in a leaflet published by the Directorate in 1993, it was announced that in the period 1983-93 it had published 5,225,009 copies of the Koran, that 486,019 pilgrims went to Mecca, that they supervised 68,203 mosques, and employed 88,533 people (of which 87,188 were employed in the countryside). It was also noted that since the foundation of the Republic, the Directorate had helped 10,918 people turn to Islam, mostly from Christianity (though the conversion of 107 atheists is also noted).[18] There is also a flourishing web-site, on which it publishes key information such as times of prayer, and religious opinions, for example, on the propriety of organ transplants.

The key role that the Directorate plays in the official religious life of the country has meant that it has enjoyed an increasingly high profile through the decades, often amid vociferous debate. Throughout, its main role has remained to provide Islamic services to the population in a controlled, ordered way, and the authorities have shown themselves extremely anxious to avoid the Directorate coming under the control of Islamic brotherhoods or other groups working from outside the state to increase the strength of Islam.[19] Some secular detractors claim that the money available to the Directorate has been increased enormously through political patronage, and this has been widely accepted as being correct.[20] Curiously, however, a doctoral dissertation by Gözaydın-Tarhanlı, part of which has been published, demonstrates that the Directorate has at no time enjoyed the exponential growth shown by the *imam-hatip* schools. Rather, it has usually taken rather less than one per cent of the national budget, and has only very rarely moved to between one and two per cent.[21] This is still a cumulative real increase because of the steady expansion of Turkey's economy, but it is linear rather than exponential. It seems that the Directorate's role has primarily been to oversee, ratify and steer the massive expansion of Islamic activity within the population as a whole rather than actually provide it.

The Directorate abroad

The Directorate is also active overseas, particularly among expatriate populations. When addressing these Turkish workers abroad, the Directorate becomes a quite explicit channel through which to support Turkish nationalism, and its teachers and mosque prayer leaders assume a loose pastoral function along with their religious duties. A fascinating report published by the Directorate in 1993 highlights this, noting various problems that Turkish workers face with integration, namely language, accommodation, economic and also spiritual issues. In the introduction to the report, the head of the Directorate, Mehmet Yılmaz writes:

> The number of our Directorate's employees working in these [foreign] countries is growing every day... They are offering religious, social and cultural services to our citizens and their children. In this way, our people living in these countries, preserving their true identities and culture, are assisted not to assimilate.

The main thrust of the report takes a similar, though perhaps less abrupt, rather paternal role. It comments on the fact that there are nearly three million Turks abroad, many of whom have gone from their villages directly to Germany or to another European country without proper training. It notes the difficulties they are experiencing with the foreign culture, and though never stating so explicitly, hints that perhaps they are falling under the spell of the more extremist Islamic currents which are found there:

> Of clean spirit, greatly attached to their traditions and rituals, our fellow citizens tried to solve their religious inadequacies

themselves, fell under the influence of inappropriate people, and saw their problems grow greater with each passing day... Without doubt, it is necessary for the peace of mind of both our fellow citizens living abroad, and for the society in which they are living, for them to be able to live in well-adjusted fashion... This 'adjustment' is conditional on their preserving their national and religious identity... It is a known fact that people who have broken away from their own beliefs and traditions are unable to unite with those of the society in which they find themselves... Accordingly, accepting that our fellow citizens living abroad have now become a permanent population, to preserve their national identity, their unity, their being in harmony with the host nation, and to ensure that they are provided with education according to the changing times is a moral duty which the Turkish state owes to its citizens.

The same official sense of the Directorate's place as a state body comes across in the links that Turkey may develop with the Balkans and particularly with the Muslim States of the former Soviet Union, known as the 'Turkic states' (*Türk Devletleri*). Whilst there is a special government agency, *TİKA*, devoted to developing business, cultural and social ties with these countries, the Directorate has also been extremely active in forming direct links with their Islamic institutions, offering the Republican model as an appropriate way for them to organise religion.

Islam and its related activities play a part in the overall responsibilities that our State will assume as its contribution toward the material and spiritual development of these brother states, and our Directorate is part of this process. We wish to work together in organising religious instruction, mosque construction and in any other areas where a need is felt by the religious leaders of these countries.

Turks brought the flag of Islam to the East and Central European countries, and to the Balkan peninsula... For this reason, as these Muslims break free from communist dominance and move toward freedom, it is an historical responsibility to help them.

In order to meet these diverse commitments, the Directorate has arranged, in consultation with the Ministry of Education for various of their personnel to be stationed abroad as religious teachers.[22]

Parallel worlds

There are then in Turkey today truly parallel worlds. The state declares that it is irrevocably secular, and reinforces this message through repeated rituals, national festivals, lessons on the life of Atatürk and the ubiquitous iconography of the Republic. It also attempts to regulate the daily practice of Islam, and in doing so provides massive resources for the inculcation, fulfilment and exploration of religious belief. It uses freely the idea of being Islamic to appeal to national sentiment, and by combining a sense of Turkish and Islamic identity hopes to appeal also to Turkish people abroad. It regards this model as a success and is currently attempting to export its conception of state-led personal piety via the Directorate to the newly freed countries of the former Soviet Union.

This parallel emphasis on religion and secularism, individually reconcilable (at least in the larger cities) according to the inclination of the person concerned has given rise to several analyses which stress the degree to which a synthesis has been made between the state, secularism and belief.[23] Nevertheless, whilst it is true that an accommodation has been reached by many people, the situation is not stable. One of the consequences of the contemporary resurgence of Islam is that the shifting, uneasy but often reconciliatory relationship with religion, which has characterised much of most persons' experience of faith within the Republic, is being replaced by a much more exclusivist, expansionist philosophy of active, committed belief.

In muted fashion, this inclination may be said to have been present from the beginning of the Republic. From its outset, the drastic secularism of the early Republic was deeply unpopular with the mass of the people. They did not revolt concertedly, or openly. One of the reasons for this, as Stirling has pointed out, is that the reforms may not immediately have affected very significantly the daily round of village life, then often still remote from the administrative centres.[24] There are other reasons too: sedentary peasants, accustomed to absolute government, do not make nearly such rebellious subjects as mountainous tribes.[25] Also, whilst some of the reforms gave rise to widespread dismay, particularly the introduction of the Latin alphabet and the call to prayer in Turkish, the foundation of the independent Republic was greeted with widespread celebration. Atatürk was revered for this resurrection of the Turkish people, and could be admired enormously for this however much his secular changes were regretted.

Yet, there was some resistance.[26] Among the most resented of the reforms was an edict that the fez was to be replaced with a European-style hat, a measure that brought home the significance of the revolution to people in a way that perhaps it had not done before. There was speculation too, that this might lead to the abolition of the veil. On 25 November 1925, an armed uprising in Rize, beginning in the sub-province named Of, supposedly led by a *Nakşibendi*, was suppressed by force. On 23 December 1930, a young conscript officer named Kubilay was beheaded in a riot in the sub-province of Menemen. This is now known as the *'Derviş Mehmet'* affair, because it appears to have been sparked by a member of the *Nakşibendi* brotherhood who had denounced the Republic, and proclaimed himself to be *Mehdi. Derviş Mehmet* is thought to have been killed after the *jandarma* fired on the riot to restore order. Nevertheless, on 31 December, more than 2,000 people were arrested and the region brought under martial law. More seriously than this even, there were major rebellions in the east in 1925, in 1927-8, and again in the late 1930s, which, on each occasion, the Turkish army only put down after extensive campaigning. It is possible to see these as early Kurdish nationalist rebellions, but they belong equally to a long tradition of tribal religious fervour inspired by perceived laxity in central rule.[27]

There is no doubt then, that however great the impetus provided by the revolution, and the undoubted enthusiasm with which it was received by some, the mass of the Sunni people would have preferred that the specifically religious aspects of the reforms had not happened. Deeply indebted to Atatürk for his victory over the Greeks, they remained stoic, occasionally losing their tempers in isolated, largely local incidents which were suppressed by the gendarmerie (*jandarma*). Those who did protest, and the Grand National

Assembly could be a vociferous debating chamber, made no impact.

Just how long this situation might have continued if left undisturbed is one of those pleasurable historical speculations. Change though it did. Some assert that the implementation of democracy was forced on Turkey by the allies, particularly by the United States, which regarded increased democracy as being a condition for providing aid. Others suggest Turkey was simply too restless to avoid a transition any longer. Whatever the reason, the immediate impetus was the definite decision of İsmet İnönü, who had become president after Atatürk's death, to continue with a full transformation to democracy. As campaigning for votes began, in spite of the repeated emphasis on ensuring that politics and religion were henceforth to be separate, politicians were hardly able to resist the offer of support for Islamic mores as a way of attracting votes. Thus, whilst the proscriptions governing Islam were in some ways widely unpopular, it was the introduction of democracy, which provided the key link between rulers and ruled, that led to their actually beginning to weaken. However complicated the situation becomes when looked at in more detail, this is the turning point.

Politics and democracy
The express aim of the Republican revolution was to establish a western, egalitarian, state that would be liberated from both Ottoman dynastic rule and the authority of religion. During his life time, Atatürk had created much of the institutional framework that was part of this vision, and even, in an attempt to achieve the final transition, had experimented with opposition parties. On each occasion he drew back, and closed down the parties that emerged, surprised, it is said, at the speed with which they grew, and particularly at their successful emphasis on religion.[28]

Atatürk's death was followed by a long period of national mourning. İnönü's presidency was made difficult by the outbreak of the Second World War, in which Turkey pursued a successful but immensely delicate neutral path. It was no time to implement a multi-party system. As peace returned, however, İnönü let it be known that he would welcome an opposition party. Accordingly, the *Demokrat Parti* was founded in January 1946, and grew rapidly. It is widely agreed that the first election, held in July that year, was not fairly conducted, particularly as it had been brought forward to take place before the *DP* were fully prepared.[29]

In 1950, elections took place again. As they approached, the Republican People's Party (*CHP*) sought to appeal to the electorate by lessening the state's control. In religion, it reintroduced Koran courses, and allowed foreign currency to be provided for Turks to go on the pilgrimage to Mecca. Just before the elections, it reopened many important tombs (*türbes*) and monasteries (*tekkes*) for visiting. In spite of these efforts, on election day, 14 May 1950, the *CHP* was trounced. İnönü refused an offer from his former military colleagues to stage a coup,[30] and the Democrat Party took its place in government.

The reason for the *CHP*'s disastrous defeat appears to be twofold. The party seemed to have underestimated the bitterness that had built up in the villages in reaction to their authoritarian behaviour. They also did not succeed in convincing the electorate that they were sincere in their relaxation of measures associated with religion. The following story I was told in a village in 1996. It is still deeply hostile, even nearly fifty years after the single-party period, and the narrator was also well aware that it showed the attitude of the *CHP* to religion in an unfavourable light.[31]

> When I was young the government collector of crop tax, then retired, used to wander around the town absolutely perfectly attired: a Panama hat, beautifully pressed jacket and trousers, a narrow tie of the early Republic style, and, in spite of his age and wrinkled jowls, cleanly shaven. In his hand, he held a stick with a silver band on which was engraved his name.
>
> He used to be feared even at that age throughout the region, and we children would take fright at his shadow as he walked past. In those days, no villager was allowed to take in his crop until it had been vetted by the tax collector. There were so many villages to be vetted that villagers would sometimes have to wait for days before taking their crops off the threshing ground.
>
> One day, the tax collector and his assistants arrived on horses in such and such a village. They went to the threshing ground and

called for sticks. In each pile of wheat they placed one of these sticks upright in the centre, and around each pile the tax collector himself drew a line with his monogrammed staff. He said, 'If this line is disturbed, or if the level of wheat changes then you will be answerable for the consequences, whether I come back a week later or a month'. The villagers slept by their wheat for day after day to try to ensure that they were indeed not disturbed.

One night, unseen by its owner, a donkey blundered on to one of the piles and ate part of the wheat, disturbing the circle drawn by the tax collector. The village council of elders met in consternation, and decided that they had no choice but to redraw the line. The owner refused, saying whatever happens I'll just explain the situation and he'll understand that there was a mistake.

Days later the tax inspector came back and saw that the pile had been disturbed. He called the man to him, and said, 'What's this?' The man replied, 'I am very sorry but a donkey stumbled into the grain and ate some'. The tax inspector said, 'That's simply no excuse. I shall have to punish you'. He beat the men, and striking not just him, but his neighbours for not taking greater care. Worse, he beat his eighty-year-old mother, hurting her so badly that she had to go to bed for days afterwards.

Ultimately, God made the tax collector pay for his terrible cruelty to an old woman, and refused to let the man die. He wandered for years throughout the town growing ever more wrinkled, and then aged so much that he had to stay permanently in bed. But he did not die. When I used to creep past his open house door as a child, terrified, I used to hear him cry, 'God come and take my life, I want to die!' But he suffered on for month after month.

The Democrat Party appears to have made its greater sympathy for religion quite explicit, even during their election campaign, and worked extremely hard to convey this message. Stirling, one of the earliest fieldworkers, gave an interview on his experiences in Turkey just before he died, and recalls being in his village during the lead up to the 1950 elections:

The Democrat Party were very clearly on the side of religion. When

they came to the village they would go off to the mosque in their
spare time. I remember a Democrat Party man came to the village
propagandising. He actually went to the mosque and they all went
with him, so that he did his prayers in front of the village and
showed that he was a good Muslim. The Republican People's Party
didn't do that. There was a rumour that turned out to be true that
the *ezan* [call to prayer from the mosque] which was legally at that
time in Turkish was going to be changed back to Arabic, that there
would be more permission for school religion and so on. These
were very small things compared with the secularism of Atatürk
and the republicans. But nevertheless it was a move in the other
direction and I think that had a great deal to do with the victory of
the Democrats in 1950.[32]

Once in power, one of the Democrat Party's first acts was to confirm
that the proscription on calling to prayer in Arabic would be lifted.
Menderes, their leader, also presided over the opening of the *imam-
hatip* schools, authorised the opening of a further important tomb, the
Eyüp Sultan Türbesi in the Golden Horn, and indicated quite
explicitly that his government was favourable towards Islam, even
early on in his time as Prime Minister.[33]

It is sometimes remarked that these reforms were very slight.[34]
Nevertheless, they had a very considerable effect. Thus, in permitting
worship at tombs once more, the *CHP* had already re-sanctioned, and
Menderes was further supporting, a social practice which is an integral
part of Anatolian Islam. Usually women, but men too, visit shrines to
pray, to sacrifice, and to make vows (*adak*). Tombs may also have
slightly different 'specialisations': to cure malaria, help a mother
lactate, provide fertility, aid the mentally ill, or enable the crippled to
walk. Still today, the enormous attraction of tombs to worshippers is
obvious to any visitor, where the largest and most important may have
thousands of people visiting, and even the smallest may be festooned
with ribbons which supplicants tie to a nearby tree to mark their visit.

In other areas of social life, the *DP* marked a clear move away from
the étatist economic policies of the *CHP*. Although Menderes
maintained public investment, at the same time he sought rapid
industrialisation through foreign investment, and above all foreign

loans, particularly from North America. Though he was successful, the lengths to which he was prepared to go to secure credit led him to be warned that he was proceeding too quickly for financial stability.[35] Within Turkey, it is sometimes said that Menderes came to an arrangement with Ford motor cars that they would build Turkey's roads in return for an absolute automobile concession. This is apocryphal, but it does give some idea of the energy with which he pursued development.

Throughout the decade, Menderes continued in power, winning elections in 1954 and 1957. In spite of his popularity, there were deep problems with his rule. The Democrat Party governments became authoritarian in their turn: seeking to separate the *CHP* from the bureaucracy which had played such a role in administering the revolution, they began a process of politicisation by placing their own men in position, and exiling or sacking those sympathetic to the *CHP*.[36] The drive to develop resulted in an inflation, which though it did not effect the agricultural producers adversely, eroded the salaries of the army officers and other wage earners severely.[37] Further, as Menderes' popularity waned, he began to use the symbols of Islam more explicitly, even claiming that he had been singled out by God when he survived a plane crash in London at Gatwick airport. The army, increasingly impatient with this state of affairs, interceded on 27 May 1960, arrested Menderes and his cabinet, and after a long trial hanged him, and the Foreign Minister, Fatin Rüştü Zorlu, in 1961.

Though it was not clear at the time, Menderes and the Democrat Party represent the only political philosophy which has, until 1999 at least, gained a majority in the National Assembly. It consists of a combination of right-wing economics, combined with overt sympathy toward Islam expressed *within* the framework of the secular republic. Although they were pro-Islam, Menderes and his supporters proclaimed the importance of Atatürk, his revolutionary principles and the secular base of the Republic. They prosecuted the *Ticani*, an extreme *tarikat* which had begun to destroy busts and statues of Atatürk. They refused a request at their party congress in 1951 to bring back the Arabic script. In 1954 they closed down the *Millet Partisi* for pursuing anti-secular political activities. Sceptics sometimes suggest that these actions were mainly cosmetic, that closing an Islamic party simply meant that they could retain the religious vote for themselves in any election. Nevertheless, there is no doubt that by forging an alliance between Islam, business and secularism, they created a broad platform that ensured electoral success.

The events of the following decades, though diverse and fascinating in detail, represent a firm continuation of this pattern. When the generals returned power to the civilians in 1963, they threw their weight behind İnönü. He was unable to form a majority government, and the very next election saw a return to that same combination of liberal economics and personal piety that characterised Menderes. The leader now was Süleyman Demirel, a technocrat, and head of the successor party to the Democrat Party, the Justice Party (*Adalet Partisi*). Demirel's time in office was even more colourful than that of Menderes. Throughout the next seventeen years he was twice deposed by the army, once in 1971, and again in 1980.

After the 1983 election, the leadership of the moderate right, and of the country, passed to Turgut Özal, a bureaucrat, who had been in charge of the privatisation programme in Demirel's governments. It very soon became clear that Özal was utterly committed both to the opening of Turkey's markets *and* to Islam. (Kenan Evren, the general who oversaw the *coup* remarks concisely in his memoirs, 'If I had known then he was a member of a *tarikat* I would not have let him in the race').[38] Özal remained Prime Minister from 1983 until 1990, when he became President, and exhibited a surprising talent for international diplomacy, guiding Turkey confidently through the difficult period of the Gulf War. Then, in 1992, just after he had attempted a serious negotiated cease-fire in the East, he died of a heart attack.

The drive and force of the Özal years in many ways changed the face of Turkey. A steady increase in the standard of living led to a vast expansion of leisure facilities in large cities, the creation of a recognisable 'yuppie' class, and huge numbers of young people who enjoyed themselves immensely in the bars, concerts and restaurants that the cities could now offer. This creation of a *jeunesse dorée* was matched by the increase in the obvious symbols of adherence to Islam, an increase openly supported by Özal and his government. In their recent work, which spans the Özal years, Hugh and Nicole Pope point out, *inter alia*, that Özal encouraged the foundation of Islamic banks,[39] that he obtained special permission from the cabinet to bury his Mother in a *Nakşibendi* cemetery in Istanbul, and that he allowed the brotherhoods to flourish as never before.[40]

In April 1991, Özal also presided over an important reform in the penal code, whereby Article 163, which forbade the use of religion for political purposes, was repealed. This reform created an anomalous situation. Although the constitutional ban on using religion for political activity remained, a key piece of secondary legislation with which the courts could prosecute active Islamists was thereby removed.[41] All this gave further impetus to the Islamic revival. Indeed, Özal's state funeral, held only the following year, was an astonishing sight, with groups of *tarikat* supporters openly performing a *zikir*, (lit. repeated, ritualized appeals to Allah) as his coffin procession passed them. Nevertheless, Özal is credited even by his enemies with bringing a dynamism to Turkey which had hitherto been absent. Many middle-class Turks today, however dismayed they were at his attitude to Islam, applaud still his intelligence, his ability to get things done and his grasp of international affairs.

The army and secularism
The complicated, and at times bewildering, intricacies of modern Turkish politics are watched over closely by the Turkish armed forces, above all the army, its senior service. From the outside, this close relationship is sometimes deplored, and has been put forward as one of the key reasons why Turkey has not been accepted by the European Union. Yet, it is often not realised by commentators just how very high the prestige of the army remains among the civilian population. Its role in the founding of the Republic is still vividly remembered. As a body, its officers are regarded as the most modern, professional, honest and co-ordinated group in the country, indeed almost the only part of the state that has not become corrupt. Whilst the universal male conscription that still obtains is cordially disliked by some youths, particularly those who are from wealthy backgrounds, the majority appear to look forward eagerly to the experience.

It is also often thought that the army made its interventions in order to act against Islam and to favour secularism. This is not quite as straightforward as it might seem. The army is committed to retaining the Republican heritage that it was left by Atatürk. This includes the secular constitution, and there can be no doubt that the army deplores religion being used to serve party political ends. However, this commitment to the Republic also includes a determination to maintain the nation's borders, and to protect the public order. However much the army despises politicians for mixing religion with government, it has been alive also to the possibility that orthodox belief may be used as a bulwark against communism (and the extent to which the army detests communism can scarcely be exaggerated). Further, the army believes that religion, if properly taught may act as a unifying force, and help to prevent sectarian, class, ethnic or political divisions among Turkey's citizens. For this reason, it has repeatedly decided that religion may in fact be a good thing if properly handled.

The third coup, that of 1980 perhaps illustrates this most clearly. Then, the political split between left and right developed to such a point that the government was paralysed. Neither side was able to achieve a majority, and as each side had recourse to alliances with smaller, more extreme parties to form a succession of coalition governments, the tension simply worsened. There were, notoriously, some two hundred violent deaths a month as people all over Turkey split between left-wing and right-wing political factions. Students and youths in particular split into large, marauding gangs and roamed the streets, beating up those who did not immediately identify themselves as being on their side. In a detailed, fascinating and vivid description to the lead up to the intervention, Birand describes how the killings gradually spread and escalated from becoming targeted assassinations to widespread, indiscriminate raids on coffee-houses, public meetings, market squares and shops. The economy collapsed. Turkey's NATO allies began to show open signs of disquiet. As the politicians continued to wrangle, the army meticulously planned its intervention.[42]

After it finally took control in a bloodless coup in 1980, the army's stated aim was to stop this unrest as soon as possible.[43] The generals appear to have done so through a combination of massive use of troops to prevent public demonstrations, legislation to outlaw political or trade union activity, taking over the administration of the country through the appointment of military governors, and condoning punishment, including torture, of extreme political groups, in particular the left. Although the harshness of their response was obviously disliked by many people, there was indisputably enormous initial popular general support for their intervention. This support waned throughout their period in power until it was at a low ebb by the time the elections in 1983 restarted the democratic process.

Before the military handed power back to civilians, it appears to have taken serious thought as to how such a scenario might be avoided in the future. It took various measures to do so, among them abolishing the upper house (senate) in order to remove blocks on the political process, pushing through a new constitution, creating a Higher Education Council (*YÖK*) in order to oversee university appointments above a certain level and perhaps most significantly, lending support to Islam through a doctrine sometimes known as the 'Turk-Islam synthesis'. Yavuz, an Islamic sympathiser, otherwise critical of the Kemalist reforms writes of this initiative: 'instead of showing a secular disregard for Islam [they] took several steps to strengthen it. The leaders of the military coup, ironically, depending on Islamic institutions and symbols for legitimization, and fusing Islamic ideas with national goals, hoped to create a more socially homogeneous and less politically active Islamic community.'[44]

In fact, the religion that they devised was still a fairly blunt tool, consisting of the familiar exhortations of Republican Islam, combined with appeals which were devised to encourage people of the Muslim faith to remain friends. Sermons, for example, from the mosque would stress the importance of good neighbourly relations among families within the same quarter (*mahalle*). In order to facilitate delivery of messages of this sort, those villages without mosques (and many Alevi villages at that time still did not have them) were 'encouraged' to build them, and to request state-trained *imam*s to be their prayer-leaders.

Until very recently, the leaders of the *coup* appeared to have been successful in preventing further political bloodshed, though the ethnic violence in the east that subsequently emerged has overshadowed this success. There have been quiet mutterings of revolutionary left

movements throughout the 1990s, though, and sadly, towards the end
of the decade clashes between politicised groups again flared up in
Istanbul University.

It is sometimes argued that the cost of these twenty years of peace
has been too high, that the army has played a highly significant role in
the subsequent success of Islam in the 1990s. It is difficult to be sure
of the causal role that it has played in this process, though it is
certainly the case that the drive towards more religious lessons and
installing mosques helped to create an ever more pervasive presence of
Islamic doctrine and practice in the public life of the country. This in
turn has helped to create an orthodox Islamic ethos upon which
activists can build for their own purposes. In the end, though, it is
perhaps best simply to conclude that the military have used the desire
for Islamic practice as a means of restoring civil peace, convinced that
they have the capability to restrain excessive zeal should that become
necessary.

Conclusions
In conclusion, Islam has been throughout the Republic at once an
enemy of the secular state, and yet a tool of social order, excluded
from the legislative apparatus of government, yet administered by the
civil service. This means that secularists have sometimes taken
succour from the fact that at least Islam is growing in a way that is
controlled by the existing legislation, and may claim that this
insurgence of belief is occurring within loyalty to Republican tenets.
Islamists may draw strength from the fact that in some aspects, their
campaign to restore Islam has been astonishingly successful. The
immediate answer as to *why* this has happened is straightforward:
there is not the slightest doubt that the re-Islamification is primarily
due to the intense desire of the mass of the Sunni people that the state
support religion. This in turn has led other groups, both in and outside
government, to avail themselves of its popularity for their own
purposes. Nevertheless, this does not tell us about the detailed
mechanisms by which this re-Islamification was brought about, and it
is to this that we now turn.

| 2 |

The Organisation of Belief

Whilst the desire on the part of the majority of the population that the state support their faith is a characteristic of the Islamic world (mass piety has crucially affected polity in countries as diverse as Algeria, Iran, Jordan, Morocco, Pakistan, and Saudi Arabia), the Turkish case has two striking aspects. A state which was predicated on the very premise that it would not be influenced by religion has, with the exception of the armed forces, embraced far more of its practice than it initially envisaged. Secondly, the transformation has, until now, been much less disruptive than one might expect. There are powerful sectors besides the army, among them the judiciary, many businessmen, branches of the civil service (notably the Ministry for Foreign Affairs), the established middle class, the political parties of a left-wing persuasion and, not least, the Alevis who are deeply opposed to the change, yet until very recently the rise of religion has not resulted in widespread civil unrest.

It is worth recalling the magnitude of the task initially facing those who favoured religion. At the founding of the Republic, Islam was blamed variously for Turkey's backwardness, for the loss of the Empire and even for the country's disastrous entry into the Great War. The party, government and inspired youth were absolutely convinced that rational organisation of the economy, education and culture (defined in the European sense as being good music, art and literature) was the key to the future. Not just this, Atatürk presented the Republican revolution as a package: nationhood was inextricably associated with republicanism and secularism. One without the other was simply unthinkable; you either took the whole deal, or nothing at all.[1]

How then was such a transformation achieved? And why has it been, until now at least, peaceful? The introduction of democracy must be part of any answer, but still only a part because it tells us little how the change in government affected and interacted with, the wider institutions of Turkish society, over which it had only varying degrees of control. I cannot give any definite explanation (indeed it would give a vastly spurious impression of the depth of our understanding of cause and effect in social change to do so),[2] but certain cultural and social factors can be shown to have favoured a peaceful incursion of Islam into the secular state. Turkish culture is resistant to head-on revolt, but susceptible to gradual reform by a person or movement building up influence slowly. In particular, by applying co-ordinated pressure, diverse groups may develop local spheres of patronage and policy within the bureaucracy which are not necessarily in ideological or political harmony with one another. Further, in seeking to influence the bureaucracy, believers have been able to avail themselves of a long-established arrangement that links the state and its citizens, whereby should a number of people require a certain project to be achieved they themselves first provide the land, capital and co-ordination for its founding, and the state may later take responsibility for its running. After the Democrat Party came to power, it authorised such arrangements for mosque construction, Koran courses and the newly founded *imam-hatip* schools. Much of this activity was channelled through legally constituted and approved associations (*derneks*) and trusts (*vakıfs*). Still today, these organisations often work together entirely legitimately with various state organs to develop Islamic worship and practice. Thus, the Turkish state does have great power, yet it may be amenable to pressure from those it administers.

Holiday haven versus terrible Turk
In Western Europe, Turkey has long had two distinct popular images. The first builds on the 'terrible Turk' of mythology, and regards it as a

country today bereft of human rights, possessed of a democracy only in name, and a state which is a heavy-handed oppressor. This view has received a great deal of publicity, particularly spurred on by the disastrous conflict in the east. Even in its weakest form it is vaguely hostile to Atatürk, implying that the army, the defender of Kemalism, is close to being the crusher of the will of the people.[3] It can be found also in wider circles. The wife of the late President Mitterand has been perhaps the most vociferous international advocate, though it emerges also in the European Parliament and in what remains of the British hard left, who occasionally attempt to impose boycotts of Turkish officials and Turkish activities in Britain.

Whatever merits this image may have when evaluating the question of the Kurdish minority, as a model for Turkey as a whole, it is clearly, even misleadingly, inadequate. Our immediate problem, the movement towards Islam, has demonstrated that there has been immense capacity within the system for the translation of belief into action. The Turkey of 1923 is simply not the Turkey of today, and one of the biggest changes is the successful re-incorporation of mass Islamic sentiment into society as a whole. On the question of religion, the government of Turkey is patently not the confrontational, inflexible force that this popular view of a reactionary state presumes. It sharpens our question simply by being so wide of the mark.

Alongside this condemnation of Turkey there is a view inspired in part by centuries of travellers' accounts in which Turkey is extolled as a fascinating country with a long history inhabited by a generous, hospitable people. In the nineteenth century, for example, this idea was caught precisely by the Lord Warkworth in his *Diary in Asiatic Turkey*.[4] Its spirit is carried on today by archaeologists, who perform a largely unacknowledged but massive contribution toward cultural links between Turkey and the West, by artistic periodicals (such as the beautifully designed *Cornucopia*) depicting the wealth of sensuous and vibrant worlds in both Istanbul and Anatolia, and it is reinforced for the wider public by the rosy hue of mass market holidays. In itself, of course, this image is too simple: though gloriously attractive in many ways, life in Turkey simply is not as easy as it implies. It does, though, capture something of the variety, warmth, generosity and spirit of the Turkish people and their readiness to enter into social interaction.

Each view is quite insufficient in itself. Yet neither is entirely wrong. Authority is strong in Turkey, as is the humanity, and readiness of so many people to create close personal links which may last a lifetime. Indeed, it is by reconciling these two points of view that the beginnings of a broad framework with which our problem can be approached will emerge.

Authority and the state

In Turkey, the state (*devlet*) has an over-arching quality which is traditionally absent from British society, closer perhaps to the French *état*.[5] It possesses the monopoly of legitimate violence and to many people it is the upholder of the moral values of the community, the leader, the guide, the keeper of order. It is also held to be rich, an infinite source of wealth: 'The state's wealth is an ocean, those who do not take from it are stupid' (lit. 'pigs': *devletin malı deniz, yemeyen domuz*) is a saying which can be heard from village to town. There is some foundation in this attitude in that the state is indeed the largest employer, employment within it is often affected by patronage, and in spite of the recent privatisations, it is responsible for more than half the economic output of the country, albeit usually at a colossal financial loss.

In recent decades, the state has lost a great deal of its attractiveness, both for employers and employees. The wages paid to civil servants are extremely small, and as the private sector expands, become comparatively even worse. The bureaucracy is clogged with clumsy, over-elaborate procedures and inflated by political appointments. Nevertheless, against the odds, there remains a residual respect for government and the state. In part, as a fascinating work by Buğra demonstrates,[6] this might be due to the fact that though state offices have largely devolved the successful production of wealth to the private sector, they have steadily resisted any relaxing of their control over the regulations which govern this wealth generation. In effect, this model suggests a separation of powers: that the private sector have to watch the bureaucracy ceaselessly to ensure that they do not get caught out by changes in the rules, whilst those in power remain modestly untouched by money, or perhaps sell themselves absolutely to no one faction or group of people.

Whatever the accuracy of this highly suggestive argument, there is no doubt that this rule-making power is backed up by the naked, direct coercive force still lying in the hands of the authorities: the police, the gendarmerie, the state courts, the constitutional court, the army and the other organs of the state. To defy these authorities openly is a dangerous game, risking a sharp reaction. Indeed, to deny authority at any level of Turkish society, with its insistence on order, is a highly risky activity: tantamount to a declaration of independence within the family, interpreted as a lack of loyalty in the work-place, and as enmity in the political arena.

On the other hand, this does not mean that what a person in authority says goes. Not at all. Whilst no one wishes his or her authority to be denied, it is fully realised that appearance is not the same as reality. If people pay lip service to the established patterns of behaviour, they have substantial freedom to pursue their chosen course of conduct, even if this may seem contradictory to the established edicts.[7] This is as true for political activity as it is for private life. Consequently, people seek to achieve their ends without necessarily making it apparent. They create contacts, make friends, lay the groundwork, exchange favours and find patrons who will help them behind the scenes. Their immediate aim is the ever so gradual accumulation of power among these contacts, and with its expansion, the achievement of their goal.[8]

One immediate result of this is that every action is seen as potentially long term. Even the smallest exchange of views, goods or services has the potential to develop into a reciprocity wherein mutually exchanged favours will benefit both parties over years, even generations, of gradually strengthening ties. This is such a strong ethic that only by the most stringent efforts can a person avoid being caught up in these exchanges, and then only selectively. Thus, a civil servant may refuse to accept hospitality in a strange village in the hope of avoiding requests for assistance when that villager comes to town, but they can hardly avoid entering into such an exchange when a close friend, relative or patron requests help.[9]

These requests, when used for a particularly significant favour – a job, contract or permit – are known as *torpil*, lit. 'torpedo' .Turks themselves occasionally claim that anything can be done with *torpil* and that without it their quest to solve a problem with the bureaucracy, to find a job, to obtain a visa, to avoid an unwanted transfer, to cope with the complex laws and tax which accompany any form of business activity, are all impossible. Again, whilst easy to exaggerate, there is some truth in this: the extensive contacts that persons build up during their professional lives mean that they can expect to establish influence to sort out the problems behind the scenes and in doing so widen the circle of people who are obliged to them. Exceptionally talented individuals may even grow in power throughout their retirement, even though they may have left formal office, as their fame as the founder of a particular movement, institution or discipline grows.

Imposing control
The readiness with which these patronage networks develop is strengthened by the nature of power in Turkish institutions. A person has the right and privilege to exert far more control over juniors than in other European countries. However, the person above him has the power to exert influence in turn.[10] This means that ministers do not shirk from political control of their ministries, general directors from similar control over their directorates, managers over their departments and so on. Consequently, all but the lowliest positions, because they may possess some power, are worth cultivating and may become drawn into the wider political process.

There are safeguards against the naked imposition of power. A person can attempt to use patronage networks just as effectively to defend his or her position as to gain one in the first place; civil servants are free to take their cases to court if they feel they have been sacked or transferred unfairly. There are ways around this in turn: rather than actually being sacked officials can be sent to a department where they have no influence, or no work to do (such as the common device whereby provincial governors (*valis*) may be appointed to advisory roles in Ankara away from their executive positions if they fall out of favour), or, in particularly stubborn cases, a new department may be created to take away a position's functions, whilst leaving the holder nominally undisturbed. Officials may also be transferred to a city or place where they have no desire to go.

The game of transfer and counter-transfer, move and counter-move can last for many years and victory go to a person in the end who has the most persistence. This type of drawn-out legalised (and legalistic) struggle is as typical for the highest in the land as it is for the lesser lights. A teacher in a secondary school once explained to me a detailed sequence of more than ten visits to different patrons (including a member of parliament, party chiefs, and officials of the Education Ministry Provincial offices), over a period of a year: first repeatedly to quash an unwanted transfer, and then to secure the one that he actually preferred. An academic acquaintance of mine had to negotiate patiently around obstacles placed in his way by political opponents for more than ten years before he was able to gain his chair.[11] Leading politicians, such as Demirel, Erbakan and the late Türkeş, have displayed throughout their chequered careers this combination of patronage, pertinacity and argument. It is illustrated also by Said-i Nursi in a complicated sequence of exile, imprisonment, exile, and further exile throughout much of his long life.

This intense interaction, in which personal contacts may be quite crucial to success in their professional and personal life, in the struggle with the bureaucratic and other obstacles placed in the way, is matched by a finely graded mutually acknowledged ranking system: a civil servant knows exactly when another person is superior, even when having to compare across professions or ministries.[12] This is true also in local government, and almost as true in the private sector. A corollary of this sensitivity to inter-personal ranking is that there are innumerable formal occasions when these fine gradings can be displayed, confirmed, re-defined and re-shuffled. Known colloquially as *protokol* almost every public concert, exhibition, visit, or event is marked by a *kokteyl*, and by having a number of seats set aside, in which only people in official positions, or who are known to people who have official positions, can sit.

Gaining power
One of the consequences of Turkey possessing this dominant but open bureaucracy, part of a huge concatenation of accumulated, cross-cutting, competing patronage networks, is that an important goal of

almost any movement or political party is to manoeuvre quietly, to build up strength over time, sometimes even over generations, in order to gain influence within the civil service. They may do this in different ways: most simply by calling in favours from friends. They may also attempt to influence the recruitment and examination process, or introduce pupils into the army or other specialist schools (such as the Political Science Faculty at Ankara University which traditionally has supplied provincial governors) who will later go on to be supportive of their cause. Religious movements, such as the *Süleymancılar* or the *Nurcular* are particularly known for this: they build hostels for poor children, help them to pass the state examinations, and later expect that they will be supported by them in turn and (as is illustrated in Chapter Three below), such activities may form part of a prosecution's case against them.

Political control has also to be seen in this double light. Of course, to win an election, to gain control of a ministry, to influence the legislative process is a key part of governing. In Turkey however, it is not the only, or even the most important, part. There is considerable momentum in Turkey's internal and foreign policy which is difficult to change in what might be only a brief time in office. Bargaining over coalition ministries is therefore less about the temporary ability to rule and rather more about the ability to gain direct control of the personnel who work in any ministry in order to push through as many specific projects as quickly as possible. Even if a party can do seemingly little openly, it may be acquiring substantial long-term influence through placing its supporters in positions of power, with whom, of course, the party will have to attempt to retain contact as best they can when again in opposition.[13] An example of this can be seen in that the Education Ministry was targeted by the National Salvation Party (*MSP*) when they were part of coalition governments in the 1970s. Later, after all political parties were banned after the 1980 *coup*, one of their most prominent members, Vehbi Dinçerler joined the newly-founded Motherland Party (*ANAP*), which came into power after the elections in 1983. Under Turgut Özal, Dinçerler returned to the Ministry of Education, even becoming its minister, and was able to build on the friendly supporters whom he had helped to put in place the previous decade. It is accepted that he was most effective in

pushing through religious reform, not least in his attempts to control
the content of school text books and their teachings on evolutionary
theory. [14]

Dividing the state

By virtue of this willingness to consider the various organs of the state
as bargaining counters, different areas of the bureaucracy may find
themselves targeted by particular groups or parties. They may also
find themselves following contradictory ideological paths. In practice
of course, different sections of the civil service may not admire, like or
condone what other parts are doing, but they have no obvious means
of stopping one other. In the coalition government between right and
left in the early 1990s, the Education Ministry, again under a
conservative minister, pursued a policy of leniency towards the *imam-
hatip* schools at a time when the Culture Ministry, under the
Republicans, wished heartily that they would simply stop giving
permission for more to be built. Likewise, however, religious activists
in the True Path Party wanted the Cultural Ministry to spend far less
on pre-Islamic research, and more on preserving Ottoman remains. It
was unable to enforce that desired policy because it had no direct
influence over the Cultural Ministry, other than trying to get their
budget cut, though it did manage to ensure that it suffered a
recruitment freeze. Distinct spheres of influence may be seen even
within ministries so that, for example, the Education Ministry
publishes text books which variously support a very secular
interpretation of Islam and others which have an activist interpretation
of the place of religion in the modern world. The possibility of this
sort of ideological bifurcation through different spheres of control
denoted by political influence is certainly one of the reasons why the
state has been able to accommodate Islam and secularism at the same
time.

Municipalities may also become drawn into these ideological
differences. Not only do they have large economic resources, but also
substantial control over the public spaces of the community which may
bring them into direct conflict with the government. There is a famous
and long-running case of this which began in the late 1970s when the
Mayor of Ankara, a member of the Republican People's Party (*CHP*),

and later a deputy in the National Assembly, authorised building a monument based on an early Hittite sculpture, one of the finest pieces in Ankara's Museum of Anatolian Civilisation. Religious conservatives felt that it was an idol, and therefore sinful. By virtue of their control of the Ministry of the Interior, they sent police in to stop it being built. The mayor, however, resisted their encroachment on the sculpture (supposedly by serving the police with trespass orders when they arrived to dismantle it) and was able to see the construction through. It has become Ankara's civic symbol, and remains today a powerful reminder of secularism in the centre of the city. In the 1990s, the situation reversed and the municipality was taken by the Welfare Party. Accordingly, as one of their initiatives, they tried to remove the symbol from the municipality's publicity, only to have their suggested substitute vetoed by the provincial governor as being overtly Islamic. The battle has been echoed in at least one provincial town to my knowledge, where local *CHP* supporters placed a copy of the statue in their town centre, less successfully this time as it was damaged during the night by Islamists.

Associations and trusts

Amidst the struggle against authority (and for power) through politics, manipulation and patronage there lies a further preoccupation, a widespread sense of the importance of co-ordinated, unanimous behaviour. This might be seen as a logical consequence of avoiding open confrontation: a person carefully seeks out those of like mind before making his or her position clear. It is more than this though. *Dayanışma*, literally 'mutual support', is an ideal in itself, regarded a social asset with any group, and, if lacking, to be restored as soon as possible. To be organised in a formal way, *örgütlenmiş*[15] is a similar and equally important concept, widely appreciated by anyone who is trying to achieve any particular aim. In a way, political parties are the prime and most powerful example of this, and indeed new political parties are opened regularly, far more so than in Britain. Equally important in bringing people together in a co-ordinated way are associations (*dernek*s), and trusts (*vakıf*s).

Both *dernek*s and *vakıf*s are voluntary organisations: they must possess an approved and agreed set of rules, and their running is overseen or inspected by government departments. Nevertheless, there is a slight difference between them. *Vakıfs* have a long history within Islam as pious foundations which existed to perform charitable deeds, to administer a specific trust or to look after a particular building. Such *vakıfs* could be extremely wealthy, and provided much of the income of the clerical class (*ulema*) in the Ottoman Empire. Aware of their power and riches, in the early nineteenth century the Ottoman government gradually confiscated all their assets, and formed a collective ministry for Sharia and '*Evkaf*', (the plural of *vakıf*). In 1924 the Republican government downgraded this ministry into two parts, forming the *Evkaf Umum Müdürlüğü*, now known as the *Vakıflar Müdürlüğü* (Directorate of Pious Foundations), and created the Directorate of Religious Affairs.[16] The *Vakıflar Müdürlüğü* is responsible for a wide range of buildings, some of great historical importance, and it publishes a journal illustrating the conservation and research that it is conducting.[17]

Today, the standard way to form a charitable trust remains a *vakıf*. In function they vary tremendously. They may simply support a library, or building of a famous figure. They may be vehicles for philanthropy for successful businessmen. They are also often linked to a wider organisation or political party. The Welfare Party runs an extensive chain of 'National Youth Trusts', *Milli Gençlik Vakıfları*, both in Turkey and abroad, particularly in Germany. Likewise, the Nakshibendi *Tarikat* possesses a large number of 'Righteous-Path' Trusts, *Hak-Yol Vakıfları*.

Whilst they may act in opposition to the state, *vakıfs* may be used also as direct support for a particular state department, and in doing so become closely integrated into its overall activities. The *Diyanet İşleri Vakfı*, the Religious Affairs Trust, which parallels and supports the activities of the Directorate itself, is a conspicuous example. Founded on 13 March 1975, the *Diyanet İşleri Vakfı* is now one of the largest in Turkey. In its constitution, its overall aim is described as follows: 'To make known Islam in its true essence, to enlighten the public on questions of religion, to support and help the Directorate of Religious Affairs, to build and furbish mosques where necessary, to open and to run foundations for the sick who are impoverished, to ensure alms that will come from our Muslim citizens go to those most in need.'[18]

One of the Trust's most prominent activities is to publish the Turkish Encyclopaedia of Islam (*İslam Ansiklopedesi*), but it also has an extensive programme of other publishing, infrastructural and aid projects. In 1993, it published a brochure giving a breakdown of these activities, including moneys dispensed, from which the table below is extracted. It can be seen that its means are substantial. The table illustrates that, in effect, the *Diyanet Vakfı* has become a means by which an active believer may have a direct input into the religious activity of the state; the larger their donation to the *Vakıf*, the more money can be spent on maintaining the Directorate's activities. Thus, whilst money does go to mosques and to the impoverished, the remaining funds are largely used for constructing the office buildings of the Directorate's personnel, for maintaining Koran courses which are under the Directorate's loose supervision, publications and for other similar activities. This conflation is reflected in the *Vakif* personnel also; its head is always the current head of the Directorate itself. Many of the civil servants in the Directorate also work in the *Vakıf*, further facilitating a close fusion of their activities.[19]

Table 2: Sample activities (with moneys dispensed) of the *Diyanet İşleri Vakfı* 1992-93.*

Activity	Approximate amount dispensed	
	1992	1993
	£	£
Contributions towards buildings including lodgings and schoolrooms for personnel of the Directorate of Religious Affairs	420,000	83,000
Aid for Mosque construction	6,000,000	6,570,000
Building *Müdürlük* headquarters	2,200,000	1,950,000
Aid for Koran courses	2,600,000	2,900,000
Grants for students	324,000	290,000

Table 2 cont.

Aid to *imam-hatip* schools	36,000	12,000
Encyclopaedia of Islam	1,700,000	1,900,000
Help for those in reduced circumstances	1,324,000	2,663,000

*Whilst the rate of inflation makes it both difficult to give conversions (and to be convinced of the accuracy of the statistics themselves), I give approximations in sterling based on the average exchange rate.

Derneks

A *dernek* is both easier to constitute and even wider in the scope that it may cover. Similar to the ubiquitous 'society' or 'association' in the West, it may have as its aim anything from chess, to sailing, or to building a school. Martin Stokes, in his fascinating monograph on the *Arabesk* movement, shows for example how *dernek*s are an essential part of the production of contemporary music, providing an organising framework for interested people to take lessons and practise together.[20] One of the prime uses of a *dernek* is that, once officially approved, its members may be given permission by the local sub-province governor to raise money for a particular cause by collecting from door to door. For this reason *dernek*s are also immensely popular among people with a specific project in mind such as a school building or a health centre. Like *vakif*s, they may often operate as the money-collecting branch of a state institution which otherwise may have inadequate resources. Nearly all the archaeological museums, for example, possess *dernek*s. Though they must return entrance moneys to the treasury, they are permitted to run a museum shop for the benefit of their *dernek*s. In this way, the large tourist museums (such as that in Antalya) may generate considerable sums of money which the museum is then free to use toward its upkeep.[21]

The use of the *dernek*s to promote religious activity has been demonstrated conclusively by Yücekök, in a piece of early research published by the Ankara Political Science Faculty as *The Social-Economic Foundations of Organised Religion in Turkey (1946-*

1968).[22] Having been given access to the records held at the Ministry of the Interior, he was able to show that there was a tremendous increase in associations formed with a religious purpose after Menderes came to power, and that this increase hardly slowed until end of the period covered by his research.[23] Within the 'religious' category, by far the largest was that of associations formed with a view to building or maintaining a mosque. (See *Table 3* below).

Table 3: Number of associations, *derneks*, founded with religious purpose.

Year	All *derneks*	Number of *derneks* with religious purposes	Religious *derneks* as % of total	Number of religious *derneks* aimed at building mosques
1946	825	11	1.3	8
1947	1072	27	2.5	23
1948	1403	58	4.1	53
1049	1736	95	5.5	88
1950	2177	154	7.1	142
1951	2546	251	9.9	226
1952	3351	406	12.1	361
1953	4422	598	13.5	538
1954	5412	809	14.9	740
1955	6887	1088	15.8	1003
1956	8630	2297	26.6	2199
1957	10111	2925	28.9	2803
1958	11960	3639	30.4	3483
1959	13613	4334	31.8	4098
1960	17138	5104	29.8	4821
1961	17482	5298	28.6	4993
1962	20065	5604	27.9	5220
1963	22002	6210	28.2	5677
1964	24180	6801	28.1	6133
1965	26677	7233	27.1	6370
1966	31051	8587	27.7	7259

Table 3 cont.

1967	34576	9745	28.2	7856
1968	37806	10730	28.4	8419

Figures taken from Yücekök (1971)

Today, Yücekök's early findings and comments remain highly relevant. Every year between 1500 and 2000 mosques are being built and opened to worshippers, so many that the Director of Religious Affairs periodically appeals to the Turkish population not to devote so many resources to their construction. Almost any mosque in the process of construction raises the great proportion of its costs from donations: part of these will be from prominent individuals, occasionally partly from the *Türkiye Diyanet Vakfı*, but the great bulk will come from local donations both in kind and cash. These donations are collected in the name of the *dernek* by supporters in the streets, by known religious figures who go from village to village appealing for timber, and by volunteers who visit shops and ask their owners if they may have, say, a tool free as an auspicious, *hayırlı*, gesture for the mosque. After the mosque is complete, the villagers (or district where the mosque is built) apply for a state *imam*, and hand over its running to the supervision of the state.

Opening imam-hatip schools
The same variable fusion of state and volunteer resources can be seen in the construction of *imam-hatip* schools, where *vakıf*s and *dernek*s play a prominent role in acting as vehicles to collect funds. The state rarely pays for their building costs, even less often for the land that they will be built on. Indeed, the real battle often begins after they have been built, when the school's supporters will have to fight strenuously to ensure that the state provides a full complement of teachers. This division between personnel and infrastructure obtained right from the outset. Reed, who published an article in 1956 describing their initial founding, writes:

> The Ministry of Education acts on the policy that no such school will be sanctioned unless a vigorous, responsible, formally organized group of local citizens first indicates its genuine interest in the new [*imam-*

hatip] school. They often purchase, or rent, a site for the proposed school... pay for equipment [and] help support needy students. The demand for religious training is so great in Turkey that the hard-pressed Ministry of Education may have to authorise the establishment of more such schools even when it is having difficulty finding suitable teachers for the existing schools.[24]

A more recent report published by the department of religious affairs in the Ministry of Education shows that such joint initiatives between citizen and state have continued to dominate the construction of the *imam-hatip* schools. In 1990, 248 such schools were paid for by *dernek*s and *vakıf*s, 76 through formal joint initiatives between the state and citizens. The construction costs were met solely by the state in just 37 cases. One of the reasons for the continuing success of such private initiatives is that if the costs are divided, it becomes relatively easy for politicians to open new *imam-hatip* schools.[25] They can quietly encourage permission to be given for their construction, and then put pressure on the Ministry of Education to set up teaching posts, *kadro*, for them. In doing so, their support, whilst highly significant, can be channelled unobtrusively through the existing state budget.

It is important to reiterate that in making the citizens pay for the building, and even running costs, of the religious schools and mosques in this way, the state has not introduced an innovatory method for the incorporation of its citizens into its activities. Normal school buildings, for example, in village Turkey were, and are today, commonly built by the villagers themselves. In the area where I first researched, the villagers built a middle school by first donating the land, then collecting the costs of its construction from guest workers in Germany. They were fond too of telling a wry story from the first years of the Republic, when no village as yet had a school building, saying that the sub-province governor called all the village heads in his jurisdiction into his office one day. The governor explained that the state could afford to pay for the running costs and teacher for a primary school in just one village. He had decided to allocate this slender provision to the village that built its school building the quickest. Immediately, the village I stayed in built an appropriate structure, working night and day. They did not win the race, though ultimately a school was opened in their village.[26]

That such an arrangement should already be present in principle reflects a fact that occurs repeatedly in the history of the rise of Islam in Turkey. The basic administrative structures of the state dominate people's lives, but the procedures through which citizens may gain access to them are established and understood by those trying to use them. If there is no overt legal impediment to a particular course of action, then obtaining state support for one's particular project becomes a matter of influence and pressure. That the project happens to have a religious base makes it more emotive, and politically sensitive, but the mechanisms by which such a project may be attained are not qualitatively different from any others; a group of people go about opening a new museum for their province in precisely the same way as they would an *imam-hatip* school. The state, through such joint initiatives, becomes almost an endlessly expandable legitimising force that can be drawn upon by different groups to pursue their particular aims.

Government and associations

Those in power have themselves been prepared to make use of the capability of associations to become vehicles for religious thought. During the first Democrat period, after 1950, fear of communism and of the Soviet Union was at its height. The Democrat Party frequently argued at that time that religion was useful as a safeguard against communism developing in Turkey.[27] This reflected feeling in the army as well, which supported the formation of a chain of *derneks* known as the 'Associations Against Communism', *Komünizmle Mücadele Dernekleri*. These explicitly used Islamic ideology to combat the growing left-wing movement, and provided counter-demonstrations when needed. Towards the build up of the second military intervention in 1971, tension grew over the visit of an American flotilla in Istanbul, which was vehemently opposed by left-wing anti-NATO groups. On 14 February 1969, a predominantly left-wing march clashed with the Association Against Communism in Istanbul. Violent remonstration between them led to two dead and many wounded.

After the 1980 coup, the generals forbade all *dernek* activity claiming that they were a contributory cause of the violent instability at that time. Though they have since been permitted to reopen, there is today a substantial body of *dernek* law, available through the stationers, which in theory at least any prospective *dernek* organisation has to follow. The *derneks* can never be quite free of political implications, as shown in the case of one of the most successful of recent *dernek*s (discussed below in Chapter Five), which is devoted to Atatürk's thought, *Atatürkçü Düşünce Derneği.* When it was in the process of being founded, the Welfare Party attempted to use its influence with the Ministry of the Interior to close it down, only for it to be successfully supported by senior figures in the army. With the exception of this type of internal power struggle, and outside the period of military rule, *dernek*s appear to operate free from official interference.[28]

Such institutions are sometimes known collectively to sociologists as 'civil society' – organised groups administered by authority but comparatively independent in their daily running. There is controversy both theoretically and practically over this issue: Hann, for example, in a recent publication points out that the term has become used too diffusely for useful analysis,[29] whilst specialists on Turkey sometimes point out that the number of associations in Turkey as against comparable institutions in the West is so small as to indicate a lack of 'civil society'. Whilst both these points are entirely justified, the residual importance of the *dernek*s and *vakıf*s in Turkey is quite clear, and the term is a useful reminder as to their possible purpose.[30] They are a way that people can organise themselves, availing themselves of the laws of the state for their own (and other people's) protection, but used in order to influence the state in a peaceful way.[31] Of course some Turks are sharply opposed to the secular Republic, but others, the majority, do not necessarily oppose the state directly: rather they are changing it, expanding its sphere in ways that they find appropriate.[32]

Whilst the absence of recent figures of *dernek* activity makes it difficult to estimate their importance, I would suspect that one of the reasons that such societies appear to play rather a lesser role in Turkey than other countries is because they are often so tightly focused. There may indeed be fewer clubs or associations dedicated to hobbies or sports, but a great proportion of the existing *derneks* concentrate directly and openly on the sensitive areas of the state's institutions and on religion, and therefore have an effect rather disproportionate to their apparently low number. Yücekök's early work certainly supports this contention, when he notes that in 1968, religiously oriented *derneks* formed 28.4 per cent, or 10,730 of the total (37,806) of *derneks* registered at that time, and by far the largest single category.[33]

Conclusions

I suggest that the relationship between the state and citizen in Turkey is complex: distant and hierarchical in that there is no doubt that the state carries great authority, yet that very same state is more open to a wider variety of influences than is commonly realised. The diffuse nature of power within Turkish institutions, widespread patronage, and powerful civil associations like the *Diyanet İşleri Vakfı*, have all combined with the introduction of democracy to help effect the reintroduction of religious practice into the body politic.

This is only part of the story. The political parties, clubs, societies and trusts mentioned so far, are the legal face of this initiative. They may become influenced by less approved bodies. Some Koran courses were, and are, held and run unofficially, with no recourse to permission or sanction. After the foundation of the Republic, those who disagreed with the official formulation of religion often had recourse to an Islamic brotherhood or *tarikat*, also soon made illegal. Some of these have become focal points for rethinking Islamic ideals in the secular Republic. In order to convey their message to the outside, they have extensively founded trusts and associations as their public face. In developing ideologies based on Islamic practice, they are likely to conflict with official policy, though unless they actually attract the attention of the state prosecutor, they may still be permitted to function. Thus, trusts and associations may become surrogate means by which the *tarikat*s may organise themselves nationally and internationally. This controversial area, along with the moves that the state has made to impede their rise, is the subject of the next chapter.

| 3 |

Tarikats, Belief and the State

The role of the *tarikat*s, and their influence on the affairs of the Republic, are among the most hotly debated of all questions, by Islamists and secularists alike. Broadly defined, a *tarikat* is a number of believers united by the respect that they show for a particular person or lineage, whom they regard as different from other human beings by virtue of their being favoured by God. *Tarikat* literally means 'way', and followers of a particular *tarikat* may hold strongly that the teachings of their founding figure are the appropriate path to achieve union with God. A *tarikat* may also have a complex internal organisation, and long initiation requirements in order to gain admittance. This hierarchical, often exclusive, configuration contrasts with worship at a mosque, where though the *imam* is the prayer-leader, he is in no way qualitatively different from the other male worshippers, and worship itself is open to all male believers.

The two positions mark a radically different way of organising and transmitting Islamic ideas. The *tarikat* approach presumes an immanent God, or at least one that may be reached from within or through a person. The more orthodox position holds that God is transcendent, beyond the reach or comprehension of believers. Strict upholders of orthodoxy may therefore regard *tarikat*s as being heretical, guilty of the sin of *şirk* (polytheism, or assuming that God may have equal partners). Part of the conflict derives also from the fact that these two approaches can become so very marked in their orientation towards central rule: within the Ottoman Empire, the orthodox clergy, the *ulema*, sought to take control through their proximity to the governing power, whilst the *tarikats*, with their charismatic leader and mobile followers often became a focus for rebellion and direct assault on the centre.[1]

In practice, *tarikats* were, and are, immensely varied, in structure, in the type of Islam they practise and in the social function that they fulfil. Sometimes, leadership is passed on from teacher to pupil by his authorisation; on other occasions, membership of a particular patrilineage may confer sacred distinction on all males within it. Usually, but not always, in those *tarikats* in which such descent and kinship play such a large part in defining sanctity, the holy lineages are not just teachers of doctrine but also mediate between disputes at different levels within the society: between lineages, families or even members of households. In Ottoman Anatolia, mobile holy figures frequently drew in displaced people from the surrounding countryside, forming bands of bandits which plagued travellers, whilst before their closure in 1928, *tarikats* in urban areas tended to be more intellectual, often powerful groups of Islamic thinkers based around a particular place of worship.[2]

This flexible organisation which could make *tarikats* centres of ideological dissent in the cities, the organising principle of rural unrest in the countryside, and, when linked with the tribal forces of the east, formidable military opponents, explains some of the vehemence and firmness with which they were condemned by Atatürk. Indeed, there seems to be no doubt that during the initial Republican reform period, the law to close them down along with the monasteries and tombs with which they were associated was actually carried out with extreme rigour. Later, very large and famous *tekke*s, such as that in Konya and that at Hacıbektaş were turned into museums. The less obtrusive structures in the countryside were abandoned or dismantled if it was felt they might become a seed-bed of opposition.

The ban on *tarikats* is still in theory in place today. Much to the frustration of left-wing secularists, it is not applied rigorously (indeed to do so would mean putting a very great many people in jail), but it has nevertheless profoundly altered the way that the *tarikat*s operate.

The vast majority of the permanent open centres of belief, the *tekke*s, remain closed. As the Republican administrative infrastructure expands, the mediating role of the *tarikat*s has diminished (though among the tribes in the east it still continues to some extent, as it does among the Alevis).[3] Instead, in appropriating the means of celebrating Islam through mosque and cleric, the Republicans have encouraged the *tarikat*s to become networks of what might be termed alternative orthodoxy, a refuge for those people who wish to reverse the reforms through more strict adherence to Holy Law (*şeriat*). Accordingly, whilst *tarikat*s vary tremendously in the intellectual position that they may take,[4] the mystical, esoteric, expressive aspect of their worship has diminished. Those *tarikat*s that now most flourish in the Republic are those which reject the extravagant rituals for which they are known in other parts of the Islamic world and maintain the importance of orthodox worship.

This can be illustrated most easily perhaps by contrasting two of the most famous *tarikat*s in Turkey, the Mevlevis and the *Nakşibendi*s. The home of the Mevlevi is in Konya at one of the most spectacular *tekke* and *türbe* complexes in the country known as the *Mevlana Türbesi*. From this *tekke*, members of the Mevlevi exerted considerable intellectual and temporal influence. The works of their founder, *Celaleddin Rumi*, were known very widely, and have provided a focus of study for generations of oriental scholars in the West.[5] They themselves developed complex economic ties with the local communities, owning and administering part of the surrounding countryside. Famously, in the Gallipoli campaign during the First World War, they had sufficient members to provide a regiment of their own.[6] After the suppression of the *tarikat*s, the Mevlevi *tekke* was closed, and later turned into a museum. Today, their whirling dervish dance is again permitted, but as a tourist attraction. The groups who perform are employed as civil servants attached to the Ministry of Culture as dancers and tour internationally. In Konya each year their dance officially takes place during the course of a festival week only. Much to the puzzlement of the assembled tourists, the performance takes place only after the most elaborate introductory *protokol* speeches, locating the event squarely within the Republican tradition.

In today's Konya, the esoteric, quiescent Mevlevi philosophy is as popular as ever. Nevertheless, in spite of this resurgent popularity, the role of the *tarikat* in spreading Rumi's ideas has become increasingly slight. The *tekke* itself, with its distinctive green tower, has become one of the most visited attractions in Turkey, with half a million foreign tourists a year. A similar number of local people, among them many women, visit also, to pray and to make vows. Rumi's sayings appear on notices and are printed on souvenir items, such as plates, throughout the city. His doctrines are passed on by word of mouth and by his publications obtainable at the museum and many small book-shops. They are reinforced by the adoption of the whirling dervish image as the civic symbol of the city, so that dervishes in mid-dance are depicted everywhere, on street signs, on souvenir items, and sold as trinkets.[7] This supremely successful commercialization of the *Mevlana* museum and Mevlevi ideas means that any organisational role of the *Mevlevi* brotherhood itself appears unimportant.

Contrast this with the Nakshibendi *Tarikat*, whose role in the Republic has recently been outlined by one of the most important of their interpreters, Professor Hamid Algar. The Nakshibendis have long played a role in Anatolia, and gone through a succession of revivalist movements in the nineteenth and early twentieth century. Unlike the Mevlevis, however, they have no centre of worship in Turkey. They are required to be close to the spiritual authority of the sheikh wherever possible, but have no need for extensive ritual. Their *zikir*, evocation of God, is silent, inward-looking, with no ostensible display. Their role within Islam is far more orthodox than that of the Mevlevis, in that they insist on the fulfilment of the *şeriat*, the establishment of religious temporal rule, as a prerequisite to any further religious experience. All this makes them an ideal repository for orthodox opposition to the secular state. Algar writes:

> There can be no doubt that the Naqshibendis have withstood the pressure of the Republican period more successfully than any other *tarikat*. The Naqshibendis, however, were particularly able to dispense with *tekkes*, performing neither the ritual dance of the Mevlevis nor the spectacular feats of the Rifa'is, they have had no

essential need for a ritual structure in which to perform the silent dhikr that is their central and distinctive practice.[8]

Unlike the Mevlevis, the Nakshibendis have, if anything, increased in importance since the Republic. They number among their members leading politicians such as the late Turgut Özal (who arranged for his mother to be buried in a Nakshibendi cemetery). They also played the formative role in the founding of the *Milli Nizam Partisi*, the religious party with which Erbakan first enjoyed success in the political arena, and dominated its successor, the *Milli Selamet Partisi*. Through their leader, Professor Coşan, they have built up an extensive network of trusts and publications, particularly the periodical *İslam*. All in all, they enjoy considerable indirect influence, perhaps the only one of the pre-Republican *tarikat* groups to do so.

The Nurcus

One of the most successful of all Islamic revivalist movements in Turkey, indeed the only one to rival the Nakshibendis, has been the loose group of followers of Said-i Nursi, known as the *Nurcu*s. Estimates of numbers are tremendously difficult to make with any confidence, but journalists' impressions are that active sympathisers in the late 1990s number several million. The *Nurcu*s claim not to be a *tarikat*, and point to the fact that they have no initiation, or formal relationship between sheikh and follower. The wisdom of such an orientation is clear: it helps to avoid the condemnation of the state on the one hand, and the possible accusations of heresy from orthodox believers on the other. It also helps them to remain close to everyday social life. Nevertheless, they do have some internal organisation, and their early history, their veneration of Said-i Nursi, and later expansion are all characteristic of *tarikat* movements. It is perhaps best therefore, to consider the *Nurcu* movement as striking an innovative mid-way point between the traditional *tarikat,* with its esoteric knowledge and exclusive membership, and the broader Islamic community: pragmatically as exploiting many of the advantages of a *tarikat* organisation (such as a close-knit group of sympathisers) but without those explicit aspects which are most likely to draw upon it the open wrath of the authorities.

Said-i Nursi was born of a Kurdish family in Bitlis, in the east in 1876, and died in Urfa in 1960.[9] Whilst his career has been the subject of an immense amount of hagiographic writing, he has also been considered in a brilliant sociological essay by Şerif Mardin.[10] In summary fashion, it is possible to divide his life into two parts. During the first, he travelled widely, and searched for a position of influence in the state through which he could implement his ideas. Thus, in 1907, he petitioned the Sultan for a university to be built in the east. Though failing in this he became active in different political spheres, founding a society for Islamic thinkers. As the political situation deteriorated, he continued to lobby for his university (which was never built), and also began to support the Young Turks, justifying his alliance with them on the grounds that they were best placed to protect the remnants of the Empire.

After the War of Independence, he supported the Republic at first. However, as its secularist reforms became clear, he began a life of studious opposition, relinquishing political involvement, but continuing to write prolifically. He was arrested, tried and exiled several times until 1950. Released on the Democrat Party gaining power, he was tried again, though acquitted. Living and working under supervision in various locations, he still travelled occasionally, and it was during one such trip that he died. Now, the movement is as popular as ever: as well as the largest group headed by Fethullah Gülen, there are also several splinter groups with identifiably different doctrinal positions.[11]

Crucial to Said-i Nursi's religious philosophy is patience and the avoidance of armed conflict among Muslims. He regards the task of believers today is to prepare for a coming leader who, benefiting from the more auspicious circumstances of the time, will be able to achieve more than they are at present able to do. He identifies distinct stages in this endeavour. Mardin explains them as first: people must lead their lives in such a way as to strengthen faith. Second: when they become sufficiently strong, they must apply the *şeriat*. Third: they should aim eventually for the unification of the Islamic world.[12] A later interpretation of *Nurculuk* identifies three stages also, though rather differently as: *iman* (faith), *hayat* (life), and finally *şeriat*.[13] The precise names are perhaps unimportant. It is the gradualness which is so crucial, in that it permits his supporters to pursue the conventional outlets of Islamic activity, to deny that they are advocating the implementation of the *şeriat* now, whilst at the same time hoping that ultimately success will be forthcoming.

In practice, this gradualism expresses itself in two main ways, the first being through the media. Said-i Nursi possessed a profound understanding of the importance of the mass media for his message. Indeed, a newspaper that he founded, *Yeni Asya*, became the focal point for his supporters throughout Turkey. He also concentrated on youths with a view to obtaining their future support. To this end, he organised educational camps with strict discipline, provided cramming schools, and helped them through examinations with the aim of enabling them to assume places of importance in the bureaucracy. Today, other *tarikat* groups do this also (notably the *Süleymancılar*): the *Nurcu*s, however, do it particularly well. The key to the technique is to select bright, but poor children, whose success lies in their succeeding in public examinations by virtue of the extra, private (but free) tuition they have received from *Nurcu* sympathisers. In this way, by welcoming these *protégés* into its midst, the state becomes the architect of its own transformation.

On the question of open political engagement, the *Nurcu* movement is divided. Though Nursi denied the possibility of interaction with the regime, seemingly on the grounds that it was more profitable initially to build up the general activity of believers, he did welcome Menderes' coming to power, sending him a telegram of congratulation in 1950. He seems also to have followed the political situation closely from afar, and according to one of his supporters, as pressure from the military was mounting, urged Menderes to declare an Islamic Republic before it was too late. Whilst Menderes did not do this, later followers have often continued to work with the Justice Party, and then the True Path Party under Demirel and later Çiller. In doing so, they appear to have been attracted to the idea of working industriously, both spiritually and materially, but without violence, through a party that remained sympathetic to the extension of Islamic practice. In turn, these later politicians have been able to turn a blind eye to the declared long-term ambitions of their movement. The state prosecutors, however, have not always been as sanguine, and it is clear that different organs of secularism, such as the army and the police have kept detailed watch upon them, occasionally bringing them to trial.

The Nurcus on trial

The succession of court cases that Said-i Nursi underwent during his lifetime illustrates the intelligence, even the genius, of his position. There is not the slightest doubt that he would have welcomed the destruction of the Republic and the establishment of a pan-Islamic community based on the *şeriat*. Yet, it proved astonishingly difficult for a legal consensus to be reached. His personal sobriety, eschewal of violence, disdain of material gain and indisputable piety influenced many people he met. His desire to suppress, rather than encourage, armed conflict, and his repeated affirmation that he was not forming a *tarikat* meant that he could at least defend himself against the obvious charges of subversion that might be brought against him. He was aided in this too, by the elliptical way in which he wrote, which meant that what might be obvious to the reader might be difficult to prove legally. Finally, his call for people to study religion within the framework of the existing order appealed to many people who felt that the secularism of the Republic had gone too far.

The fact remains, however, that his philosophy is hostile to the Republic's constitution, and it is instructive to examine the authorities' reaction to his movement. Early writers, such as Tunaya, before it became clear to them just how successful Nursi was to become, were critical and dismissive as they would be today with less subtle, and far more aggressive *tarikat*s such as the *Aczmendi*.[14] Today, the reaction of the authorities is more reasoned. It appears to be that, to the extent that being a *Nurcu* constitutes no more than pious worship, they make no difficulties. The authorities do not seek to restrict the circulation of the *Nur Risaleleri*, his corpus of works. However, they do attempt to keep a close watch when groups of *Nurcu*s begin to confront the secular system in a systematic way. In this case, studying or proselytizing Nursi's philosophy can be held against such groups as an indication of their subversive intent. The trial deposition below, taken from a case which took place in 1985/6, gives an insight into this process.

The prosecutors' statement opens with an account of Said-i Nursi's

Nur Risaleleri, claiming that he rejects Turkish nationalism, wishes to found an Islamic state with its centre in Mecca and its language Arabic, regards the nation as having no need for a constitution other than the Koran and its secular rules as transient.[15] The prosecutor adds that Said-i Nursi wishes to ban the present banks, to forbid charging interest, and to dismantle the modern system of courts of law. He also emphasises Nursi's Kurdish ancestry, and accuses him of wishing to form a distinctive Kurdish community. Finally, he notes the laws that all these activities controvert. The defendants (named and drawn from Istanbul, Izmir, and other towns in Anatolia) are specifically charged with:

> Various activities aimed at spreading the ideas of *Nurculuk* in the nation as a whole, ultimately with the purpose of obtaining yet more followers. In order to obtain people who will later take jobs in key positions, they created ties with successful final-year middle-school pupils, children of a convenient age to be influenced by their ideals. They took these final-year school pupils and gave them free tuition, turning apartments into cramming schools. They used university students already members of the *Nurcu* movement as teachers, so that these successful school pupils would pass the entrance examinations to the science-based and military lycées. During these courses, separately from the academic teaching, they gave lessons in religion, performing the *namaz*, and explaining from time to time Said-i Nursi's *Nur Risaleleri*.

The prosecution sums up its case:

> Thus the ideas of the *Nurcus* were beginning to be inculcated, along with arguments against the present regime and praise for the *şeriat*. Some of the pupils about to sit the examinations were conducted personally to them by members of the *Nurcus*. All their accommodation and subsistence costs were met by the *Nurcus*. When a student had been successful in the military examinations, they used all means at their disposal to ensure that they did not fail the health checks, including replacing their identity photographs on the relevant papers. When these students began their studies at the

Izmir Maltepe Army Lycée, they took them in groups of four and five to selected places in Izmir, gave them food and drink, and showed them videos and other computer games in order for them to pass the time pleasantly. They then showed them videos of religious subjects which favour the *şeriat*. Even in their summer holidays they left them no free time. They took them to summer camps on the seaside and even taught them there... In this way they pursued their activities aimed at indoctrinating pupils secretly into the *Nurcu* movement.

The defence did not rebut the factual description offered by the prosecution, but replied to the charges individually. They maintained that they were motivated by hospitality, that they had no intention of reading the *Risale-i Nur* in a way that could be construed as being hostile to the state. They rejected the charge of being a *tarikat* or attempting to recruit followers in any formal way, saying that, as the *Nurcu*s have no initiation procedures, they could hardly be accused of attempting to find acolytes, otherwise when 'any two people come together there would be a *Nurcu* group'. They stressed that, since 1965, variable decisions had been made by the Republican courts as to the propriety of the *Risale-i Nur*, and that there was no indication in the prosecution's case anyway of exactly which passages had supposedly been read. During the trial, the prosecution countered this defence with varied evidence of systematic organisation, including photographs taken by the National Intelligence Service (*MİT*), and detailed witness' statements.

In his summing up, the judge reaffirmed that the constitution of the Republic demanded a separation between the laws of the land and matters of religion. He emphasised that individual religious freedom demands that the state itself remains independent of religion. He pointed out that it was absolutely clear that the defendants were attempting to contravene this separation. With regard to sentences, of the large number of accused. some were released through lack of evidence or by virtue of their youth. Others were fined. Several, who were drivers or chauffeurs by profession, were deprived of their driving licences for a certain period. Others were sentenced to a few months and, those regarded as the ringleaders, to between four and six years in gaol.[16]

In spite of this high-profile case, and others similar concerning the activities of the *Süleymancılar* and of the *Fethullahçılar*,[17] the prosecution service has not attempted to obtain a blanket repression of *Nurcu* activities. The Directorate of Religious Affairs maintains its high profile, the army writes continuous and detailed reports on the activities of the brotherhoods' followers, the secularist basis of the Republic is reaffirmed continuously, but the overall level of Islamic activity continues to mount. The seeming inability of the civil process to control the sheer extent of the Islamic inclinations of the mass of the people has led to intense frustration among secularists, who are forced to witness the piecemeal Islamification of the public social life of the nation.

Sacrificial remnants

To give one example of many. An increasingly controversial question is the right to collect and exploit the skins of the sacrifices after the Annual Feast of Sacrifice (*Kurban Bayramı*). At the outset of the Republic, the Turkish Air Foundation, the charitable arm of the Turkish Air Force, was endowed with the right to gather these pelts in perpetuity. They base their appeal on *zekat* and *fitre,* the giving to charity which is one of the five pillars of Islam. Whilst initially, it appears that most people were content to tolerate this concatenation of state and religion, throughout the 1980s, there came a slow fall in the number of skins that the Turkish Air Foundation received.

In 1992, the law was tightened up. The sole right of the Turkish Air Foundation to collect money was reaffirmed, and the money thus gained split between 45 per cent for the Turkish Air Force, 5 per cent for the *Diyanet Vakfı*, with the remaining 50 per cent divided between three different charities. In spite of this new regulation, the number of skins collected by the Turkish Air Foundation remains far less than they would like. The following often choleric quotations illustrate this:

From a directive from the Denizli governor, 10 May 1993:

It has been forbidden [by law] for individuals and institutions except for the Turkish Air Foundation to collect sacrificial pelts and intestines or annual alms [*fitre zekat*]. Announcements (hand-written notices, distributing envelopes, advertising in the press or media, posters and bills and so on) by people or institutions other than the Turkish Air Foundation... are also against the law.

That is why, in order that there be no cause for mistakes during the 1993 sacrifice period, I request firmly that citizens are informed of these facts during the sermons to be given in the mosques, that the attempts to collect the skins are unimpeded in any way, and that officials are given any support that they need.

From a letter from the Denizli Turkish Air Foundation, 14 June 1993:

> In spite of all the precautions taken by our office, from an estimated 60,000 sacrifices in the province of Denizli, only 8,300 skins were collected. Just as in 1992, as a result of active and widespread activity by individuals and institutions other than the Turkish Air Foundation, 52,000 sacrificial skins were collected illegally, representing a [great] loss of KDV [Value Added Tax] to the state. [The writer goes on to suggest that the accounts of all *derneks* and *vakıfs* be examined in order to locate the culprits.]

From a letter from Turkish General Headquarters of the Turkish Air Foundation to the Under-Secretary of State in the Ministry of Finance, 27 August 1998:

> If we take 1992 as an example, the Turkish Air Foundation was able to collect hardly 20 per cent of the sacrifices. The remaining sacrificial skins and intestines, that is about 3,000,000, were collected by people, *derneks* and *vakıfs* who were not entitled to do so (such as camps, Associations for the Assistance of Pupils to attend School and Courses, for Constructing and Maintaining Mosques, for Constructing and Maintaining Schools, Sports Clubs, *Akyazılı Vakfı* [a *vakıf* run by Fethullah Gülen], *Milli Gençlik Vakfı* [the main *vakıf* of the Welfare Party], *Server Gazi Vakfı* and others. In this way, approximately 200 billion Turkish liras [very approximately £20 million] have gone to extremist

religious groups, to the PKK in the east, and to the Hizbullah [terrorist extremist Islam]. This is a fact that will have been noted by the Ministry as well as shown by the documents in our possession.

The battle for people's minds

Part of the intense frustration shown by the secular authorities stems from genuine puzzlement that the Republican reforms have not been more respected as a serious attempt at religious reform. This claim to be a movement from within Islam might seem surprising, but in certain aspects it is justified, and its defenders are quite serious in their claim. Both Kemalism and many reform movements wish to rid religion of intermediaries between God and believer, insist that the Koran is the paramount manifestation of God's message, and that worship in the mosque is the only appropriate collective outlet for religious expression. Orthodox believers often act directly against the *tarikat*s, accusing them of heresy. Both Kemalism and orthodox Islam attack alternative 'folk' Islamic practices: worshipping at tombs of saints, belief in the healing power of holy men or their relics, acceptance of miracles, or writing charms. The connection is made quite explicitly by Yorukan, a Professor in the Faculty of Theology, in a work on Islam published first in 1957, and reprinted by the Directorate of Religious Affairs in 1961, when he (without any irony whatsoever) draws support from Saudi Arabia in his commentary on Republican measures:

> Today, we must learn what is really part of our religion, discard what is not, fight against bigotry, ignorance and laziness, and take a path that will improve the nation. This is the duty of every Muslim...To nurture a *tarikat* is above all against the law. As well as this, it leads the nation to laziness, a love of bigotry, and the people to ignorance. Virtuous and wise people, those who are sensible, do not become involved with such things. This is not asceticism, it is not esoteric knowledge. To become bound to a sheikh, to enter a dervish order, to interpose the sheikh as a vehicle between the supplicant and God, to congregate in secret is to leave the common road and to enter a community apart. Esoteric

knowledge is a personal matter, it is psychological, not
sociological, it cannot be attained in such a community. To lead a
separate path, to give oneself to another person, has been forbidden
by the Koran.
In some Muslim nations there are no sects or *tarikats*. In Saudi
Arabia to proclaim a sect or *tarikat* is forbidden, and they expel
members of *tarikats* from the country... To set oneself apart from
religion is forbidden and the penalty severe.[18] [in a footnote on
same page]

A similar idea was put forward by a general at the time of the 1971
coup. As a plea for orthodoxy, it is as harsh and as firm as anything
proclaimed by an impassioned cleric.

> Atatürk, without a doubt, was respectful of religious sensibilities
> and beliefs, and appreciated the importance of religion more than
> anyone else. I have examined each of Atatürk's revolutionary acts
> one by one, each of them, and compared them with the sayings of
> our Prophet and the knowledge imparted in the Koran. I have
> attempted to show how he rescued our religion and brought it
> salvation, Atatürk has fulfilled the commands of the Prophet better
> than any other. Where in this is anything contrary to religion?
> Atatürk did not destroy our religion in accepting secularism. On the
> contrary he had the foresight to pass the business of religion to the
> Prophet's true house [*ehli-beyt*]. Atatürk performed a service to
> religion by cleansing it of those who through practicing sorcery
> were rushing into heresy. Come, see how those who blow on the
> sick [claiming to cure them] and write charms call Atatürk an
> infidel! If we want to save Atatürkism and the poor wretches who
> fall into the maelstrom ideologies of the Maoists, Castroites,
> Marxists, Leninists, Rightists, Leftists, *Nurcus*, *Süleymancıs*, and
> so on, the one and only explanation of Atatürkism must be spread
> from the pulpits of the mosques and the lecterns of the schools.[19]

Modernisation and Islamic belief

This overlap between reformist Islam and Kemalism has been
important. It has been the foundation upon which those who have

embraced the Kemalist revolution defend it as being a reform, rather than an anti-religious movement.[20] It means that at least some of those who work for the Republican religious institutions can feel that they are behaving according to the tenets of Islam. It also means that persons and groups who are against the reforms, such as the *Nurcus* or the *Nakşibendis* can nevertheless co-operate with the state to build mosques, print copies of the Koran and increase faith as a partial step towards ultimate fulfilment. In doing so, it both gives them hope that ultimately they will be able to change the regime, and also satisfaction that they are doing their best in difficult circumstances.

Why then, have the reforms only partially persuaded part of the population? This is not quite such a clear-cut question as it might sound. To assert simply that people have always wanted the *şeriat* is quite wrong. Whilst it is now becoming an important issue, at the founding of the Republic, the vast mass of the people of Turkey, then largely rural, had little conception of holy law, and disliked intensely having interaction with government courts, whether religious or otherwise.[21] Further, Turkey is a profoundly ordered country still, and many people are often quite prepared to come to differing degrees of religious accommodation with the secular authority, as the Tappers have stressed.[22] In practice, different explanations have been stressed by different researchers, such as the desire to establish an Islamic political community, the inadequacy of the Kemalist regime in replacing the ritual satisfaction that Islam provided, and the way that Islam may reinforce gender hierarchy.[23]

I think that this diversity of suggested solutions reflects the reality of the situation. There is no one reason for the rise of Islam. Rather, multiple factors interact in complex ways, and it is extremely difficult to assess when one is more important than another. Indeed, here I would add one factor to the list. A striking difference between the official, Kemalist interpretation of religion and the dominant tone of the religious revivalist movements is their respective orientation toward modernity. The Kemalists were convinced that it is only by relegating belief to the inner self that the physical universe could be studied dispassionately. Their attitude towards religion was very much that of Fraser in *The Golden Bough*, obscurantism that stops people from perceiving their surroundings in an appropriately detached way.

They were (and are) convinced that it denies progress and prevents the country from exploiting the fruits of science in order to attain affluence. This utter certainty that it was through scientific knowledge that Turkey would industrialise provided the basis for the founding of the network of schools, universities and research institutions of the Republic. Of course, so far as the secular authorities are concerned, this view does not actually prevent the Republic from supporting religion as well as science, as long as the two are kept separate within the system. One can support the other: a particular vision of personalised religion taught by the state can, through that vision, extol people to leave the secular parts of the state as they are.

In spite of the vigour with which this view of religion has been put forward, in the last few decades, a more popular interpretation has gained sway among the mass of the people. They have adopted the idea of progress and consumer affluence with a willingness and enthusiasm that is often surprising to visitors. They are aware, too, that the cognitive base of firstly the industrial, and now the technological revolution that they are importing from the West is seemingly directly contradictory to a traditional interpretation of Islam. Faced with this dilemma, rather than minimise the role of the faith, they have actively sought to develop an intellectual understanding of religion that embraces the physical, as well as the spiritual world. In other words, they have sought to seek ways of expanding religion to embrace, rather than retreat from new knowledge. In conversations I have had in provincial towns whilst travelling, many active Islamic believers have pointed to the days when Islam was a world-leader in science, in astronomy, in philosophy and in medicine. They also may assert, as each discovery is made, that it has already been anticipated in the Koran, that all the books that ever have been, or shall be, written are to be found within it.

This type of approach has produced an abundant literature which is quite different from the moralistic, plain faith that has been encouraged throughout much of the Republic. Rather, it is expansionist, exclusivist and all embracing. Above, in Chapter 1, I describe the textbook written by Fiğlalı used in schools in their moral learning (*ahlak*) lessons. However, the Directorate of Religious Affairs, the *Diyanet İşleri Vakfı*, and the Ministry of Education also send books to schools for their libraries. Among these are works which assert that, far from being contrary or opposed to the modern world, Islam has anticipated its inventions, that the discoveries of science merely confirm the revealed and infallible nature of the Koran and the wisdom of its tenets. Thus, a work on health and Islam is divided into chapters, each showing the way in which the researches of the West have confirmed that to perform the ritual ablution is healthy, that pigs are unhealthy to eat, that praying is good exercise and that to fast is good for the body. One on education begins by quoting parts of the Koran and sayings of the Prophet in favour of science (*ilim*), then illustrates the size of the libraries of Islam in former times. It goes on to consider the strength of Islamic thinkers in astronomy, mathematics, geometry, physics, chemistry, and medicine. In its confidence in Islam's absolute success, its emphasis on the exoteric aspects of Islam and the universality of its message, it is quite different from the sentiments expressed in the *ahlak* textbooks.[24]

Thus, I suggest that the original Republican formula, stoic inner belief whilst getting on with one's public duty to serve the nation, thus separating the absoluteness of faith from everyday, practical experience, has turned out to be unacceptable to a large part of a population which has by and large retained its literal faith in divine creation and intervention in all things. Nevertheless, they sense the difficulties raised by technology keenly. They do wish to talk about them. Many find the contradictions thrown up important, vital even in their lives. They wish to discuss these matters in detail, to be led and to lead in ways that will resolve them. Paul Stirling, in an interview held near the end of fifty years of research in Anatolia, described this issue as follows:

> One of my favourite examples is this: Ali Osman [one of Stirling's informants] is reading the Koran while I write my notes one morning. He looked up and said, 'It says here that the sun goes around the earth, but they teach my grandson in school that the earth goes round the sun. What do you say?' That is just one example. Every time people come back to the village from Germany there are tremendous conversations, everybody asking questions, discussing, just as a matter of course.[25]

Said-i Nursi, the most successful of the ideological reformers, did talk about these issues. Indeed, perhaps Nursi's most obvious achievement is his providing a body of doctrine which helps to convince his followers that it is possible to be a good Muslim and a follower of the secular sciences at the same time. He addresses this issue throughout his work, and on a number of levels. For example, he turns the Republican attack on the Ottoman Empire on its head. He asserts that it is because the Ottomans strayed from the path of religion that they weakened, that within the Koran can be found the secret of both temporal and spiritual worlds, and therefore they could have modernised within its benificence rather than turn their backs on its secrets. He stresses, too, that it is the duty of all believers to study the world with the best means at their disposal, and that no contradiction between a creator and the material world can emerge from the findings of empirical science. Rather, science simply reaffirms the order, the beauty and the rhythm that can be found in nature that has been created by God.[26]

He was a master too at examining specific doctrinal questions and problems that were addressed to him by his followers. We may take in illustration his solution of the puzzle posed by Stirling's informant, the conundrum of the place of the sun in the universe:

> For example, the Qur'an speaks of the sun as *a moving lamp* because it does not mention the sun for its own sake, but because the sun is the mainstay of the order and the centre of the system in the universe, and order and system are two means of obtaining the knowledge of the Creator. When the Qur'an says, 'And *the sun runs its course*', it suggests the well-ordered disposition of Divine Power in the revolutions of winter and summer, and day and night, and therefore implies the majesty of the Maker. Thus, whatever the reality of this 'running' is, it does not harm the intended meaning, which is the observed order woven into the structure of the universe.[27]

This message is also pursued with admirable clarity by the successor to Said-i Nursi, Fethullah Gülen, now the most prominent of his followers. Gülen too is a prolific writer, and has written a series of works on reconciling modernity with faith. Whilst influenced by Nursi, he has internalised contemporary science also, and draws equally on allusions from the Koran and examples from physics, biology and astronomy. Thus, in his *Essentials of the Islamic Faith*, he begins with the necessary fact of belief, as does Nursi. He continues by contrasting the rules of God (*şeriat*) and those of science, saying that we should lead our lives according to *şeriat* to develop our spiritual position in the afterlife, and according to science (both in the sense of technical investigation and knowledge as a whole) to build our lives in this. He connects the two by affirming that it is through science we are able to study the immutable, the fascinating and the ordered universe that God has created.

Gülen offers several further explanations of the relationship between the revealed knowledge of the Koran and the scientific world. He affirms that the Koran is written for all ages, both for those with a less developed scientific understanding than ours, and for those in the future. For this reason, in order to be able to be appealing and comprehensible to people in all periods, its verses talk in hints rather than direct correlations. In a neat application of Popperian philosophy, he stresses that the rules of science are continually changing, as well as being manifestly inadequate in many ways. Therefore, they should not be confused with reality, the actual ordered creation of life, whose secret belongs to God, and is reflected in the immutable, unchanging verses of the Koran. Nevertheless, as much as we can do so, it is incumbent upon us to strive to understand the universe in our own way.

Clearly, ideas such as these are immensely comforting to a people who would rather not give up their faith as they modernise, and it is hardly surprising that they should find solace in them. Simple empirical observation indicates that many Sunnis in Turkey find the Nursi (and the later Gülen) formula of expanding belief to embrace technological innovation convincing, and vastly preferable to the internalising secularism propounded by early Kemalism. Once this step is taken, and accepted, the way is clear to struggle both to modernise, and to proselytise further the Faith itself. It thus becomes possible both to be a citizen of the modern world, and to be a pious believer.[28]

Conclusions

In sum, the model that I have put forward in this and the previous chapter is straightforward but has complex implications when viewed in the context of the religious revival. Authority must be respected. Yet, to subvert authority is as much part of Turkish society as its imposition, and most people are busy doing both, in ways that are ordered, mutually known and well-understood. Different aspects of social life are more amenable to such subversion and imposition than others. Kurdish independence has met with sustained opposition. Communism, or far left-wing ideas have likewise failed or been crushed.

Islam is different. Here, the Turkish State has not given the same unambiguous response.[29] The state claims to be both secular and also to respect personal piety; it wishes to free the state from religion yet is not above using it to facilitate social control. Consequently, unless there are repeated calls for the return of the *şeriat*, the courts intervene only selectively. This ambivalence, whilst it has hardly affected the state's ability to react to frontal declarations of revolt, has left it particularly susceptible to subversion via patronage networks, mutual-support organisations and the careful accumulative weight of active but peaceful believers. Indeed, there has developed a shifting boundary: as the practice of Islam has expanded the Kemalist state has gradually redrawn its position, but has found, until now, no anchor point. Commensurately, the particular cultural pattern whereby authority may be gradually subverted has positively encouraged the development and strength of a religious philosophy of slow retrenchment through the existing organs of the state and society.

The organisations of civil society such as *dernek*s, and *vakıf*s play a vital role in this development. Whilst it is forbidden to found a *dernek* specifically in the name of religion, *tarikat* organisations have in practice built up complicated and extensive chains of such associations, providing legitimate ways in which they may co-ordinate and publicise their activities. An examination of the temporal career of Fethullah Gülen illustrates this model once more. According to various descriptions of his life, he began his career as mosque preacher in Izmir. Whilst he did not meet Said-i Nursi personally, he appears to have become converted to his views after hearing him speak. Though without money, he opened a *vakıf*, consisting of no more than an apartment, to provide Islamically-inclined students with board and lodging. Successful in this, he opened further *vakıf*s, and as his reputation grew, also ran summer camps for youths. Later, he branched out further in the education sector, opening *hazırlık*, preparatory schools, which helped to prepare students for their state examinations. Then, he developed media interests, becoming the proprietor of *Zaman*, the Islamically-inclined mass newspaper. Finally, during the Özal period, he branched into financial affairs and became part of a wider sector of banks and institutions devoted to bringing Islamic banking to Turkey.

In the 1990s, Gülen, usually known as *Fetullah Hoca* (lit. 'teacher'), has, if anything, grown in influence. As well as his activities in the financial sector, which frequently bring him into contact with political figures, he appears to have become an unofficial part of a government inspired initiative to expand Turkish influence in the Turkic states, the government helping him to develop a chain of high schools in those countries. In spite of this high profile, he has been favoured more in the political than the military sphere. Though, until recently, tolerated by the courts, the army does not approve of the *Nurcu* movement he represents, placing them, just as did General Olçaytu above, alongside Marxists, and other fundamentalists. Nevertheless, he has been an important part of the fabric of the Republic. He is a peaceful man, insistent that his followers shun any sort of civil violence against the established order, but nevertheless one whose philosophy is not, ultimately, compatible with it.[30]

I have considered this model in detail only with regard to the *Nurcu*s, but it appears to be applicable to others as well. Take the *Süleymancılar* for example. They are a popular group, not as widespread as the *Nurcus*, but still present in Istanbul, and in most other regions of Turkey, particularly central and western Anatolia. Ideologically, they appear to stress the absolutely central place that the Koran must play within any religious activity, and combine this with highly disciplined study and attention to religious duties. There have been a number of court cases in which they were accused of going further than this, and inculcating a systematic hatred for Atatürk.[31] Their activities are based in a number of hostels and schools for poor children scattered around the country. These schools are supported by voluntary associations which are in turn linked through a federation known as the '*Kurs ve Okullara Yardım Dernekleri Federasyonu*', 'The Federation of Associations for the Support of Courses and Schools'. In a general meeting held on 21 May 1979, in the Istanbul Sport and Exhibition Centre, their leader Kemal Kaçar, is quoted as outlining their strength as follows; 'In this hall, we are meeting as a general council representing more than a hundred thousand pupils studying courses in more than a thousand private buildings from a variety of towns and cities in Turkey, and, in Europe and Germany, spreading like a net, 215 Cultural Centres for Islam.'[32]

The different areas of social life: authority, organisation, and belief, that I have chosen to discuss only explain part of the story. One of the outstanding questions is why has the army permitted the rise of religion to be handled by the organs of civilian society in the first place? Though military leaders are patently not happy with the situation (however much they may have contributed to the process through their acknowledgement and occasional support of religion as a means of supporting the social order), they have notably not resorted to violent reprisals. They still prefer to rely on the state prosecutor where they can, calling him to do his job ever more rigorously where there is actual evidence of Islamic conspiracy. They spend considerable resources on compiling reports and collecting evidence to this end,[33] and it is notable that the religious trials seemed genuinely to be handled on the evidence: they certainly have not descended into being show trials.[34]

Perhaps the moment the army might have employed direct coercion against religion passed when it accepted İnönü's assurance that the democratic process should be allowed to proceed after the first Democrat Party's stunning victory. On the other hand, it might also be argued that the religious question has only come gradually to the fore, that there has been no one point when a person, or a body of people, during the decades of subsequent slow change could actually have decided *this* is the point when enough is enough and no more. Menderes' victory may therefore simply have not appeared the threat to the foundations of secularism that secular Republicans now regard it as having heralded.

Alternatively, it might be that the military, faced with religion's revival, decided definitely that to be faced with active Islam was far preferable, and manageable, than being faced with a divisive communism. It might be also, that, when it comes to disagreements within orthodox Islam (as distinct from questions of nationalism), Turks, whether in authority or not, by and large do heed appeals not to shed blood, and would genuinely rather not do so. Once this decision is made, then the way is clear for a deadly serious but largely peaceful struggle through the civil process. Whether or not these notions are valid, they are certainly put to the test by the more recent rise of overtly political Islam, and the tension that has stemmed from it, the subject of the next two chapters.

| 4 |

Political Islam: The Rise of Erbakan

In 1957, in a seminal article entitled 'Politics and Islam in Turkey 1920-1955', Rustow tentatively suggested that are three sorts of people in Turkey: the out and out 'Secularists' who wish to have very little to do with religion, the believers or 'Moderates' who are prepared to accept that the state is secular though retaining their faith, and a much smaller number of 'Clericalists', who dislike the reforms, and wish fervently that they would be gone.[1] This simple three-fold distinction was also used by later analysts,[2] who often assume that the apparent chaos in Turkish politics masks broad stability: that the moderate right-wing parties dominate, that the left, more sharply secular, are the main opposition,[3] whilst there is also a small Islamic political movement which is largely ineffective.

The presumption that religiously-inspired political movements could not be successful long appeared justified. Whilst throughout the Republic there have been repeated attempts to set up explicitly Islamic parties, they were closed down by the authorities or in themselves unsuccessful.[4] Necmettin Erbakan's fate at first appeared to be no different. By trade an engineer and academic with a reputation for piety, he set out to join the Justice Party, led by Demirel. On being refused, he stood as the independent candidate for Konya in the 1969 general election. Campaigning extensively and openly in the name of Islam, he succeeded in being elected. Once part of the Assembly, he formed the *Milli Nizam Partisi* (National Order Party) at the beginning of 1970, sponsored by two other deputies. It is widely acknowledged that the party was supported by the Nakshibendi *tarikat*, with whom he had made close contacts at university as a student in Istanbul. Unsurprisingly, the constitutional court closed down his party on 20 May 1971, just after the second military coup.

In October 1972, Süleyman Emre, a leading member of the defunct *MNP* formed a new party, the *Milli Selamet Partisi* (National Salvation Party). It entered the October 1973 elections, and enjoyed a surprise success, gaining 11.8 per cent of the vote, 48 deputies, and 3 senators.[5] A week after the elections, Emre resigned the leadership, and Erbakan took his place. No party had a majority, and there followed a period in which Turkey remained without a government. Ecevit, head of the Republican People's Party, had the largest number of deputies. He offered Erbakan the chance to join a coalition, but Erbakan appears to have been unable to convince the rest of his party to join in with the Republicans, whom they regarded as being against religion. After long fruitless discussions, finally, on 26 January 1974, Ecevit and Erbakan did come to an agreement, Erbakan becoming Deputy Prime Minister.[6]

The coalition that followed was uneasy and short. It came to an end just after the successful Cyprus intervention only nine months later. Ecevit, vastly increased in confidence and a national hero, refused to pass on the title 'acting prime minister' to Erbakan for the duration of a visit to Scandinavia; in response Erbakan refused to sanction his going. On this low note, the coalition dissolved. Ecevit was unable to form another government. Nevertheless, Erbakan survived in power to become Deputy Prime Minister in the next government, this time headed by Demirel in a broad-based coalition, known as the 'Nationalist Front'. At the next general elections, held in 1977, Erbakan and his party were rather less successful, gaining 8.6 per cent of the vote, and the number of *MSP* deputies fell to twenty-four. Even then, they played a brief part in power, as part of a further coalition led by Demirel.[7]

That Erbakan's first party, quite explicitly based on a religious ideology, should have been closed down is entirely normal in the history of the Republic. That he was permitted to sustain a reincarnation of that Islamic party throughout the next decade, and even play a major part in government, is unprecedented. In attempting to explain this conundrum, contemporary writers in Turkey often refer to the military. At the time of Erbakan's re-entry into politics, Turkey was still under the indirect influence of the second army coup. They suggest that the military authorities, confident in their ability to limit Islamic militancy, saw Erbakan both as a potential opponent to Demirel's Justice Party, and a means to impede the spread of communism. Such writers also often note a specific visit made by two military figures to Erbakan, who had judiciously removed himself to Switzerland, appearing to invite him back to Turkey with the promise that he could act freely.[8] Whatever the exact circumstances, and motives, behind Erbakan's being permitted to function, 1972 marks a watershed in the development of Islamic party politics in Turkey.

Once in power, was Erbakan able to achieve very much? During his campaigns for office, Erbakan had developed a particular approach known as *milli görüş* (national viewpoint), described and referred to frequently in his publicity and speeches. The *milli görüş* had the broad aim of state-led economic development within a populist Islamic framework that was centred on the moral unity of the family. This was reflected in the successful programme that he brought to the coalition governments, which among other things was aimed at raising the number of *imam-hatip* schools, introducing the *ahlak* (religious morals) lessons into middle schools, and increasing the numbers of state-funded *imams* in villages. He also demanded economic measures, such as the establishment of a Ministry for Industry and a simplification of taxation (the former was achieved more easily than the latter). Erbakan did not push through the more revolutionary changes that he had promised during his campaigns. Though avowedly against charging interest, he did not make a stand when the government felt it necessary to raise interest rates. More radical reforms, such as teaching Arabic lessons in all normal state secondary schools, whilst generating an immense amount of publicity, failed to carry his coalition partners.

In retrospect, it is perhaps best to see this period as continuing the process of a gradual accumulation of Islamic practice. When looked at independently of Erbakan's rhetoric, many of his efforts built on the activity that the Democrat or Justice Parties had themselves presided over in previous years, and are quite compatible with them. This is shown clearly by the fact that when Erbakan began to work with Demirel's 'nationalist front' coalitions, his party appears to have experienced little of the ideological discomfort that marked the *CHP* coalition.[9] Indeed, between 1974 and 1978, the number of *imam hatip* schools jumped in astounding fashion from 101 to 334. The time in power also established a precedent. Later, in the 1990s, it was immensely useful for the Welfare Party to be able to hark back to a golden period of success.[10] Erbakan himself was able to build on this period in order to strengthen his claim as someone who possessed a progressive but distinctively Islamic view, a view that he was later to develop into the concept of an *Adil Düzen* (Just Order).

The 1980s
During the decade that followed, the successor to the National Salvation Party, the Welfare Party (*Refah Partisi*), was not closed down but, rather, excluded from the political arena. Though the generals returned the country to democracy they controlled the process tightly. All previously active political parties were banned and their leaders, including Erbakan, barred from taking part in politics for ten years. Through procedural blocking by the National Security Council, attempts to found the Welfare Party were delayed until 21 September 1983, leaving it too late for them to enter the general elections. Özal's victory in 1983 finally came in an election in which only three parties, none of them of ostensibly religious, had been permitted to enter.

As the time for the next elections approached, Özal, seemingly motivated by an opportunity to establish his legitimacy as leader, decided to hold a nation-wide referendum to ask the electorate whether the banned leaders should be permitted to return immediately to politics. Narrowly, in 1987, it approved their doing so. Erbakan returned to the fray by taking over leadership of the Welfare Party. At the general elections soon afterwards, Welfare gained seven per cent national support. In spite of this, they were unable to enter the Assembly, because a new election law had been introduced insisting that any political party must pass a barrier of ten per cent support.[11] Thus, by virtue of the *coup*, restrictions on parties, exclusions on individuals permitted to stand and changes in the electoral law, Erbakan and the Welfare Party remained outside parliament for the whole of the decade.

At this point, even some of those within the Islamic movement appear to have grown discouraged. Coşan, for example, the head of the Nakshibendi movement, writing in *İslam* deplored the way that internal strife and friction had prevented them from combining together to pass the election barrier, pointing out that the election law favoured movements which were able to maintain unity and express themselves through one party. At a conference in Istanbul in 1990, he was more explicit, and accused Erbakan of deserting the Nakshibendis, who had helped to set him up in the first place. He also accused him of banning the Welfare Party supporters from buying his journal, or from making donations to the trust, *Hak-Yol Vakfı,* through which the *tarikat*'s activities are supported. He went on to criticise Erbakan's policy, particularly his ineffectiveness saying:

> After 20 years, 46 [*sic*] representatives and 3 senators... we are reduced to nothing, something like seven per cent, ten per cent. What do you guess will be the case in the next elections? I ask for the most optimistic predictions: ten per cent, fifteen. But Turkey is 99 per cent Muslim. Why was he unable to realise this unity, this togetherness?... [Erbakan] says that Friday, the day of prayers, should be a holiday, but people do not come to his party, the Friday holiday doesn't happen. If in the Assembly, this many deputies would raise their fingers, then Friday would become a holiday. Everybody would go to the mosque... and one of Allah's commands would be fulfilled... But he doesn't do this. Allah will look to ask questions of one who struggles for 20 years and fails to get any sort of result. Will they not ask 'In 20 years, what have you done? You have been in politics for 20 years, what point have you reached?'[12]

The 1990s
In the event, Coşan's pessimistic picture of the political success of the

Welfare Party turned out to be wrong. During the 1990s, still under Erbakan, the Welfare Party made spectacular gains. In the general elections held in 1991, by combining with the Nationalist Action Party (*Milliyetçi Hareket Partisi*, a far right-wing party led by the late Alparslan Türkeş) and the much smaller Democratic Reformist Party (*Islahatçı Demokrasi Partisi*), they succeeded in passing the 10 per cent barrier and gained 62 seats in the Grand National Assembly. The election alliance separated soon after they entered parliament, but this still left Erbakan with 40 deputies. Building on this higher profile, the party took the metropolitan municipalities of Ankara and Istanbul in 1994, as well as more than 300 others in small towns and cities across Turkey. In the general election held on 24 December 1995, they grew further and emerged as the largest political party of all with 158 deputies, and 22 per cent of the vote overall. Though now the largest party, they did not have enough seats to form a majority: the Welfare Party was closely followed by the True Path Party, now headed by Çiller, and the Motherland Party headed by Yılmaz.

Having gained this breakthrough, the next question was whether Erbakan would be able to become prime minister. Initially, Demirel, now president, followed protocol precisely, giving Erbakan the opportunity to form a government as the leader of the party with the greatest number of deputies. Erbakan did his best, but failed to reach agreement with Çiller, then almost persuaded Yılmaz, who pulled out at the last minute. After a storm of protest from the press, Çiller and Yılmaz came together to form a coalition government in March 1996. Highly skilled tactics by Welfare accentuated the divisions between them. The coalition effectively ground to a halt within three months, with Yılmaz openly trying to have his coalition partner Çiller impeached for financial irregularities. Then, in June 1996, Erbakan agreed a surprise coalition with Çiller – it is said by offering to protect her from further investigation into her affairs.[13] Not everybody in her party agreed with this action. Two deputies resigned within days of the coalition, and ten more refused to vote for her. Nevertheless, supported by the votes of the small Great Unity Party (*Büyük Birlik Partisi*)[14] the remaining deputies were sufficient to ensure a vote of confidence, and the coalition came into being. Thus Erbakan became the first leader of an Islamic party to head a government in Republican Turkey.

Almost as quickly, his luck began to change. A visit to Libya ended disastrously, with Colonel Gaddafi calling repeatedly for autonomy for the Kurds in Erbakan's presence. A popular attempt to bring headscarfs back into the universities became snarled up in the courts. Despite his anti-Jewish rhetoric, Erbakan ratified a major security agreement with Israel. Faced with mounting criticism from within his own party, an erosion of support for the coalition among the True Path Party, widespread civil protest, and explicitly pro-secular moves from the army, national security council, and state prosecutor, he resigned in June 1997, hoping to pass the premiership to his coalition partner, Tansu Çiller. Surprising almost everybody, President Demirel asked Yılmaz, now in opposition, rather than Çiller, to form a new government. Worse was to come for Erbakan. In January 1998, along with two of his leading supporters, he was found guilty of acting against the secular constitution. This carries an automatic prohibition on taking any further active part in politics for five years.

In the light of these dramatic events, the dominant argument among commentators has changed. From maintaining that the political groups that favour Islam are doomed to failure, they have begun to argue that even if the religious party of the day does succeed in governing, it will remain impotent. In support of this argument, they point to the difficulty that Erbakan experienced with the legal authorities, his failure to introduce any major measures against the secular republic, the hostility of the armed forces, and the lack of support offered even by those other Islamic countries whom he claimed would support him. They sometimes add that, even if the religious party has emerged with a large parliamentary representation, they nevertheless only have gained, until now, just over 20 per cent of the total vote, leaving nearly 80 per cent who are against. Some even argue that it would do nothing but good if Erbakan were to take power on his own, because it would confirm the inadequacies of his leadership.

Much of this is true. Erbakan clearly had great difficulties in implementing his programme, and the intense embarrassment of his being snubbed by Libya will not be forgotten for years to come. Nevertheless, this argument conceals neatly the fact that the early model has been utterly falsified. Even though the picture is complicated by changes in the electoral rules, it is quite clear that political Islam has gone through three distinct phases. First (1924-1972) it was permitted to operate not at all, or in only brief bursts of activity. Secondly (1972-1991) it became a sustained, tolerated minority group, playing a part in power for the early part of this period, contributing considerably towards the general growth of Islam, but with no real hope of gaining an electoral majority. They did, however, successively establish, rethink, then regroup their position whilst in opposition. Third (from 1991 onwards), political Islam has become a mass force.

How effective it will be in this new context is another matter entirely. The sheer size that it has attained brings into play a whole new set of variables: the extent to which Islamists will be able to exploit coherently those parts of the state that they control at any one time, the capability of their opponents to neutralise the larger number of supporters that they will be able to put into positions of influence, whether the other parties will be forced to combine together effectively against them thereby effectively creating a secular front, and whether a direct, violent civil confrontation will emerge in the way that it did in the pre-1980 period. This change in scale may even affect the calculations of the authorities; it is comparatively easy to ban a party when it has no particular identity, or it has not captured the public's imagination. It becomes a different proposition altogether when it represents the aspirations of some millions of people, possesses an established philosophy, and a coherent, diverse grass-roots organisation. The 1980 coup, even if it later lost support, at least enjoyed initial popularity. A coup without mass goodwill might be altogether more difficult to execute and to sustain.

There is a further, equally significant issue. The arguments about the efficacy of the Welfare Party and political Islam have helped to conceal the fact that the transformation is not just a matter of votes, it is also social. The increase in population, infrastructural improvement, the communications revolution, and, above all, massive migration have produced a dislocated rural population that has created a huge challenge to the existing urban ethos. This movement brings with it a rural way of life that is far more entrenched in Islamic cosmology than is the case among those who have been brought up in the old Republican urban centres. Being sensitive to this conjunction of the rural and the modern and the problems that it has thrown up was one clear factor in the Welfare Party's success and helped them to outflank the more conventional figures and parties, each buttressed by their extensive patron/client support groups that until now have dominated and often led to inertia in the democratic process.[15]

Social change
This can be demonstrated most simply by contrasting the situation at the outset of the Republic with that today. In 1923, Turkey's population was largely rural. Transport infrastructure was rudimentary. The limited railway system was the only way of moving comfortably around the countryside. Whilst of course some people did make journeys for all sorts of reasons, the localised nature of the communities and the almost entire lack of developed industries meant that outside periods of military service there really was very little opportunity or reason for the vast majority of the population to move around. In part because of this restricted mobility, and in part for other reasons (such as the traditional central Anatolian obeisance to central authority), the Kemalist elite really could be sure that any opposition to their plans for the new way of life in Turkey would find it difficult to coalesce and even more difficult to succeed in any effective way.[16]

This comparative lack of mobility also meant the Kemalists could train school teachers, university graduates, and bureaucrats safe in the asssumption that, whilst some change was occurring in the villages, the rural world was comparatively constant and available for them to influence. The significance of Makal's early description lies partly in the fact that he was a Kemalist teacher in a sceptical village, but it also indicates so very clearly that he is almost the only representative of the industrialised world to come into contact with them. This meant that a very few initiates, trusted to have understood and learnt the message correctly, could go into the countryside and immediately become important figures, even if their message was undoubtedly on occasions disliked. In turn, this missionary approach included the presumption that, but for providing material for folklore, village life was totally obsolete and insular, contributing almost nothing towards

Turkey's modernisation.

By the 1990s, however, the situation was quite different. The very success of the initial modernising mission means that Turkey's population has multiplied fivefold, from about 12 millions to more than 60 millions. The balance between the rural and urban areas has altered drastically. Today, Turkey's towns take up about 60 per cent of the population, as distinct from 14 per cent in 1927. Transport infrastructure, job mobility, social contacts, political relations, economic relations and production techniques have altered social life so radically that there is no village in Turkey that has not in some way been affected by this transformation, and no village which has not contributed at least some of its population towards it.[17]

The consequences of this rapid development are many, difficult to conceive with any accuracy and still more difficult to describe. One crucial fact, however, is that the very speed with which urbanisation has occurred means that the majority of Turkey's urban inhabitants are of village origin. This should not be understood as an obstacle to a person achieving success and fame. The Republic was in great part built by incomers from rural areas who internalised western urban norms, regarding them as an integral part of the Kemalist programme. Indeed that the Republic should have had such an open policy to its citizens, discriminating on the basis of neither ethnic group nor class is in itself extremely important. However, at some point in the Republic's history, I suspect around about the early 1960s, the number of people arriving became such that the cities were unable to absorb newcomers and inculcate them into the approved Kemalist urban lifestyle. This process has continued, accelerating throughout the decades.

Ankara, for example, was planned as a capital city of about half a million inhabitants, and now has probably six or seven times that number. What was once a quietish bureaucratic city has now become choked with people struggling to make a living within an infrastructure hopelessly inadequate to meet their needs. Istanbul likewise has become a sprawling conurbation where the life of the great majority of its nine or ten million occupants is dominated by inadequate food, air, water, electricity and housing. The poorest are begging for their daily bread in the streets, and all but the very wealthiest are unable to escape from the effects of over-population. Even those who have a job cannot be sure of being able to live: the monthly rate for a flat in almost any area is now substantially higher than most wages.

This lack of access to very basic services is matched by the paralysis, over-manning and under-funding which affects almost all civil service departments. In Istanbul, as to a lesser extent in all large cities, this leads to the state's incapacity to discharge its functions in anything but the most stuttering, spasmodic way. The schools for example, key to inculcation of the nationalist ethic,[18] faced with too many potential pupils, have taken to charging ever larger sums for parents to register their children at them. These charges are semi-official, intended to cover repairs to the school, heating bills and so on. There are also consistent rumours that under-the-table payments are made by parents desperate for their children to attend the school of their choice, or even sometimes any school. Further, such is the pressure on further education places that pupils are unlikely to gain a place in a university without intense and often prohibitively expensive private tuition. Even then, the chances of success are slim: more than a million candidates entered the national university entrance exams in 1995, competing for about 400,000 places. Perhaps a tenth, or even less, of these places genuinely represent an established university education.

Small wonder then that faced with the difficulty of integrating into the economic and social life of the town, villagers often retain links with their rural roots in many different ways. They may move back to the village for part of the year, obtain food parcels from the village, send their children to school in the village if the school there is better than those to which they have access in the town, retire to the village as their life draws near its end, and choose to be buried there. Now, indeed, there is no sharp break between village and urban life. There is a continuum: all villages, however remote, have taken on some of the attributes of urban life, with piped water, televisions, refrigerators, washing-machines, cookers, improved roads, telephones, schools, electricity and health-services now common-place among the more wealthy, whilst even the poorest have seen some benefit. In turn, the increasingly mobile village populations drift in and out of the city: sometimes moving to it but not quite cutting off their links with those who remain, sometimes moving back when an urban venture fails. The city itself, with its decreasing well-established elite steadily loosing ground, is unable to inculcate its old morals or culture. Instead, rural accent, dress, food, and manners now dominate much of urban life, often to the despair of the longer-established residents who deplore the 'villagification' of their environment. The upheaval that it has brought has resulted in literally millions of new incumbents falling back on their own devices, recreating their own life-style and norms among a jumble of blaring often transitory music fashions, stark nationalist enthusiasm, flourishing reformulations of Islam and a buoyant black-market economy.[19]

Once the existence of this amazing *melange* is taken into account a host of questions spring to mind. The most important of these is, 'How is modern Turkey influenced by the fact that the clearly dominating urban elite culture (which used to control both government and state) has been replaced by a massive influx of people vastly more mobile, economically, physically and socially than before, all learning a host of new approaches to life without being willing (or often being unable even if they are willing) to give up the philosophy, contacts and associations with their rural past?' Part of the answer to this problem is that the people *en masse* are choosing reformulations of Islam rather than Kemalism to achieve it. At the same time however, the tremendous difficulty which many have in leading their daily lives, their intense frustration with blatantly corrupt political practices at the national and the local level mean that they are drawn to any political philosophy which offers to guarantee them relief from pain, and an honest government.

The Welfare Party
The Welfare Party offered just such a synthesis to meet this new demand. It promised efficiently organised services for the masses, a political ideology based on Islamic mores, and bitter hostility towards the corrupt politicians and 'crooks' who were depriving the workers of their just rewards. Even so, it was not at all clear that they were going to be able to convince quite so many voters. Before the party's manifest victories, several writers questioned whether it had sufficient flexibility to make the transition to a party of mass appeal.[20] In

practice, there appear several circumstances that helped the Party over that awkward, indeterminate middle size that has destroyed other political movements. It was aided by a decision of the first Republican People's Party/National Salvation Party coalition to permit guest workers abroad to cast their votes in the Turkish elections, an electorate from whom it has consistently gained a higher proportion than other parties.[21] It appears to have been supported also more strongly by Sunni communities in areas where there already existed local conflict between Sunni and Alevi groups.[22] It was also helped by the rise in conflict in the east. Just at the point when the party was attempting to reform itself in the late 1980s, disaffected Kurds in the eastern provinces began to see Welfare as an alternative to the Republican regime. This provided a large source of votes that has continued until today, though it has made the party doubly suspicious in the eyes of the army. [23]

Welfare also made a self-conscious attempt to modernise, to change its image from being a 'reactionary' party. Party policy was to reject privileged links with the European Community in favour of a more Islam-oriented foreign trade regime. Nevertheless, it was quite clear that it sought western-style consumer wealth for the poor as the foundation stone of its policies. Indeed, whilst 'Welfare' has become the standard way to translate *'Refah'*, there are many contexts in their speeches and writings when 'affluence' is what is meant, and it would not be mistaken to refer to Welfare as the 'Affluence Party'. In pursuing this modern image, the core of the party's leadership was careful to change a widespread impression in which it was caricatured as being supported mainly by 'backward' villagers dressed in woolly caps and playing with worry beads, and against technological innovation. It ensured that its spokesmen were always well dressed, often very fashionably, and during the late 1980s even startled viewers with the sight of Islamic fashion dress shows on television.

Party members were also self-consciously outward oriented, and often very well read. Leaders were able to argue their position with urbanity and fluency. In the National Assembly, their members of parliament were curious for systematic knowledge about the world to a degree not noticeable in other parties. I remember years ago, a secular librarian in the parliamentary library telling me that the most depressing part of his job was that the only members of parliament who had the faintest idea of how to use a modern library were the representatives for the Welfare Party. Again whilst this is no doubt an exaggeration, it gives an idea of their direction and thirst for information.

Just after the results of the 1994 general election, I held a fascinating discussion with one of the Welfare Party's leaders, who described this process in detail. According to my informant, the National Salvation Party, when considering how to build its voter base, decided initially to concentrate on those who went to mosques regularly: that is, those worshippers who attended at least the Friday prayers if not the full five occasions daily. In doing so, the party leaders were encouraged by the thought that if all who went to pray voted for the party, they would easily win a majority. However, during the period in opposition during the 1980s, they realised the disappointing fact that although people may go to mosques, when it comes to elections they often give their votes to other parties.

In order to get round this problem, the party decided in the future to broaden its voter appeal by going out into the community as a whole to solicit votes even in the most seemingly inauspicious places, those which might normally be thought of as entirely secular, even anti-Islamic: they congregated on the beach, on the lawn of the Bosphorus University, in night-clubs. My informant explained that they would attract attention by finding first a prominent place to pray, and then justify themselves to remonstrators, slowly attempting to convince them of the importance of their mission. He described also the difficulty of being so open: that at first people laughed at them, but that in the end they started to listen. He further added that the success of the mass Islamic movements in Iran, in Algeria and then in Egypt, encouraged them greatly, and made them feel that they too might be able to base a movement on genuine general popular appeal. He added that, of course, this change of emphasis was beginning to lead to greatly increased support, and that this meant that they no longer felt the need to hide their convictions.

Erbakan's philosophy

In achieving a message with general appeal, the Welfare Party was helped enormously by Erbakan having devised a system of economic reform which at once blamed the other parties for Turkey's woes and offered a solution within the framework of an ostensibly Islamic programme. Erbakan referred repeatedly to this system in his pithy speeches, and published it in a booklet *Adil Ekonomik Düzen, A Just Economic Order*, distributed by the Welfare Party. In it, his philosophy is blunt and sharp. Quite unlike the *Nurcu*, and later the Fethullah Gülen ethic of devoted study, co-operation and peaceful activism, it appeals directly to the sense of confrontational deprivation felt by those who are suffering as Turkey modernises.

First, Erbakan's explanation of Turkey's woes is simple. He claims that the whole world is in the grip of a Zionist conspiracy: that they control the major banks in New York, and through them the World Bank and the international monetary system. They lend money to Turkey, to the Islamic world, and to other countries, and then by charging interest on the money ensure the continuing impoverishment of all debtors. He comments on the widespread income discrepancy within Turkey, and claims that those who do have money are allied to these Zionist elements. He regards the political parties, be they right or left wing, as fraudulent in whatever they claim because of their links with these groups and the western imperialist nations.

> The slave regime that is part and parcel of the economic system in Turkey did not come about of its own accord. It is a consequence of systematic, planned and deliberate modern colonial initiatives of the Imperialist and Zionist forces of this earth. The Zionists have taken control of world Imperialism. Using the vehicle of interest-bearing capital, they have colonised the whole of humanity. By means of the Imperialist states, they control the world's governments.
>
> Turkey's false parties are supported by Imperialism and Zionism. With all the opportunities at their command, they work to bring them to their bidding. The result of these labours is that for forty years, essentially identical counterfeit, western parties have been to the fore.[24]

He further sums up his argument in a series of 'microbes' which are responsible for the present position as follows: interest, tax, the mint (i.e. money supply), exchange and credit. His argument against interest is that it bears no resemblance to the value of the work which is being conducted with the money thus obtained: against tax that it impoverishes people who have worked hard: and against the money supply that printing money without any economic basis simply fuels crippling inflation. He also asserts that the exchange rates are manipulated by the Zionists and Imperialists to devalue the best efforts of Turkey's workers, and that to give credit without linking it to the production of the article concerned is merely an excuse for extortion. From the point of view of the worker, Erbakan claims that for every salary, a third is lost in tax. A third more is lost in national interest payments, and further proportions through devaluation of the lira against foreign currencies and by contributions to social insurance. For this reason, workers only benefit from a sixteenth of their labour.

Erbakan's description is wild and abhorrent in its racist overtones, but many of the other comments that he makes are telling. It is true that conditions have been difficult for many, that they are forced to work for low wages which are taxed, whilst it is notoriously easy for owners of property and businesses to evade paying any tax at all. Though studiously ignored by the parties in power, international (and domestic) interest repayments are one of the biggest economic problems Turkey will have to face in the future, and inflation has been fuelled by printing money to excess.

His suggestions for replacing this system are rather more difficult to follow. He explains that the 'Just Economic Order' which the Welfare Party will institute 'contains elements of both capitalism and communism, but with the valuable, and without the harmful aspects of both'. He amplifies this by saying that there will be a healthy mix between private and public industry, that profit will be permitted but not interest, that the people will be protected from monopolies, that income tax will be substituted for production tax, and that credit will be issued when it is provided with suitable backing.

Whether or not these individual points add up to a sensible system, it is clear that Erbakan's overall philosophy relies on creating a mandate for radical change with millennial overtones. The crucial, ever repeated, idea in his economic theory is that interest is the root of the evil of the capitalist system because in itself it is non-productive. He claims that there is no guarantee that people will be able to increase production with the money they have borrowed sufficiently to cover the interest that they will have to pay on it, leading them often further into debt and ultimately closure. He asserts again and again that when the evil of interest is banned, production will expand many fold, exports will boom, unemployment will end. Once realised, this will take Turkey past the level of development in Europe within ten years.

From outside, Erbakan was seen sometimes as a dangerous windbag: by the other parties he was often regarded as the Welfare Party's liability. This was simply (and demonstrably) not so. Erbakan is a master of the simple rhetoric which appeals to the mass of the Turkish electorate. During the campaigns that he fought so effectively, it was the other parties who were handicapped by their continuous bickering and criticisms of each other whilst seemingly allowing many of the population to go hungry. Increasingly in his press conferences, Erbakan stressed the number of unemployed, the national debt and the terrorist conflict in the east and linked this with the 'fraudulent' parties and the 'regime of slavery' under which Turkey was living. This message was a powerful one, especially when linked to an ideology with which the broad mass of the electorate is in sympathy. For example, there is a frequent idea among the less well off that there is a great deal of wealth in Turkey, but that corruption and profiteering are preventing it from trickling down to their level. Erbakan's argument for a 'Just Economic Order' was often interpreted by them to imply that corruption is now so endemic that the only way to remove it is to bring back the *şeriat*, which would permit the severe punishment sanctified by Holy Writ, and they then might be able to reap the fruits of their labour. This open assertion was rare even in the 1980s, but it became increasingly common as the position of newly-moved immigrants to the cities, even if they managed to find a job, became ever more desperate.

Moreover, however curious and anachronistic the 'Just Order' might seem, it did at least serve as a basis for a wealth of doctrinal literature and provided a convenient contrast to the other parties. It could even be talked up to a level of metatheory: the intellectuals of the

Welfare Party were fond of meeting with Western journalists, and saying to them 'name one economic theory which has demonstrably solved any significant problem! No one knows better than anyone else how the economy actually works. Given that they are so over-confident, why shouldn't we suggest alternative, if radical theories?' This was a line with which they were frequently successful, at least in gaining the attention of those reporters who were weary of the fantasies of free-market economics.

The organisation of the party

The Welfare Party was further helped by having what is without the slightest doubt the most advanced and modern party organisation in Turkey. Until 1983, as did the other parties, it had a headquarters at Ankara, then further province and sub-province branches which were responsible to one another in an ascending chain leading back to the headquarters at Ankara. During the next years, helped by efficient fund raising, particularly through their *vakıfs* in Germany, the party appears to have created a novel organisational structure which made its smallest unit the catchment area of each ballot box. It appointed an officer in charge of each such area, and furnished him with a list of all the respective voters, and access to a computer terminal. This information, and the names of the respective ballot box 'heads' were kept on a data base in Ankara, along with an identification number. The party expected the man to keep close tabs on the balance of votes in his particular area so that they could call him at any time for an exact assessment of its standing with the electorate.[25]

This coherent organisation and sense of purpose gave the party many advantages. As little examples of this: two days after the election, on the 26 December 1995, it published a brochure outlining the Welfare Party's 'Great Victory'. In this leaflet, a press release was provided by by Erbakan summarising the share of the electorate which the Welfare Party had won, an announcement of the provinces which had won the Welfare Party's 'Golden Electoral Medal' for the most votes, a breakdown of the Party's vote in different regions of Turkey and a list of the names, education level and profession of every single one of the Welfare Party's new representatives. Compared to its rivals, this was a feat of preparation and presentation of accurate, useful material of astonishing efficiency. The party was prepared also to go to great lengths to bring voters to the polls, even those from abroad who had come to Turkey's borders to register their votes. The same brochure that was published so quickly after the elections indicates that the Welfare Party won a far greater share of these votes cast at the border than any other party.[26] The party was also prepared to gain votes by providing voters with presents – coal, coffee or money – so long as they promised on the Koran that they would cast their votes for Welfare at the ballot box.

The same sense of innovative organisation served them extremely well in their quest to dominate the municipalities. All over Turkey, municipalities have often been regarded as opportunities for the rank and file of the party to gain rewards for their faithful service. Mayors have often been good at public speaking, adept at finding supporters, but not possessed of a particularly clear policy of what they will do in office other than siphon off funds illegally. One way to achieve this is to award building contracts to friends and take half the money off them again at a later date. The problem may not emerge at all, or only when the building constructed from the depleted moneys remaining is clearly inadequate to meet the demands on it. Once the mayor in charge runs affairs like this, then it becomes very difficult to prevent employees all the way down the organisation from requesting bribes, even for the smallest tasks. This gives rise to the sad sight of municipalities clearly not performing their tasks adequately, and enormous cynicism among the voters. There is a very widespread presumption for example, that everyone steals what can be got away with, beginning from the most junior clerk, who may take a pencil, the desk manager who takes a pad of paper, and so on, each person stealing as the opportunity offers.

The Welfare Party differed. In both Ankara and Istanbul, it is held to have maintained services more efficiently than their predecessors. This sense of purpose is confirmed by Çakır in his later researches into the district municipalities in Istanbul in the early 1990s, where he found that municipality services before Welfare came to power were often in enormous disarray. The Welfare Party combated this with a combined sense of purpose. First, they banned employees from taking backhanders, displaying a sign on the door saying 'no bribes taken here'. Next, they exploited the international community of Islamic sympathisers, particular expatriate workers in Germany, to persuade them to donate equipment to the municipality. They also held meetings to meet locals on a regular basis, providing opportunities for feed-back among the local population. The combined effect of these measures was that people began to be convinced that the Welfare Party could help their lot.

Of course, there are efficient party workers in other parties and other districts. The difference between them and the Welfare was that among the conventional parties, such efficient organisers emerged more or less at random: party workers may have a clear idea of a decent policy, but they are just as likely to have their eye on the main chance. By successfully incorporating their supporters into a wider ethos, the Welfare Party made it much more difficult for individuals to divert funds for their own ends. This does not mean of course that individuals became more honest in any Platonic way; rather they had to put the team first or be rejected. The wider goal of gaining power overcame the immediate lure of petty corruption.

Welfare in power
Having been successful, supplying the prime minister, and becoming the senior party in government, how did Welfare fare? Erbakan did not succeed in changing any of the founding laws of the secular Republic. Nor did he implement the 'Just Economic Order' or anything approaching it. Erbakan's frequently expressed desire to form closer ties with other Islamic nations was disastrous. Not only was his trip to Libya marred by his humiliation by Gaddafi, as outlined above, he also failed to receive the welcome he wished for when he visited Iran. By the end of his premiership, he was sending Abdullah Gül, the closest the Welfare Party had to a Mandelson, to America to reassure Washington of the party's secular credentials, a move which while politic, was hardly commensurate with his avowed destruction of the capitalist system.[27] The party did, however, institute wholesale changes of personnel in the bureaucracy, particularly attracting attention through its attempt to change senior legal figures – judges and prosecutors. The Government authorised an enormous number of *imam-hatip* schools: their number appears to have jumped by 70 in the official statistics for 1996-7.[28]

Erbakan himself behaved bullishly, even provocatively. He announced further initiatives throughout his premiership, such as affirming the support of the Government for building mosques in Taksim Square, in the centre of Istanbul, and in Çankaya, seat of the governmental residences in Ankara. One of his most daring actions was to hold a *Ramazan* banquet at the Prime Minister's residence, bringing together *tarikat* leaders, the head of the Directorate of Religious Affairs, and leading professors from the Theology Faculties to dine at the break of fast, *iftar*. This made a huge impact. The foundation of the Republican control of Islam lies in ensuring that the state-led orthodox centres of Islamic activity provide a plausible buttress against the *tarikat* groups. At one level, the television pictures of turbaned sheikhs attending a meal in the Prime Minister's house is a visual nightmare for committed secularists; more profoundly it reflects a potential redistribution of power whereby Islamic forces, both within and outside the state, combine openly against avowedly secularist groups. The possibility of an open split that this might in turn provoke corresponds to the worst fear of authority: *bölücülük*, or movements which divide the body politic. It is hardly surprising that this open flaunting of Islamic credentials in a society accustomed to covert change led in February 1997 to the special measures of the State Security Council, and subsequently to Erbakan's fall.

Conclusions
In this chapter, I have attempted to outline the way that coherent organisation, alternative, appealing ideologies, and sensitivity to social change enabled a political Islamic movement to come to the fore in Turkey. That it should have been so successful has confounded many people both inside and outside the country, who regard the movement still as being in some way irrelevant to Turkey's main concerns. This can now be shown to be quite wrong. In effect, the Welfare Party marked a reorganisation of the preoccupations of Turkish society. In the past most parties were content to pursue re-Islamicization through Kemalist ideologies and still claim to be secularist. Under Erbakan, re-Islamicization was achieved through asserting the right to found an Islamic state, whilst actually achieving only a small part of this aim.

The latter approach is, not surprisingly, far more likely to result in overt clashes with the secular authorities.

The Welfare Party itself possessed a powerful sense of being a persecuted minority, convinced that it was being deprived of its lawful right to govern by a series of conspiracies by the Kemalist 'establishment'.[29] This led the party to interpret its closure in terms of a breach of human rights, and its representatives have declared their intention to apply to the European Court of Human Rights to overturn the decision of the Constitutional Court. In this, they have been supported by the Western press. The Welfare Party's closure was met with a storm of newspaper comment which focused on 'democracy' and 'human rights', very much the terms in which Welfare would like to see itself discussed. Indeed, the former members of the Welfare Party have conveniently collected dozens of overseas press extracts on a single web-site file for sympathisers to peruse.[30]

This comment, much of it hostile to the decision for closure, has made writing the next chapter particularly difficult. Though the press coverage is perhaps sometimes not very well informed, it shows how very difficult it is to write about the crucial question of closing democratically elected parties without taking a moral position. Further, as well as being against human nature not to wish to express an opinion, these are issues of such substantive relevance to the political relationship between Turkey and Europe that it hardly serves or illuminates these matters to avoid commenting on them entirely. In the next chapter, I have accordingly phrased the argument in terms of a conventional liberal question: did the Welfare Party serve to support, or threaten, the plurality of ideas and ways of life within Turkish society?

Immediately, however, I should offer two qualifications. The first is that I do not know what the consequences of the closure will be. I fully accept that though it might be the intent of the state prosecutor to defend plural liberalism as best he can through his decision, any such volatile social measure is insufficiently predictable to be sure of achieving its goal. There is a strong, and plausible argument that it may provoke more than it may quieten. Secondly, my discussion does not touch on the Welfare Party's replacement, the Virtue Party, *Fazilet Partisi* or whatever party may follow *Fazilet* in turn if the later application to close it also succeeds. There are activists within the political Islamic movement who quite explicitly see their rightful task as impeding 'fundamentalism' (their term). They may succeed in doing so, and it would be quite premature to make any comment on the direction that they may take.

| 5 |

Erbakan: Fall and Reaction

Though long anticipated, the manner of Erbakan's fall is fascinating. After his accession to power, senior military officers had been making quite clear their displeasure through press briefings and curtly-phrased warning speeches at formal occasions. In the summer of 1996, they denied members of the Welfare Party access to an army graduation ceremony on the grounds that their Islamic beards made them inappropriately dressed. Ominously, in January 1977 the joint forces held a major conference of staff officers.[1] At the beginning of February, in Sincan, a district of Ankara, pro-Islamic demonstrations held to mark Jerusalem Day became riotous. A secular newspaper reporter was assaulted, and the nation was able to watch a bearded man strike a western-dressed woman on its television sets. The army reacted by sending tanks 'on exercise' to the area.

Then, on the 28 February 1997, the National Security Council presented Erbakan with a series of demands which they described as being designed to protect secularism (Appendix 3). At the meeting, Erbakan refused to ratify the proposals, though he finally capitulated and signed later. On 20 May 1997, though Erbakan was still Prime Minster, the head state prosecutor applied to the constitutional court to have the Welfare Party closed down. On 11 June, the army announced the formation of a new group the 'Western Working Group' (*Batı Çalışma Grubu*) aimed at investigating the infiltration of fundamentalist sympathisers into the civil service. Faced with these concerted blows from the authorities, deputies began to leave the True Path Party, and the coalition fell below the level needed to maintain support. Erbakan was left no choice but to resign. Worse was to come: even after a meticulous defence of his position and his actions to the Constitutional Court amounting to nearly 500 pages, in January 1998 the Welfare Party was banned by the court, and Erbakan suspended from politics.

It is sometimes held that these events constitute a fourth coup. This is not true in any straightforward way. The National Security Council, consisting of the President of the Republic, the Prime Minister, the Ministers of Defence, Interior and Foreign Affairs, the Chief of General Staff, and the four heads of the services (Army, Navy, Air Force and Gendarmes), is made up only partially of military figures. The Constitutional Court is the apex of the civilian legal system and is renowned for its independent upholding of its authority whatever the government in power. There seems no reason to doubt that many of the deputies in the True Path Party genuinely opposed the further Islamification of the country. It is better seen as a co-ordinated action, the military combined with the bureaucracy and senior political figures. As of so many of the manoeuvres surrounding Islam and authority in the Republic, it was achieved without any violence at all, however real the threat of coercion if the powers that be had been ignored.

The measures of 28 February 1997

The fears of the generals and the National Security Council, as expressed in their detailed measures on the 28 February are varied. They are concerned that there might be a direct attack on the secular basis of the Republic. The revolution in Iran, the situation in Algeria, and the Talibani success in Afghanistan are perceived as genuine threats, even if at present such a forceful armed confrontation within Turkey appears to be unlikely to succeed. To this end, they identify links between *tarikat* groups, Iranian training, and the ease and availability of weapons in modern Turkey. Their further concern is lest the slow changes in the Islamic milieu within Turkey will eventually lead to a result just as fatal to the Republic, even if not necessarily achieved through a violent revolt funded from the outside. This is quite clear in their comments on the rise of the Welfare Party, whom they accuse of infiltrating the civil service, and using religious education as 'the surest way to ensure the survival of its ideology'.[2]

Their suggested remedy is to draw Islamic activity more tightly under the umbrella of the state. They suggest that the state prosecutors should become more incisive at acting against breaches of the law, and that the law itself should be tightened. They propose that all Koran courses should come under the direction of the Ministry of Education (rather than be loosely supervised by the Directorate of Religious Affairs as they are at present), and most ambitiously that *imam-hatip* schools should be absorbed in a wholesale change in the Turkish education system whereby all pupils go to similar, non-vocational schools for eight years.

Major reform of the education system had been discussed by previous governments, but the implications are considerable. Especially, reform is extremely expensive. When Yılmaz took over as Prime Minister after Erbakan's fall, he announced special taxes to raise money to pay for the measures intended, but it is doubtful that these will be sufficient, even if subsequent governments do not wish to implement the changes fully. Further, it is unlikely that there would be the political will for a complete absorption of the *imam-hatip* schools. That they have traditionally been paid for through private subscription means that their supporters will be vociferous in trying to retain them for their original purpose, even after the laws theoretically marking their demise are passed. Further, because the supporters have originally gained permission to open them largely through their senior contacts in the political system, they will equally be able to use those contacts to lobby to keep them open. Whilst the issue has still not been resolved entirely it looks as if, as of autumn 1999, the closure of the middle school level will go ahead, with the whole senior Lycée level remaining open.

The reaction
Reaction to these measures, to Erbakan's fall, and to the subsequent closure of the Welfare Party has been mixed. Official spokespersons in European countries expressed their concern openly, whilst the

international press were almost all vociferous in their condemnation. Even in Britain (traditionally more sympathetic to Turkey than mainland Europe) many commentators felt that they were inadvisable, and at least one international seminar, held in London at the Royal Services Institute just after the Welfare Party was banned, contained many participants who felt that the moves harmed Turkey's prospects in the European Union.

However, within Turkey, the measures were met with a huge sigh of relief among secularists. Discussing the situation with me, one activist even compared 28 February 1997 as the point at which the Republic was saved, as important to them as the distinction between BC and AD is to Christianity. Whilst this is a little theatrical, it does give some indication of how secularists were looking for decisive action from the Republican authorities.

Of course, this feeling is by no means universal. Even leaving to one side politically committed Islamists, there are a number of intellectuals who take a different view. Whilst deploring violence, they counter the secularist position by saying, 'Should Turkey become a moderate but Islamic state, would it matter terribly?' This view is linked to the presumption that the initial imposition of the Kemalist reforms was authoritarian, therefore a mass rejection of those reforms (if peaceful) must be a good thing. These people often go by the name of 'Second Republicans', *İkinci Cumhuriyetçiler*. This is not a paid-up organisation, but rather a loose coalition of intellectuals, journalists and believers who think that a moderate synthesis between Islam and modernity could be reached, and imply that the repressive secular state is preventing them from achieving it.[3] Interestingly, some outside commentators take this view as well, and journalists, European Union officials, and even diplomats, number amongst them.

Pluralism

Defenders of the secular system argue that increasing Islamic activism has not, in fact, led to an increase in personal freedom or even cleaner politics.[4] They maintain that the Welfare Party, at the top at least, was not more honest than the next party: certainly, Erbakan is no poorer than many other leading politicians. They note that whilst the ethic of the party may have ensured that members low down the scale behaved in honest fashion, such a strong culture brought its own dangers. It is widely rumoured that bribes were still necessary to gain contracts in Welfare-controlled municipalities, not however to individuals but as donations to the local party organisation. The readiness of the Welfare Party to make gifts to voters, of sugar, coffee, and sometimes cash, in return for their votes has been repeatedly testified.[5] Further, whilst nothing was legally proven, the election to the municipality in Ankara in 1994 appeared quite definitely to have been manipulated (in this case through substituting completed ballot papers). All this, whilst testifying once more to the efficiency of the Welfare Party, does not accord well with its belief in democracy.

More subtly, at present, whether or not this was originally intended by the founders of the Republic, there is indisputably in Turkey an astounding variety of social philosophies available with which to guide one's life, some very Islamic and some patently not. Take marriage as an example. There is a legal requirement to go through a simple and brief wedding ceremony administered by an official of the town municipality where the couple reside. Many people in addition, also hold an Islamic service, *nikah*, by asking the local *imam* to officiate. In villages, they may still further hold a traditional celebration with music and dance. In towns and cities, they are likely to hold a large celebration lasting a few hours, which takes place with music in a large purpose-built wedding hall.[6] Those who are more Islamically inclined often decline to use musicians for a marriage gathering, and may substitute instead a *müezzin* (caller to prayer) or other suitably qualified persons to intone hymns, *ilahi*, often verses from the Koran. Yet again, those who are not at all interested in Islam may seek different traditions with which to celebrate: in the early 1990s, I witnessed one ceremony at the Hilton Hotel in which the management arranged for the couple to be ushered into the room to the accompaniment of loud drum music. They were then placed on a stage surrounded with flunkies dressed in Roman togas holding torches above their heads. This way of supplementing the bare civil marriage rite appeared to be very successful.[7]

Whilst it would be absolutely mistaken to assume that all members of the Welfare Party (and now its successor, the Virtue Party) are against this diverging plurality, there is a mass of evidence to suggest that it is deplored by Islamic activists, from whom the Welfare Party derived much of its support. Even the briefest of excursions among Welfare Party rallies illustrated this, where a common theme in speeches was to regard women who wander freely without their heads covered as sinful, and a symptom of the shortcomings of the secular Republic. In their speeches, and in their actions when they were in power, the Welfare Party consistently attempted to move against women who dressed with insufficient modesty. The Welfare mayor of Konya famously wished to reintroduce separate buses for school boys and girls, and to build a hospital at which all those in the building would be women. After the Welfare Party captured the Ankara Greater Municipality in 1994, I was trapped in the traffic created by their victory parade along the Eskişehir Road (a main thoroughfare leading off Atatürk Boulevard). Our car was buffeted and spat at by Welfare Party supporters: the women were entirely dressed in black, whilst the men with beards shouted 'Whores!' to the women in my car, who were unveiled.

These attempts to deplore activities that do not conform can be seen in other areas as well. One of the measures that the Welfare Party did succeed in passing closed down casinos throughout the country. They also pursued a series of measures designed to restrict the sale of alcohol, particularly in village grocery shops. Another measure, though this time a failure, was aimed at reorganising civil service office hours in order to fit in with the times of the *Ramazan* fast. A leading Welfare Party member of parliament suggested that the Byzantine walls in Istanbul be taken down to provide stone bricks for the shanty towns, and the famous underground cistern '*Yerebatan*' at Sultanahmet be turned into a car park. The mayor of Konya closed down authorised brothels within the city precincts – with disastrous results to the social fabric of the city, because it splintered the trade and sent it underground into the hands of a largely Kurdish *mafya*.

These measures are sometimes regarded as being cultural, as having little effect on the lives of people. A report by the *Observer* in 1994, for example, regarded assaults on women by religious activists as being of little importance.[8] A popular account of Islam in the modern world by Oliver Roy with the suggestive title *The Bankruptcy of Political Islam* has even suggested that a preoccupation with such adjustments of social life has become the norm for Islamic political movements.[9] He is correct in noting this trend, but utterly mistaken in suggesting that they are 'cultural' in the sense that the word is usually meant to mean effusions of art or music or dress that have little to do with the organising powers or hierarchies of society. The imposition of cultural uniformity through legislation is intimately related to power. The rise of political Islam in Turkey has created a situation where plurality of religious belief is not bolstered, but threatened. In effect, this means that where people do not wish to conform in matters of religion, they may be threatened, forced to accede against their will, or at worst killed. It is painful to liberal sensitivities to spell these things out but absurd to ignore them.

There are many examples of this. Pupils in *imam-hatip* schools are frequently bullied, or victimised, if it is felt that they are slacking in their religious duties. One boy, reported in *Sabah* newspaper, was beaten and hospitalised because he admitted that he had failed to carry out his *aptes*, ritual cleansing, properly before prayers.[10] Prominent critics of Islam have been regularly killed. Dursun, who wrote a series of books demonstrating that the Koran could be seen as being based on pre-historic texts was shot. Bahiye Üçok, a lady professor in the Faculty of Theology at Ankara University, later a deputy, (who suggested, among other things, that there was nothing in Islam that required women to be covered, and that there was no reason why Arabic should in itself be more sacred than other languages found in the Islamic world) was assassinated. A barman in Istanbul who appeared on television with an 'Allah' tattoo on his chest was killed for bringing God's name into dishonour (yet it turned out that he was a follower of the *Mevlevi*, and was so tattooed out of respect rather than insult). Uğur Mumcu, a prominent secularist writing for *Cumhuriyet,* was murdered in a car bomb by unknown assailants.

The Welfare Party did not play a neutral part in the background to these events, nor did it attempt to restrain them. Whilst there can be no doubt that many of their leaders in Ankara may personally have deplored them, the fact remains that the legislation promoted by the Refah Party encouraged rather than diminished the chance of the occurence of these events. For example, the abortive attempt to change the times at which civil servants work during the *Ramazan* may seem a neutral desire to reflect the will of the people. It was not. *Ramazan* is a tense time at which violent outbreaks are already comparatively common. During this month it used to be absolutely usual for people to fast if they wished, not to do so if they were disinclined. Now, however, in all sorts of settings (eg. in schools, previously one of the hot-beds of Kemalist reform) those who eat or smoke during the fast are regularly threatened. To attempt to enforce changes of office hours can only reinforce those who believe that they have a right to attack someone who does not wish to fast.[11]

A similar point can be made when examining the speeches of Erbakan. Even allowing for political licence, Erbakan's rhetoric when in power was not that of a peaceful man. He explicitly accused a particular group, the 'Zionists' of controlling the whole world. He accused every other political party in Turkey of utter, co-ordinated corruption. He stated quite openly that Europe and America, having been bought out by the 'Zionists', have enslaved Turkey. Left-wing intellectuals in Turkey often laugh when they recall the wit with which he speaks. At the same time, however, that same freedom of locution may become very extreme, as when he claimed, 'We shall come to power. Whether it will be peaceful, or whether it will be bloody is not yet clear', a comment that later was instrumental in the request to the Constitutional Court to close the party.[12]

Nor is it the case that riots have failed to occur. The riot at Sincan was caused, in part, by inflammatory speeches. The most famous, and destructive, example of this in recent times has been that of the massacres at Sivas. There, a group of Alevis, folklorists, and intellectuals, including the late Aziz Nesin, a prolific atheist philosopher, met for a convention in a hotel. Aziz Nesin had already attracted attention for beginning to publish Rushdie's *Satanic Verses* in Turkish, and even before participants arrived for the meeting, circulars had been sent around attempting to whip up feeling against the congress. When they were actually in the hotel, outside a crowd began to form, gradually growing and preventing them from leaving. Over the next twenty-four hours, the crowd became more and more agitated, finally setting fire to the hotel. Thirty-seven people were burnt to death. Many of the events of the night were caught on video-tape and television cameras. One of the most distressing aspects of the riot was the way that it built up so slowly, slogan chanting gradually turning into massacre.[13]

The Welfare Party denied responsibility. Again, whilst there is no doubt that many people in the party would have been horrified at the deaths, it is also the case that the municipality at Sivas was controlled by the Welfare Party. Achieving public order within cities is partly the responsibility of the municipality who have official constables, *zabıtas*, employed by them. In the event, their attempts to disperse the crowd, to lower the rising temper of ill-feeling, to rescue the people within the hotel were entirely ineffectual until the provincial governor intervened, by which time the hotel was well alight and many people dead. It later emerged that, when he realised his identity, the fireman, an employee of the municipality, who rescued Aziz Nesin, beat him on the ladder when he was being brought down from the flames, on the grounds that he was an atheist. Thus, whether or not the Welfare Party representatives in Sivas were complicit in the riot and arson, they manifestly failed in their duty to protect citizens from religious hatred in an area where they were in power, and their own employees were shown to have condoned it. As a final irony, one of the leading members of the Welfare Party offered himself as defence lawyer for the accused. Again, this does not imply that he felt personally that the murders should have taken place. It was however, an extremely unfortunate signal to the rest of the population, giving a message that the Welfare Party condoned the action of those who felt that murder is an appropriate way to treat those who do not wish to believe in religion.

The secular opposition
A further strand of thought, again exemplified by the 'Second Republican' movement, is that because the secular reforms were imposed by the state, they must necessarily be opposed by the vast mass of the people. This view tends to see the rise of Islam in Turkey with a sort of grim satisfaction, as if the state at last is getting its just deserts as the masses claim their rightful heritage.[14] It is true that much of this work has indeed been concerned with people who, in varying ways, have disagreed with the reforms. However, it would be quite wrong to extrapolate from this that only the army and a few

senior bureaucrats embrace secularism. The Islamic revival is taking place within a society that has always been diverse, and is now ever more so. A host of different positions, the self-consciously secular, the indifferent, the actively religious, the adamant atheist, are tempered in different ways according to generation, sect, politics, interest groups and gender, a variety so great that modern Turkey, however powerful the religious upsurge may seem inclined towards encouraging a cultural uniformity, strikes the researcher by its heterogeneity.

There are many ways of demonstrating this. To look first at party politics, it is sometimes held that in Turkey, parties are no more than mechanisms to channel resources – in effect client/patronage organisations within which ideology is not significant.[15] Almost the exact opposite has turned out to be the case. The many parties demonstrate combinations of religion, secularism, liberalism and nationalism which reflect, and appeal to, different sectors of the population.[16] For example, one of the central groups in Turkish life is the first or second generation urban Republicans. These people, now nearing the end of their working lives, would most likely have been at the political centre: members of Demirel's True Path Party or the old Republican People's Party (*CHP*). They may be pious, but they have reached a successful accommodation of belief and faith whereby they hold that the state's secularism should not be undermined by religious politics.[17] Though they have no objection to religious practice, they do not wish to change the governing principles of the country.

Usually slightly younger, more private-sector orientated, there are those who wish for a greater participation in religion by the state, but are not in themselves against the secular rules partly because they do not see how an accommodation can be made between business, and *şeriat* law. Such people would most likely be members of the Motherland Party in the late Turgut Özal's time, when it was pursuing Turkey's financial integration with the West alongside its pro-religious policies.[18] Then there is a strong minority which asserts that Turkish nationalism should come before religion as the dominant way that Turks express themselves. Usually prominent in small towns, but with a larger following altogether in the eastern cities, they distrust the pan-nationalism and anti-Kemalism advocated by many advocates of the *şeriat*. Such people are most likely to be members of the far-right Nationalist Action Party (*MHP*), the 'grey wolves' led for many years by the late Alparslan Türkeş. In 1999, headed by Devlet Bahçeli, they became coalition partners in government for the first time.

Then there is the left wing, which in itself has many different positions that people may take up, from old-fashioned pre-politicised *CHP* to out-and-out Marxism. They include also Çankaya (Turkey's equivalent of the left-bank) socialism, and radical feminism. By inclination, many of these people would have voted for the Social Democrat Populist Party (*SHP*) under Erdal İnönü, and are happier than most to vote for the re-incarnated *CHP* under Baykal. Though they sometimes enjoy flirting with religious intellectuals ('so interesting'), invite them to their drinks parties, and enjoy the sensation of being anti-establishment alongside them, they do not actually vote for the Welfare Party, as the fact that Çankaya municipality has a *CHP* mayor indicates. Also on the left is the curious combination developed by Ecevit of nationalism and socialism together in the Democratic Left Party (*DSP*). Coincidentally or not, his two brief periods as Prime Minister have included national triumphs: during his first, the intervention in Cyprus, and his second, much later, in 1999, the arrest of Öcalan, the PKK terrorist leader. In between, his doggedness has appealed to old trade unionists in small towns and villages, with firmer pockets of support on the Black-Sea Coast, though his honesty in itself is an asset across a wide section of voters. He also enjoys particular support among the Alevis, who are attracted to his vision of a social-democrat life on the Scandinavian model.

Of course, not all views can be tied into politics. Turkey has a very young population. This youth has brought all sorts of hidden benefits in terms of economic dynamism, expanding consumer markets and cheap labour. Throughout the last two decades, it has also manifested itself through an explosion in popular music, both drawn from the West, and from Turkey. Music has always been part of Turkish life, but stars such as Sezen Aksu, Sertap, Demet, Deniz, and above all Tarkan produce catchy melodies, video-clips and stadium concerts which draw tens of thousands of admirers. Far from being religious, these performances and their lyrics are suggestive, even overtly erotic.

Whilst the pious may occasionally enjoy this movement vicariously, at heart it is profoundly rooted in a consumerism that has no more to do with religion than vaguely expressed allusions to fate, love and fidelity.[19] It is hardly surprising then, that actively religious people attempt occasionally to impede its spread, most conspicuously by trying to ban Tarkan concerts or attacking the transmitters of MTV, an international youth music channel. This popular music culture merges also into a life style of leisure, access to summer houses on the Mediterranean and Aegean coasts, restaurants, night clubs and alcohol that used to available to only the very wealthiest. Now, to varying degrees, it is simply part of many persons' lives.

Turning to gender, the emancipation of women was one of the planks of the Kemalist revolution. Sceptics may argue that this movement has been no more successful than feminist movements in other parts of the world. Whilst it is true that it is has not always been an easy struggle, millions of women have entered public life in the professions, civil service and other areas. Many of these women today feel that they owe to Atatürk this ability to play a full part in the economic and business life in the country. There is no doubt that sexual harassment in the work-place is as big a problem in Turkey as it is in other Western countries. Nevertheless, a great many of these women do not wish to adopt the veil and headscarf, something which they have never known nor wish to. Indeed, they regard its prospect with explicit fury and repeated dismay.[20]

Then there is the seamier side of life, the nightclubs, gambling and the rise in transvestite prostitution. This last group, claiming the right to lead their lives as women, should they so wish, frequently reported violent intimidation at the hands of the Welfare-controlled Istanbul municipality. People in these areas of social life too, if they are politically committed at all, are unlikely to regard secularism as a regime imposed by an authoritarian state. Indeed, the *mafya* who share their world and come out themselves largely at night, but who form such a powerful interlocutory function between politicians and business, are involved most deeply with the moderate right wing rather than with religious groups, as the renowned *Susurluk* affair (discussed below) has demonstrated.

Divided secularism

It might be asked, given that there are such disparate groups wishing to maintain the status quo, why have they not acted more firmly against the Islamic revival? Partly, the reason appears to be that the power and vigour of the Atatürk revolution meant that, after its initial imposition, it was felt that secularism did not need to receive complex intellectual justification. The educated elite, who still make up a substantial proportion of the urban middle class, correspondingly failed to realise the intensity and sheer determination of the Islamic movement to create a way of life that would offer an alternative to Kemalism. Indeed, for many years, for those living within urban Turkey a full-blown Islamic revival seemed quite out of the question.

They were reinforced in this belief by two factors. The first was an almost universal inclination among the urban middle class to assume that village life itself is unpleasant, dirty and backward. There are the beginnings of a movement to romanticise the countryside in consumer advertising (*country-fresh butter*), but most established urban dwellers refuse even today ever to enter a village, to talk to villagers unless they be a taxi driver, maid, concierge or workman, or to visit the poorer areas of the cities. This is matched by a curiously prevalent contemporary academic lack of interest in village life.[21] All this hinders understanding Turkey's problems, and the reaction of rural people as they move into the cities.

A second reason is the army. Outside Turkey, it is not always realised that the army has a particularly favourable image among Turkish people. By many, it is held to be the guardian not just of the country's borders but also of the civil peace, and the Republican heritage. In this, the military have taken on some of the perceived role of a police force in Europe: a body that stands outside society, but can be relied upon to protect it from social disorder. Contrariwise, the police have a very low reputation as being corrupt, ready to employ indiscriminate violence, and themselves prone to the crimes that they are supposed to be cleaning up.

In spite of this reliance on the military, there is a tension between intellectuals and the army which it is difficult to surmount. Many of the middle class incline, even if mildly, toward the left. On the other hand, the army, whilst protecting secularism, is happy to encourage controlled religion at the expense of the left, whom they regard as 'communists'. During the terrible troubles of the late 1970s, many left-wing people felt, quite correctly, that they were singled out for brutal treatment by the armed forces and police, far more so than the right wing.[22] The army then, are protectors, but not protectors with whom the urban middle class have been able to strike a comfortable intellectual affiliation.

A similar argument can be applied to the Alevis who, it is sometimes suggested, might become a model for Kemalist secularism.[23] The Alevis' secularised, internalised mysticism, discussed in the next chapter, has long clashed with official insistence on the paramountcy of mosque and Koran, however moderately interpreted. This makes the Alevis extremely reluctant to regard the army with anything but ambivalence. For them, it is a reactionary tool of orthodoxy, even if, inasmuch as it opposes the political re-Islamification of the country, a good thing.

Leaving aside these difficulties, perhaps the most important factor of all is the virtual inability of secular political parties to work together for any length of time. Turkish politics have always been vociferous, but as democracy began to crystallise, and the creation of competing patronage groups became part and parcel of the political process, they found it increasingly impossible to co-operate, even when the absence of inter-party co-operation was detrimental to the country. During the late 1970s, for example, the main political groups clearly exacerbated the bad feeling between extremist gangs which were openly shooting each other in the street. As the clashes worsened, and law and order became hardly achievable, the political parties quarrelled with such passion over who would be the next president, quite unable to reach a decision, that the business of governing seemed to have come to a halt.[24] A similar *impasse* was directly responsible for the Welfare government coming to power. If the two centre-right parties, the Motherland Party, and the True Path Party, who were quite able to create and maintain a majority government, had agreed to share power, then they would have had an absolutely assured rule until the end of that parliament. An equal accusation could be made against the left, whose refusal to combine under one party means that they lost what chance they had to play a co-ordinated part in power. Of course,

political unity in itself would not simplify the deeper impulses that
have led people towards Islam, but it would make the whole process
of reaching an accommodation in the future far less potentially
disruptive, and far more achievable within the existing canons of the
Republic.

Associations for Atatürkist Thought

Brought sharply into focus by the success of Erbakan's government,
there are signs that the splintered resistance to the rise of Islam among
the civil population may be beginning to coalesce. One sign of this is
the emergence of a chain of associations known as *Atatürkçü
Düşünce Dernekleri*, 'Associations for Atatürkist Thought'. In 1998,
they were reported to consist of 378 branches, with more than
100,000 members in Turkey and among the Turkish population in
Germany.[25]

They are sometimes thought to be irrelevant. This is too hasty a
judgement. Part of their importance is that they claim to be an apolitical
secular front, one that gathers members from across the party
spectrum. Whilst, as in any other association, there appear to be
internal arguments about the degree of political intervention they
should pursue, in the one branch association that I know well, they
have succeeded in achieving the aim of attracting people from all
mainstream parties. They have also drawn people in without respect
for their sect, there being a high proportion of Alevis among their
numbers. Their activities too deserve to be taken seriously. Whilst
they do operate simply at the iconic level, by selling Atatürk's picture
or photographs, they also mark the beginnings of a genuine movement
to discuss the intellectual content of Atatürk's programme in a much
more sophisticated way than has until now often been the norm.

Erbakan's government also gave rise to a quite unprecedented level
of peaceful protest. One of the first signs of this was a demonstration
held in November 1996, on the anniversary of Atatürk's death, when
tens of thousands of people marched together to his mausoleum.
Those doing so were condemned as 'provocateurs' by the Welfare
government, who also pointed out that they had marched without first
applying for permission to do so from the Welfare-held city
municipality. A much wider protest began in February 1997, when

thousands of people began to switch their lights out for one minute at nine o'clock each evening. The protest began as a reaction against a series of revelations that emerged after a car crash on 3 November 1996 on the Istanbul motorway. Known as the *Susurluk* affair, after the town where it occurred, it turned out that those in the wrecked car included a wanted assassin, Abdullah Çatlı, along with a police chief and a deputy in Tansu Çiller's party. Astonishingly, Çatlı had an official passport only given to those who have been of service to the state. As the investigation continued, it seemed to reveal systematic links between right-wing politicians, police chiefs, *mafya* and hit men possibly even employed by the government to eliminate unwanted figures.

As the protest spread across Turkey, the Welfare government became visibly unnerved. This encouraged the one-minute demonstrations to spread even further, among those who now felt that it expressed a struggle for secularism rather than against corruption. The Welfare Party was not helped too, by one of its senior Ministers, Şevket Kazan, likening protestors to the Alevis by making a derogatory reference to a custom among some Alevis groups of extinguishing a candle, *mum söndürmek*, during their ceremonies, and continuing worship in the dark. Later, the public prosecutor announced that he would open proceedings on the basis of inciting religious hatred.

The situation today then has a curious fluidity. Any pro-Islamic party may be closed down at any time, yet there is an immense groundswell of support for a political party based on Islam which will hardly disappear. On the other hand, there is equally enormous popular determination to oppose any further Islamification of Turkish society, as the rise of a secularist movement during Erbakan's time in power demonstrated. Whilst the army support the *Atatürkçü Düşünce Dernekleri*, they are likely to be extremely concerned at the split that is emerging between overtly secular and non-secular approaches because of the increased possibility of a violent confrontation between holders of the two positions. Their response, to stress Atatürk's memory whilst at the same time reiterating the importance of moderate religious practice, whilst reminiscent of their measures in the post-1980 period, functionally fulfils a different role in today's Turkey.

Then, religion was aimed at building a bridge across violent party differences, and, whilst it is impossible to be categorical, it does appear to have contributed to the diminution of violence. On this occasion, it is designed to bridge a gap between secularist and Islamist views, and may end up by satisfying nobody, being too much for one group and insufficient for the other.

The elections of 19 April 1999

In the event, the general elections in April 1999 provided a quick test of the State Security Council's actions. They were held at a particularly awkward juncture. After Erbakan offered his resignation in June 1997, he did so thinking that the President would hand over the right to be Prime Minister to his coalition partner and Deputy Prime Minister, Tansu Çiller. However, surprising everybody, President Demirel instead offered the chance to form a government to Mesut Yılmaz, then in opposition. Yılmaz did so, with Ecevit as Deputy Prime Minister.

After their party was banned, the ex-Welfare Party deputies were permitted to retain their seats as independents, but Deniz Baykal, leader of the *CHP*, supported the coalition from outside government, giving it a working majority. For a space, this arrangement appeared to be working rather well. Then, Baykal insisted that general elections be called in April, twenty months earlier than they needed be, in return for his continuing co-operation. Things became even more confused when Yılmaz was forced to resign after allegations that he favoured a business associate during the awarding of a television company licence. Turkey was once again without a Prime Minister until, finally, Ecevit became caretaker Prime Minister in order to lead the country to the elections, by then fixed for 19 April, as Baykal had desired.

During the run up to the elections, it was difficult to gauge how successful the newly founded Virtue Party, the replacement for the Welfare Party might be. Erbakan was no longer the leader, banned automatically from politics as a consequence of the Welfare Party being confirmed guilty of acting against the constitution of the Republic. He continued to exert influence from outside the party, however, much to the disquiet of those within it who saw their chance to break free from his flamboyant style of leadership. The state prosecutor, meanwhile, maintained his initiative by arresting the powerful ex-Welfare mayor of Istanbul, Tayyip Erdoğan, who was found guilty of anti-secular activities and given a prison sentence.

All this appeared to indicate that it would be difficult for the Islamic political movement to do as well as it had done in the past. Nevertheless, political parties do rise and fall quickly in Turkey, and to be recently conceived does not necessarily mitigate against success. Indeed, in 1983, the brand-new Motherland Party under Özal was elected by a surge of cross-party support that appeared to stem greatly from a desire to express opposition to the wishes of authority. It was perfectly possible that its wishes on this occasion might be similarly defied, which would have produced the nightmarish scenario of an Islamist majority elected government and a resolutely secular military.

Then, in the midst of this uncertainty, a parallel plot reached its *dénouement*. The army had already declared to Syria in 1988 that it absolutely had to expel Öcalan, the PKK leader, or face military consequences. These threats did succeed in flushing him out, apparently to Russia. Then Öcalan appeared in Italy, seemingly welcomed by the Communist Party. He left Italy and disappeared from sight momentarily, though there were rumours that he had attempted to land in the Netherlands, only to be turned away by their airforce planes. Then, astonishingly, on 16 February 1999, the news broke that Öcalan had been arrested in Kenya by Turkish commandos, it seems, after having been under the protection of Greek Embassy officials there. He was escorted back to Turkey, and was paraded in triumph on the nation's television screens. Stimulated by widespread international demonstrations by Kurdish supporters, the international media concentrated on questioning whether Öcalan would receive a fair trial. Within Turkey, public euphoria concentrated more on the relief of having captured the PKK leader, and the hope that it would bring an end to the violence in the east. Buoyed by his newly affirmed nationalist credentials, Ecevit, the caretaker-Prime Minister, entered the elections a hero.

The results confirmed Ecevit's success, his party, the Democratic Left Party (*DSP*) gaining the most seats. They also marked the rise of the Nationalist Action Party (*MHP*), the extremist right-wing nationalist party, under the comparative unknown Devlet Bahçeli. The

Virtue Party (*FP*) came third. The fractured moderate right, *ANAP* and *DYP*, were respectively fourth and fifth. The *CHP*, surely marred by Baykal's precipitate action in pulling down the coalition, suffered a disastrous failure, and failed to pass the 10 per cent barrier to enter the Assembly for the first time in the history of the Republic.

Table 4: 19 April 1999 General Election Results*

Party	Leader	Main Orientation	Number of votes gained	% of votes won	Number of seats
Democratic Left (*DSP*)	Ecevit	Left (Nationalist)	6,919,670	22.19	136
Nationalist Action (*MHP*)	Bahçeli	Far right (Nationalist)	5,606,583	17.98	129
Virtue (*FP*)	Kutan	Religious	4,805,381	15.41	111
Motherland (*ANAP*)	Yılmaz	Right	4,122,929	13.22	86
True Path (*DYP*)	Çiller	Right	3,745,417	12.01	85
Independents			270,265	0.87	3
Totals			25,470,245	81.68	550

* These figures ignore parties (and their votes) which failed to pass the 10 per cent barrier, notably the Republican People's Party (*CHP*) under Baykal, who gained 8.4%.

The new government

During the Erbakan period, a new axis had begun to appear by which the moderate right split according to its orientation towards religion. The *DYP* under Çiller had aligned itself with the Welfare Party in order to keep them both in power, whilst Yılmaz worked with Ecevit to form a government with the left. This *ad hoc* co-operation between right and left continued in the post-election period. Ecevit with the largest number of seats became Prime Minister, and Bahçeli the Deputy Prime Minister. This still did not quite produce a majority, so Yılmaz joined in the coalition, also as Deputy Prime Minister. This left the Virtue Party, with 111 seats, and the True Path Party, with 85 seats, as the opposition.

Thus, seemingly neutralized, the religious question appeared momentarily to disappear. The secular left, particularly the shattered *CHP*, fraught with the images of the 1970s when many of them had fought with the *MHP* became concerned about an entirely new problem: the extent to which a party that might once have appeared (to them at least) to be extremely nasty, even fascist, would be able to moderate if in government. First indications are obviously unclear, though beatings do appear to have taken place on the streets of Ankara and other south-eastern cities in the immediate aftermath of the results.

Just as soon again, however, the religious debate returned to the fore. One of the new members of parliament for the Virtue Party, Merve Kavakçi, refused to remove her headscarf as she entered the Assembly to take her vows to the Republic at the beginning of the new session. The session was adjourned in confusion, and the resulting controversy extended even to comments from Demirel. Then Savaş, the public prosecutor who had successfully argued for the closure of the Welfare Party, threw the Virtue Party into complete disarray by applying for its closure to the Constitutional Court, claiming that they were 'blood-sucking vampires'. This time, he called not only for the party to be closed but also for its deputies to be stripped of their parliamentary status.

It is too soon to evaluate these recent events properly. Nevertheless, if the Constitutional Court closes the Virtue Party and expels its deputies, then there will need to be parliamentary by-elections to fill the vacated seats. It is very unlikely indeed that an overtly Islamic-favouring party would be allowed to stand. If so, we may have seen the conclusion of a cycle that began with Erbakan, whereby groups that overtly favour Islam are not allowed to create popular parties, and a major experiment in Turkey's modern history would be, seemingly at least, at an end.

Conclusions

In conclusion, the relationship between political Islam and the wider institutions of Turkish society is much more complex than a simple confrontation between secular authority and religious expression. The earlier chapters in this book have demonstrated that the state itself may become diverse, the supporter of different ideologies, and drawn into conflict through its closeness with the people it administers. Urban Turkish society is so heterogeneous that political Islam can only be considered as one among a number of different approaches that people are adopting as they modernise. The military themselves are not so much against Islam, as against the use of Islam in the political arena. Nevertheless, they are increasingly becoming conscious of the amount of leeway that the state has already offered Islamic movements, and are thinking carefully of how to prevent them from gaining further ground.

It is certainly likely that the courts, and the legal device of suppressing parties, will remain part of any future programme. We should be cautious before judging. Ensuring that religious practice is free but not dominant over others is a problem that we do not, in general, have to face in the West. Indeed, the relationship between orthodox religion and society in Turkey is in many ways a mirror image of that in Europe. In Britain, for instance, the state is forced to legislate for an ever less religious society, Accordingly, it has been changing procedures so that those who live together (in what used to be known as 'in sin') are increasingly administered in the same way as the decreasing number who still prefer 'holy' matrimony. In Turkey, the reverse is true: the institutions of society are presented with expanding and strengthening belief, albeit in an otherwise heterogeneous environment. It may very well be that the Turkish solution of controlled, but permitted, worship is a better solution than is commonly realised.

One part of the population that the initiative aimed at achieving this quiescence will definitely not placate is the Alevis. Whilst they themselves are by no means homogeneous, most of them would prefer that the state did not support religion at all. This firm secular orientation means that, in the future they are likely to play a significant role, often fusing with the remnants of the Republican left wing to constitute a key part of the confrontation between secular and religious approaches. This in itself though, raises a further question. What is it about their particular way of life that leads them to become so resolutely secular? In order to offer an answer, even if a preliminary one, we consider them in some detail in the next chapter.

| 6 |

The Emergence of the Alevis

Periodically within Turkey there have been attempts to 'discover' the Alevis. These accounts usually followed a pattern: the reporter would stress certain qualities, their humanism, their loyalty to the state, the equality of men and women in their communities, and the 'hidden' or occluded rituals which lie at the heart of their society. The Alevis then appeared lost to the public view until the next writer, who would produce something fairly similar. Now, the situation is different. Whilst there is no lack of journalistic interest, there is an ever-growing spate of publications covering diverse aspects of Alevi society, their history, relations with the state, ceremonies and doctrines. These are not just articles but major publications, going through many editions. Unlike the previous accounts, many of them are written by the Alevis themselves.

These works are sometimes regarded as being rather repetitive, and perhaps not very useful. This is unfair. They represent and display varied and important aspects of Alevi life: explorations of attitudes and beliefs which have previously been spoken rather than written down, deliberations on what it means to be an Alevi today in both fiction and prose, odd pieces of anecdote and research and more coherent sweeps of different aspects of Alevi social history and ethnography.[1] That they constitute in great part an oral tradition made literate explains both their seeming similarity, and their immediacy. Indeed, they should be viewed as part of a general trend. The past decade has seen an unprecedented rise in Alevi cultural associations, periodicals devoted to exploring the nature of 'Aleviness', television programmes, discussion groups debating the 'Alevi question' and higher political exposure than they have known before. In short, a people who until recently were mute on the national stage are creating a modern, public cultural heritage.[2]

The Alevis have always been regarded by their Sunni counterparts as being deeply unorthodox, often even as not being Islamic at all. Nevertheless, one of the great triumphs of the Republic has been to ensure that both Alevis and Sunnis were able to feel allegiance to its tenets and live at peace. This may no longer be the case. Before the 1980 coup, there were serious attacks on the Alevis in Kahramanmaraş, Çorum and other towns in Anatolia. More recently, the Alevis point to the massacres at Sivas in 1994, which they regard primarily as a sectarian attack on them by Sunni fundamentalists. The atmosphere was still tense when in 1995, two Alevi religious figures were machine-gunned to death in a coffee-house in Istanbul. The resulting reaction from the Alevi community was sharp: rioting over two days was only quelled by a large police presence, during the course of which more people were injured and several of the demonstrators were killed by police. For several days it looked as if the conflict would spread to the rest of Turkey, though thankfully it did not. A little after this, however, a reminder of how sensitive the situation remained came through an unguarded but highly offensive remark by a television presenter concerning an Alevi guest who appeared on his programme. The broadcasting station was besieged by angry Alevi youths, who threw stones at its windows. Several threatened to sue. In 1998, the sectarian issue came to the fore again, when a leading figure in the Virtue Party was indicted for remarks calculating to incite religious conflict.

The Alevis have always been known as supporters of the Republic. This is still the case; they revere Atatürk's memory, and many regard the period of single-party rule under İnönü with unabashed nostalgia as a golden age. Nevertheless, their relationship with the state is ambivalent. They have never been explicitly acknowledged in state policy. There is a small but highly educated minority that wish for this to change, and the state to explicitly support 'Aleviness', *Alevilik,* through the Directorate of Religious Affairs as a legitimate interpretation of faith. The majority, however, appear to desire the opposite. For them *Alevilik* is a minority culture that has spent centuries suffering under a dominant central authority, and they see no merit in approaching it now. Among this latter group, many, though by no means all, are sceptical as to the literal truth of religious knowledge. These people are often active supporters of the left-wing political parties, parties which though secular, have an equally uneasy relationship with the authorities.

In short, then, the Alevis are a highly significant minority that is actively exploring, and becoming aware of, its own culture in a way that it has not done before. Many (though not all) among them are becoming less religious within a society that seemingly is becoming increasingly more religious. Depending on how circumstances unfold, they may come into violent contact with Sunni activists in overtly sectarian conflict, they may become embroiled on the secular side of the increasingly volatile religious/secular divide, and they may forge a diverse, confusing and perhaps, by virtue of their internal divisions, acrimonious relationship with the state.

Lack of Alevi research

In spite of the Alevis' importance, until very recently curiously little has been known in detail of their society, particularly in the earlier Republican period.[3] There are a number of reasons for this. Traditionally, they have been almost entirely rural. The lack of official recognition has discouraged research into their communities. Their own, only lately changed, reticence has made it difficult for outsiders to live among them. Partly due to their rural location, fewer of their number than might have been expected are occupying important positions in the bureaucracy, business or the media. Further, the general historical studies written by Westerners about Turkey, works that influence strongly our image of the country, such as those by Bernard Lewis or Geoffrey Lewis, or later Stanford Shaw, hardly mention the Alevis. Even recent studies such as Erik Zürcher's still have not yet incorporated such knowledge that is becoming available.[4]

Given this potentially critical but occluded background my aim in this chapter is to offer a brief account of Alevi social organisation and religious doctrines, and then to discuss their integration into modern Turkish society. Of course, I can only offer an abstract, vastly simplified model of the far more complicated and intricate reality that individual people and groups live through. Within this overall realisation of its inadequacies, my explanation assumes that the prevailing Alevi ethos is linked to the transition from sedentary, rather remote villages to being part of a modern nation-state. Specifically, it assumes that their traditional communal, hierarchical society can only modernise with great disruption, a disruption that is greater for the Alevis than for their Sunni counter-parts.[5] A few seek new structures for that belief in the administrative organisation of the state. Most do not. For many Alevis, religion begins to serve less as a system of belief in which they have absolute faith and more as a culture: a distinct body of sayings, poetry, music, traditions and song which can be researched and studied as a thing in itself. *Alevilik* becomes predominantly a moulding ethic of everyday life in which the literal statement of belief is becoming less significant.

Whilst this model of culture and social change may need extensive elaboration, justification and qualification, I believe that it is broadly accurate. If it is so, then it helps us to understand why the Alevis are changing in such different ways from the Sunni population, why they are so conspicuously resisting the resurgence of religion and why they are likely to be such determined supporters of the Republican, secularist cause.

Though I have paid systematic attention to the Alevis over a number of years, I have conducted most of my ethnographic research among one particular group, and it is from that group I draw my examples in the account below. Not, I hasten to add because I think that all Alevi communities necessarily conform to my experience (though the literature available does appear to parallel those instances I offer),[6] but rather because it is better to provide specific material where possible. I regret in particular, that I have not had the opportunity of working among the Kurdish Alevis, and at present at least, there is still little published detailed ethnography available (particularly concerning their religious traditions) which would help to fill the gap.[7]

The Alevis

In brief, the Alevis are a heterodox minority in Anatolia who know themselves by that name. *Alevilik* crosses the ethnic boundary: there are major Alevi Turkish and Alevi Kurdish populations. There are also smaller, mainly nomadic groups, where the boundary between ethnicity and religion is rather less clear, like the *Tahtacıs* or the *Abdal*s.

The number of Alevis who inhabit modern Turkey is uncertain, made the more so because, like other minority groups, they are not included in the ten-yearly census run by the State Institute of Statistics. Any suggestion of numbers is also fraught with the danger of political claim and counter-claim. Tentatively it would appear that the Alevis number slightly less than 20 per cent of Turkey's total population. Assuming that Turkey's population is 64 million this would give a total figure of perhaps 10-12 million. Of these, the largest group is that of the Turkish Alevis, consisting of perhaps 8-9 million. The next largest is that of the Alevi Kurds, consisting of perhaps 2-3 million. It should be stressed that unless a full census is taken, this can be no more than a highly provisional figure based partly on my limited field research, and partly on general impressions.

Their distribution is equally difficult to establish. In modern times, there have been only two serious attempts at establishing the whereabouts of ethnic and religious groups in Turkey. The first, the 'village inventory', *Köy Envanteri*, was conducted in the 1960s. Seemingly driven by a number of academics and Republican officials who believed that information about Anatolian villages was one key to helping their development, it finished a victim of political disapproval, and though completed, was not published. Whilst interesting, the information provided in the various volumes is often of doubtful accuracy. The second attempt, this time by Dr Peter Andrews, working from Germany, has resulted in the synoptic *Ethnic Groups in Turkey*. Derived from a combination of printed sources, questioning émigrés and commissioned articles, it is of the greatest use, though it has not yet been possible to check its details through fieldwork.[8]

This uncertainty may change quite soon: Alevi groups, driven by the tremendous momentum that they have generated for research into their own culture, are for the first time conducting field investigations into their own distribution. Until the results of this are known and assessed, it seems impossible to say (more or less in accordance with Andrews) other than that in modern times, but before the rapid migration to urban regions, the Alevis have inhabited most densely a belt which begins at the province of Ankara, and passes through Çorum, Yozgat, Amasya, Samsun, Erzincan, Tokat, Sivas, and Kahramanmaraş towards the north and east. They are also found in lesser concentrations throughout Turkey, particularly in the Aegean region. Traditionally, at least, as one would expect, the Kurdish Alevis appear to be found in greater concentrations in the provinces further east, such as Bingöl, Elazığ, Erzincan, Tunçeli and Malatya, with a number too in the south-east, in the Diyarbakır and Gaziantep region.

Today, given the rapid migration from all parts of Turkey (migration which appears to affect the Alevi population even more than the Sunni), it is likely that at least half the Alevi population is to be found in large urban conurbations, particularly Istanbul. There are also many Alevis among the emigrants to Western Europe, particularly Germany. Whilst the full history of the conflict in the east has yet to be written, it seems particularly likely that the Kurdish Alevis have suffered bitterly from the unrest, and that their numbers in traditional locations are therefore greatly depleted.

Diversity and resemblance

Many, even the great majority, of Alevi communities regard their patron saint as being *Hacı Bektaş Veli*. They refer to visiting his tomb and monastery (now a state museum) at the town of *Hacıbektaş* in Kırşehir province as going on the pilgrimage (*hac*). Some have maintained a relationship with lineages living in the town itself (whom they know as *efendis*) and regard them with respect as being directly descended from Hacı Bektash. In spite of this potential unity, the Alevis today appear extremely diverse. Their costumes, nomenclature, dances, prayers, rites and even annual ritual calendar often differ substantially among groups and locations. They have no church, no codified doctrine, no accepted clergy and no school to teach Alevi customs. There is, though, a certain underlying compatibility. All the research that has been conducted until now indicates that in rural Anatolia traditional Alevi society is based on locally inherited religious leadership (often known as *dede*, lit. 'grandfather'; *baba*, 'father' or *pir*, 'saint', 'leader', on collective rituals (which include both men and women, and at which outsiders are not permitted) and on a preoccupation with the importance of the inner life of the individual and the community.

This preoccupation with the inner essence of being, which the Alevis often know as *tarikat*, gives an important insight into the organising principles of Alevi society. Brotherhoods, and their accompanying mystical lore, *tasavvuf*, are found throughout Islam in Turkey. However, in Sunni communities, the various *tarikat*s and their teachings are a supplement, a buttress or a foil to orthodox worship, but they do not replace it. In contrast, the Alevis have turned their conception of *tarikat* into the guiding principle of their lives and it becomes the ethic by which most people judge religious fulfilment. In the Sunni communities, men may take up with a *tarikat*, but in the Alevi communities all people, both men and women are born into one. This reversal creates a preoccupation with hierarchy, descent, and mysticism in Alevi society. It has profound implications for their communities' internal organisation and for the construction of the self, and helps greatly to explain the similarities between apparently diverse Alevi traditions.

Within this framework Alevi religion is made up of a number of strands.[9] In broad, during their exegesis the religious leaders, *dedes*, may draw on the Koran and on different events in Islamic history, particularly those traditions which concern Ali, the nephew of the Prophet. There is no one sacred text, but many *dedes* know and quote from a work, the *Buyruk*, which, they maintain, was written by the sixth *imam*, *İmam Cafer*. In many areas, the actual prayers and poetry employed appear to be extremely similar to those of the Bektashis, and some Alevis go so far as to say that there is no difference between their communities.[10]

There are other influences too. They draw on the wider minstrel, *aşık* tradition of Anatolian Islam, represented by figures like *Yunus Emre*, whose songs and poetry are in Turkish rather than Arabic, or *Pir Sultan Abdal*. In other areas, Alevis may draw on many other,

more contemporary folk poets, such as *Aşık Veysel,* or they may
themselves create their own variations on Alevi themes. They may
have absorbed ritual traditions from their previously neighbouring
Rum (Greek Anatolian) communities. Some Alevis claim that their
ceremonies are pre-Islamic in conception, and may take pride in this.
This has made them a focus for people, such as Hasluck, whose
researches into historical continuities in religious practice remain of
interest today.[11] This eclectic and multi-layered complex of belief and
practice is one of the reasons that they appear heterodox to a Sunni
activism which seeks to simplify and place boundaries on what
is permissible within the faith.

The Alevis and Shi'ism
It is often asked whether the Alevis are Shi'ite. The Alevis themselves
do not use the appellation *Şi'i.* Indeed, they associate the use of the
word with 'those fanatics in Iran'. The Alevis have no social or
spiritual links with Iran, and the Turkish Alevis without a doubt see
their primary social allegiance as to the Republican State.
Nevertheless, as their name implies, their doctrines do give enormous
weight to the importance of the Prophet's nephew, and they are clearly
influenced by a Shi'ite perception of the development of Islam in
history. Ali is exalted continuously in poetry and in song. Their key
rituals celebrate the martyrdom of *Hüseyin,* Ali's son, at the Kerbala,
and the Alevis fast during the month of *Muharrem,* rather than at the
Ramazan. Indeed, as outlined by an important work by Moosa, it
appears to be that they would be classified theologically within the
Shi'ite tradition as a 'ghulat' sect: a group so 'extreme' (Moosa's
term) in their worship of Ali that it is doubtful that they would be
recognised by mainstream Shi'ite peoples.[12]

These aspects of the Alevi canon come out very clearly in the text
named *Buyruk,* which is just beginning to be studied by Western
scholars.[13] Many *dedes* possess a copy in modern Turkish, and
consult it frequently, using it as a basis for their teachings. It contains
no codified law, but rather is a series of descriptions of different facets
of religious life, anecdotes, ritual prescriptions, and definitions of
appropriate conduct. Many of the events it describes are mirrored in
Alevi ritual and song, and it offers a profoundly illuminating insight

into their cosmology.

For example, at the heart of Alevi ritual life is a collective ceremony known as the *cem*. In the villages, it takes place only during darkness, mostly during winter months, and both men and women attend. It is long, with several distinct stages, but culminates in a slow dance known as the *kırklar sema,* dance of the forty, in which both men and women take part. Whilst the *sema* is being danced, a minstrel intones a ballad (known as a *miraçlama*) celebrating Muhammed's ascent to heaven, where God's secrets were imparted to him. This event is one of the canons of orthodox Islam, but the Alevis' version is unusual. They say that God imparted knowledge to both Muhammed and Ali, awarding Ali the inner secrets of life. Muhammed is not aware of this but, on the night of the Miraç, he comes across Ali, who is teaching his forty followers these truths through the *sema*. The Prophet joins in their dance and, after a series of miraculous signs, becomes convinced of Ali's place in God's favour.[14]

The *Buyruk* tells this story also, dividing it into a number of episodes. The sample extract below is taken from the second section. In it, we are told how Ali is favoured with the duty of leadership by the Angel Gabriel, and that Ali and Muhammed became physically united as one body.

Extract from *Buyruk* – Second Chapter

> After joining in the forty's *sema*, Muhammed rose and returned to his house. All his disciples came to visit him. The disciples said to Muhammed; 'O, emissary of God... Explain what God said to you, we also would know'. On this Muhammed commanded: 'O believers, God's secret is reality [*hakikat*].... Come! Be followers of *hakikat*.
>
> The disciples asked, 'What is *hakikat*, O emissary of God?' Muhammed commanded: '*Hakikat* is to confess with the tongue, affirm with the heart, believe and have faith. To love yourself, and the community. To submit yourself to a leader [*pir*] and obey his commands'.
>
> Then [the angel] Gabriel came. Gabriel said: 'O Muhammed. God has decreed your giving this position to Ali'. But Muhammed

wanted to avoid doing this. Gabriel came again. 'O Muhammed why do you not fulfil God's decree?'

Muhammed replied: 'There is no *minber* [pulpit]'. Gabriel said; 'God commanded you to build a pulpit on a giant scale, climb it and fulfil your duty'. On this Muhammed gave a sign. The believers built a pulpit on a giant scale. Muhammed climbed to the top of the pulpit. First he read a fine sermon then he decreed:

'O believers Shah Ali has arrived at the *hakikat*. Come, strive after Ali', and he took Ali's right hand. He brought him to the pulpit. He opened his sash with sacred hands. He pressed Ali to his breast. The two entered into one gown. The two showed their heads from one collar. Two heads, but one gown appeared.

And Muhammed said: 'Your blood is my blood, your flesh is my flesh, your body is my body, your soul is my soul [*ruh*], your spirit is my spirit [*can*]'.

Muhammed's disciples, who were watching this event, were surprised. One from among them requested jealously; 'O emissary of God, take off your gown, we would see also'. On this, Muhammed took the gown off from his body. All those present saw that Muhammed and Ali had become one body. 'We have believed, O emissary of God', they said. The Prophet donned his sacred gown. 'Ali and I are one fruit of the same tree' he said. Then he took Ali's hand. He placed one thumb on another. He said that Ali should be his deputy. He read the following verse; 'O Muhammed, without a doubt those who bow their heads to you are as if they have bowed their heads to God'. Then he read the following prayer for Ali; 'My God. Help those who support him, and be an enemy to his enemies. Help those who give him help, weaken those who trouble him'.

Alevi and Sunni Islam

In spite of this clear reverence for Ali, the Alevis' greatest point of comparison remains with the Sunni communities amongst which they live. Almost every aspect of their worship and religious practice is expressed as a contrast with the Sunni way of life. For example, all the Alevis whom I have met emphasise that there are three conditions of Aleviness, *Aleviliğin üç şartı*. These are '*Eline, diline, beline sahib ol!'*, 'Be master of your hand, tongue and loins!'. Whilst interpretations vary, most people take this to mean, 'Do not take what is not yours, do not say what you have not seen, and do not make love outside wedlock'. They compare these with the Sunni 'five pillars', saying that they are the Alevi equivalent, sufficient in themselves to attain personal fulfilment in the eyes of their religion. Again, whilst these three conditions are known throughout mystical Islam in Turkey, as *edep*, the Alevis are distinguished by the enormous emphasis they place on them, so that they become one of the main defining attributes of whether a person is an Alevi.

Doctrinally, their link with the Sunni communities and their different way of life is expressed through a device which again, though familiar within Islam, has its own Alevi interpretation. They claim that there are four ways to God. These are *şeriat, tarikat, marifet* and *hakikat*.[15] The Alevis in the area I worked understand the terms in the following way.

> *Şeriat* is the first stage. Alevis claim that most Sunnis are at this stage. At this point, a person has done no more than learn the rules of Islam and remains on the surface of existence. Alevis also use *şeriat* to signify the daily practice of orthodox Islam in a Sunni village (the five pillars, ritual separation between men and women, attending the mosque) and associate it with that Islamic tradition that gives importance to its Arab inheritance, with its centre lying at Mecca.
>
> *Tarikat*: They maintain that most Alevis are at this stage. Here a person has begun to seek the understanding that lies beneath the surface. Collectively, they associate *tarikat* with the *cem* ceremony, with the complex lore, music and traditions which accompany it, with obeisance to a holy figure, a *dede*, and with the inclusion of both men and women in social life. They regard this form of Islam as being distinctly Turkish, and as deriving from the Turkic Sufi schools such as those of *Ahmet Yesevi*, and his pupils.[16] For many, its spiritual centre lies at the tomb of *Hacı Bektaş*.
>
> *Marifet*: '*Marifet*' literally means 'spiritual knowledge'. This expression is not widely used. Though it is recognised as a

necessary stage in a person's development, the villagers I know
attached to it no particular explanatory exegesis.

Hakikat is the final stage, to be desired by all, but attainable by
few. At this point, a person has become one with God. The
physical rules of the universe loosen their bonds, and a person can
achieve miracles. A person on this level is sometimes known as
'developed', *ermiş*. Ideally, religious leaders, *dedes*, are at this
stage. Certainly, the prophets and great saints like Ali, and his
descendant, *Hacı Bektaş Veli*, are so.

It is important to realise that, in the village setting, the Alevi
cosmology is quite clear that the Sunni way of doing things is a
legitimate, even necessary, first step towards God, though ultimately
an inadequate one. This means that outside the village, for example,
when Alevis are stationed in a Sunni village as civil servants, they may
go to pray at the mosque, or keep the fast without any sense that they
have betrayed their own religious tradition.

This dualism is also reflected within the Alevi communities. Most
Alevi villages have a mosque. Whilst some villages maintain that they
only installed them at the behest of the state, others appear to have
embraced them more willingly. All the villages that I knew had a
Sunni, state-appointed mosque *imam* with whom the villagers were
friendly, though they varied in the extent that they actually used the
mosques and the *imam*'s services. Where I stayed, the mosque was
not popular, and there was rarely the sufficient minimum of three
people to hold the Friday prayers. It would, however, be full on the
two annual festivals: the feast of sacrifice, and the 'sugar' festival,
Şeker Bayramı, which marks the end of the *Ramazan*. Other villages
placed more importance on mosque worship, and the Friday prayers
might be quite well attended. Likewise, whilst where I stayed very
few men fasted during the *Ramazan*, but in other villages there
sometimes were more.

This use of the orthodox tradition can be seen also during funerals.
The villagers I knew best deliberately performed the actual interment
of the body as it would be according to Sunni ritual. After their death,
a person, whether man or woman, is washed, placed in a shroud and
laid out in front of a purely male congregation in the open air, just as

they are in a Sunni village. Usually, the mosque *imam*, then pronounces a service which the villagers regard as being part of orthodox Islam, common to both Alevis and Sunnis. Whilst I could not be sure of the accuracy of this claim, certainly the fact that the state-trained mosque *imam* may conduct the ceremony gives it support. The body is then taken to the graveyard, and interred to the intoning of *ilahi*, Arabic hymns by the *imam*.

The same readiness to embrace the orthodox aspects of Islam can be seen in the formal roles that are available for men to fill within the community. Only those who are born of a *dede* lineage may teach Alevi prayers or lead an Alevi ritual. Village men who wish to follow a religious path who are not *dedes* may instead learn the orthodox liturgy, in which case they are known as *hocas*. A *hoca* may be called in at any time when a villager asks for a prayer, though in this case it will be in Arabic, rather than the Turkish used by the *dedes*. The first funeral I witnessed in the village, for example, was conducted by the village *hoca*, because the person who had died had become estranged from his relatives, and no one had money to pay the state-appointed mosque *imam* on his behalf to conduct the service. The *hocas* also have a prominent role in a ceremony which the villagers hold three days after a person has died, known as *dar çekme*. At the *dar çekme*, neighbours and relatives collect in the deceased villager's house. In the main room, twelve people, six men and six women line up in a horseshoe formation. They face a number of *dedes* lined up in front of them, and the spouse or close relative of the deceased. To their left, the *hoca* recites a collective prayer, known as *halkçılık namazı*, and a verse is read from the Koran. I was unable to attend this brief ceremony, but I was kindly supplied the text of the prayer. It consists chiefly of repeated supplications to the one God, begging for mercy and asking for forgiveness. After the ceremony, the villagers share a sacrifice in which the whole community is expected to partake.

In spite of this syncretism, it would be mistaken to say that there is an easy relationship between *Sunnilik*, and *Alevilik*. Though men vary to the extent that they are able, or indeed wish to articulate their religious beliefs, many draw a contrast between the depth of the Alevi, and the supposed superficiality of the Sunni, religious experience. They may maintain, for example, that among the Sunnis belief in God is based on fear of a God who exists on high, but that the Alevis base their faith in love, a love which is within all people. They illustrate this by saying that in the beginning, God created the world, and gave creatures life (*can*), but that on looking down from on high, God saw nothing which truly reflected His/Her Being. Accordingly, God gave all humans a part of Him/Herself:[17] this part is our soul (*ruh*). Now, when we pray together in the *cem*, we do so face to face, and through the collective worship, see into one another's hearts and so become part of God.

Some men also stress that mosques have been imposed on them, against their will by the state, particularly citing the period after 1980, maintaining that the military commanders of that time tried to ensure that all villages built a mosque even if they had not done so before. Occasionally, the Alevis would express deep fear, even hatred of the Sunni, particularly after watching the national news, which during the 1990s routinely depicted riots at mosques after the Friday prayers by sympathisers of the Welfare Party, particularly after it was closed down.

Otherwise, they may turn orthodox Islam into a humorous subject. They told a story, for example, of a teacher stationed in the village who, when drunk, used to recite a marvellous *ezan* (call to prayer from the mosque). One night, he did so, beautifully and loudly, from the window of his house. An old man in the village struggled to get to the mosque, calling his wife for his trousers as he did so, thinking it was the first *namaz* of the day. Many men found recalling this scene highly amusing. When one or two men decided to keep the *Ramazan* fast whilst I was in the village, they were roundly ribbed for their sudden piety, though no one attempted to stop them doing so. They also were fond of making jokes at the *imam*'s expense. On one occasion the mosque *imam* seeing the chance for a transfer to a Sunni village (where, he remarked, he might have a chance to build up a decent congregation) left in a hurry carrying a sack of onions. After a few days, he was disappointed in this hope, and came back, though still bearing the sack. The villagers thought this was highly amusing, for though he had not gained his transfer, he had not lost his winter supply of onions.

The Alevis and Christianity

Occasionally, both in the press, and in political debate, a potential relationship between Christianity and the Alevis is mooted.[18] Usually it is posed as a threat, whereby it is maintained that the Alevis will convert *en masse* to Christianity. I do not think this is likely. Most Alevis are quite clear that they are Muslim. Further, there is no one organisation or leader who has the power to represent them or persuade them to take such a drastic step. This said, the village Alevis whom I knew declared themselves sympathetic to Christianity, saying that they had various things in common: in particular that just as the Christians have twelve disciples, so do they have twelve *imams*, and a trinity also, Allah, the Prophet Muhammed and Ali. They also have fond memories of the *Rum* villagers who used to live next to them, and it is likely that among their religious traditions there are ceremonies borrowed from them, though they did not seem now to be aware of this.[19]

Christianity did occasionally crop up as a foil in their ambivalent relationship with the local Sunni, as is illustrated by the following event during my fieldwork. One afternoon, late in the summer of 1989, three Sunni men came in a jeep to the tea house in the village, outside which I was sitting at the time. One man was a retired Koran course teacher, the other a *hacı*, the third, their driver. They explained that they were collecting poplar trees (*kavak*) to use when constructing the new town mosque in the sub-province centre, which they expected to be given as *hayır*, a charitable gift. No man in the tea house offered any trees, though one said that if they would build a church then he would be happy to donate trees from his land. Great laughter followed, and the men drove off in irritated fashion to the village above ours. They had more success there, though it was also Alevi. However, the *hacı*, who was old and frail, was knocked down and killed by one of the poplar trees that were being felled for the mosque. Some of the men expressed no regret at all on hearing this, saying that he was a *yobaz*, fanatic. Others were shocked at the idea of a man being killed whilst working for a pious cause.

Being a dede

The *dedes* play a key role in village life: they are at once the leaders of religious ceremony and the transmitters of sacred knowledge to the community. However, the right to practise being a *dede,* passes from one generation to another by patrilineage. If a man is not born into a *dede* lineage, he cannot become a *dede.* In the villages I know best, lineages consist of no more than about fifty households, and sometimes much less. About one in ten of these lineages were accepted by the community as being *dedes.* This acceptance of a lineage as being *dede* is based on a number of mutually supporting factors. Most important is a sign that they have been favoured by God at some point in their history, that they are *keramet sahibi,* possessor of 'keramet'. *Keramet* is usually translated in the literature as 'charisma',[20] but in this context it means more specifically that the *dede* or his lineage at some time in the past have performed a miracle. There are other ways too that a *dede* lineage may become accepted: through their ancestors having attended the school of Hacı Bektash, by being descended from a famous figure in Islamic history (one lineage claimed *Muhittin Arabi* as their forbear) or by having an endorsement, *vasiyetname,* from the contemporary descendants of Hacı Bektash (*efendis*) that they are fit to lead Alevi rituals. The following was shown to me as such an endorsement by one of the *dedes:*

> A, descended from the sons of B, of the lineage C, illustrious son of D, now resident in X village, is in every respect a worthy model and guide. This *vasiyetname* assures that in the event that those belonging to this hearth transfer their allegiance and respect to the said licensed seventh son of D, sure and peaceful love (*muhabbet*) will come to the community.

The hierarchical relationship between lay and sacred lineages is formalised in that each *dede* lineage possesses a number of lineages that are regarded as their followers, *talips.* The number of follower lineages that a lineage has varies, but may be up to sixty or seventy, and perhaps in the case of a famous lineage, substantially more. The relationship between *dede* and follower varies greatly. At its closest, *dedes* may perform a number of services for their followers; they may help out in wedding negotiations, offer advice on daily matters and frequently be invited to preside over a *cem*. More distantly, they may come only once, for a more formal pastoral visit, each year, or even, if the followers are not favourably inclined, have no contact at all.

All lineages, whether *dede*s or not, must follow a *dede* lineage in their turn. This means that no person is without a *dede* to whom to turn if so desired. In theory, these links do not change over generations, being held by many men to have been made by Hacı Bektash himself. Nevertheless, if a *dede* lineage wishes to appoint another *dede* lineage to represent them (perhaps through their becoming too depleted or disinclined to fulfil the responsibility themselves), they may do so. It is also recognised that the follower lineages possess the right to change their *dede*, or even their *dede* lineage, if they demonstrate that they are grossly unsuitable.

Settling disputes

The Alevis justify their claim to being able to manage their own affairs by asserting that they have their own, distinctive means of settling disputes.[21] Part of this system revolves around the *dede*s, who are empowered to mediate in conflicts. In a *tarikat* ritual, with the help of the community, they must ensure that all present are at peace with one another before worship begins. That religious ritual must be held in an atmosphere wherein all have declared amity for each other may sound insignificant: it is not. In the Alevi community, *tarikat* worship embraces all its households, so it is a ritual that affects everyone. Further, it is a characteristic of Anatolian village life that when people quarrel, they may become on 'non-speaking terms', *küs*. This sort of stand-off is particularly amenable to solution by mediation. A *cem* therefore provides the opportunity, the occasion and the mechanism for long established conflicts to be resolved.

Specifically, in the area where I worked, a *cem* only takes place when a *dede* is offered a sacrifice, usually a sheep or a goat, by one of his followers. A sacrifice may be so offered for various reasons: as a demonstration of unity among the community, to mark an important *dede*'s visit, to honour one's fellow villagers, or to make or to fulfil a vow. The ceremony takes place in the largest room of a house, which is often built with the idea of holding such ceremonies in mind. It is usual for all those in that village quarter (*mahalle*) to send two people to represent their household, one man and one woman. The sacrifice is cooked at a hearth at one end of the room. Next to the hearth, on its right, sit those who are from a *dede* lineage. Behind them sit their wives and unmarried daughters, known as *ana*s (mothers). Opposite, sit the men of the community. Behind them sit the remaining women and children. Facing the hearth sits a minstrel, usually a man but sometimes a woman, with a *saz*, an eight-stringed instrument similar in shape to a mandolin.

The ceremony opens formally by unrolling a prayer rug, known as 'Ali's space', *Ali'nin meydanı*, before the assembled company. Before going further, the *dede* invites the couple who have offered the sacrifice to appear before him on 'Ali's space', and questions them as to the happiness of their household, and whether they have a quarrel with anyone else in the community. Having asked them this question, he turns to the rest of the assembled community and equally asks them whether they are satisfied with these responses. Only on receiving an assent can the ceremony go ahead. If it does turn out that there is an unresolved conflict, then the *dede* sets out to reconcile the parties in conflict through stressing the importance of everybody in the society being at peace with one-another, saying that the Alevi way is based on disturbing no other person, and on a person being responsible for his or her actions. If the parties refuse to come to terms, then worship cannot take place until they leave the ritual. Usually punishment consists of offering compensation for the wrong done. However, in extreme circumstances, a person may be ejected from the community, refused the co-operation of his or her neighbours in going about daily tasks, and ignored – not be offered a 'selam', by everybody in the village.[22]

Outside this ritual framework *dede*s are only expected to intervene in a quarrel when they are invited to do so by their followers. Which individual *dede* emerges as a key figure from his respective lineage depends on a number of factors: on his age, on his tact, honesty and ability. It is unseemly for a *dede* to appear covetous or quarrelsome, and much of the respect that he may gain in his life depends on the gravitas that he maintains and accumulates.[23] It also depends on his ability to bring disputants to peace. If so accepted in a mediating role, the *dede* again resolves quarrels and disagreements through a strong emphasis on bringing the two sides together by persuasion and appeal. One *dede* explained their system to me in the following way:

> Now, if there are small sorts of encroachments on another's boundary or problems of elopement, we solve them, bring them to peace... The *dedes*... do not send every subject to the [state] courts. Whether in village or town, except for serious assaults, we make peace among people. We make two hearts one, *iki gönül bir ederiz*. They [the villagers] thus live in a humane way. This is the defining characteristic of the Alevi-Bektashi Niyazi *Tarikat*. Those who go to the *Tarikat* of Hacı Bektash Niyazi never permit a division in their midst.
>
> I would give you an example. I went to a village a little the other side of... This village had split into two over the question of the *muhtar* [elected village head]. The two sides had complained about each other [to the authorities]. I don't know what they hadn't done... there was going to be a murder. For some years they had been unable to come together to hold a sacrifice [i.e. conduct a *cem* ceremony]. Ah! There were some followers of mine on the present *muhtar*'s side. I met with them. After that I met with the opposition's side. 'You', I said, 'If you don't make peace amongst yourselves... these are your children, you have children, [to the other side I said too] you have children, if there is a murder, if you do not prevent this murder [then you will be responsible]. I would bring you to peace. Muhammed's way is the way of the heart, *gönül*. The way of God'. I worked for four days, on the fifth I brought them to peace. I was presented a peace sacrifice. They embraced, kissed, we ate their sacrifice and the sacrificial morsels. 'Let Allah be content with you', they said, and I departed.

Dispute reconciliation and theory

That a society may be controlled through mediation by holy figures within a lineage structure has been a well-known, if controversial theme among fieldworkers in Islamic societies.[24] The controversy in part is over how frequently quarrels are actually solved through such mechanisms. This is a good question, because it raises the possibility that the researcher is reifying a theoretical system of social control at the expense of a more complicated reality.

In response, I would suggest that, among the Turkish Alevis, mediation by *dedes* between warring patrilineages is a part, but only a part of a wider system of social control that relies also on a sense among people that it is appropriate to be on good terms with others, to rub along where it is at all possible, one which is an inherent part of their ritual practice and sense of self. It is a frequent boast among people that they offend (*incitme*) no one or that they abuse no-one's rights: *kimsenin hakkını yemem*! The foundation of *Alevilik*, the three conditions, similarly is a prescription of good behaviour: 'Be master of your hands, tongue and loins!'. The *Buyruk* also provides confirmation of this attitude, calling quite explicitly for quiescent, forgiving responses to adversity or difficulties. The sample extract below is taken from Chapter 7, entitled *Sofu*. 'Sofu' is a usual Turkish word, referring to a novitiate in a brotherhood. It has connotations of a poor, modest believer. Other words: *Hacı* and *Gazi* are laudatory terms, referring to a person who has successfully made the pilgrimage to Mecca, and someone who has successfully fought for the faith respectively.

From *Buyruk* Chapter 7

> Those (*sofus*) who embrace one another on their thresholds become *hacıs*, *gazis* a thousand times, they escape from great and minor sins, become purified, without sin. Then the *sofu* among the people resembles the angels in the sky... the moon and sun among the stars, and brings to mind God's messengers.
>
> If a *sofu* goes to another *sofu*'s house then they are saved from the sins they have committed with their feet. If they kiss a hand, they are saved from the sins they have committed with their hands. If they look from their heart to the other's face they are saved from the sins they have committed with their eyes. If they love a *sofu* they are saved from the sins they have committed with their heart and their soul. And if they give food of this world to eat to a *sofu* then in heaven God will offer them the food of heaven. If a *sofu* goes to a *sofu*'s village, province or country then they gain a hundred-thousand mercies, a hundred-thousand abundances and a

hundred thousand merits.

Returning to the question of how much the Alevis actually run their lives through their independent mechanisms of social control, of which the patrilineage is a crucial part, but only a part, I would say that in previous years, and to a lesser extent still, they can genuinely regulate a great deal of their lives according to this method. It is highly sophisticated. By virtue of the *dedes*, they possess the means to mediate feuds and arguments within and between the community lineages. During the collective rituals, also run by the *dedes*, buttressed by a coherent theology, they appeal to individual relations within the household and to the wider community. Finally, through the emphasis on a quiet, esoteric mystical conception of the self, they appeal to individual restraint. This is an entirely plausible way of resolving a very substantial proportion of the difficulties that a sedentary, quiescent comparatively isolated rural community is likely to encounter.

The Alevis and the Republic

Many Alevis venerate Atatürk. They may claim that he was a creator of an ideal way of life, and often regret the elections in 1950 which led to the demise of the Republican Peoples Party. Some *dedes* even say that they love him as much as they love *mehdi*, the twelfth, vanished *imam*, who is supposed to return one day to rule. They are adamant that the Alevis were instrumental in providing him support during his travels in Anatolia to inspire the Republican cause, and there are several published books devoted to researching this issue.[25]

That the Alevis should have supported Atatürk, and now revere him is obvious in that he offered them security from religious persecution. There are other reasons also. The Turkish Alevis, who make up the bulk of the Alevi population, are thoroughly in sympathy with the Republican interpretation of Turkish history.[26] The minimisation of Arabic and Persian influences in the new historiography and the nationalist reforms devoted to cleansing the language of non-Turkish words accord closely with their own conception of their past and culture. They regard *Alevilik* above all as the real Turkish Islam and maintain that Sunni Islam came to Turkey only when the Arabs invaded Anatolia.[27] In their ceremonies, *dedes* speak almost entirely in Turkish. Their prayers also are in Turkish, not Arabic, and they say sometimes of the voice of the minstrel: 'The Koran in Turkish' (*Kuran' ın Türkçesi*). Thus, the systematic construction of a nation based on a Turkish heritage is one with which they could readily identify.

Whilst welcoming the Republic, the Alevi villagers do not appear to have changed life within their communities in any rapid way, nor were they forced to by the state. They continued to hold their ceremonies, which even though theoretically illegal, were not actively suppressed by the authorities. Inasmuch as certain administrative measures, such as the village law, or the appointment of village heads, affected their lives, they appear to have absorbed them by making a clear contrast between their own concerns and those of the state.

In the area where I conducted fieldwork, even though the state is secular, the villagers articulate this distinction using the terms *şeriat* and *tarikat*.[28] *Şeriat* encompasses not just the Sunni practice of religion but anything to do with the state: the *jandarma*, police, law courts, and those orders that may drift from on high via the sub-province governor. It also includes services provided by the state, such as the school, health centre, and bank co-operative, even when the villagers have helped build them. *Tarikat* refers to anything to do with the life in the inner part of the community, including its ceremonies and customs, both those that are secret, closed to outsiders, and those more open, like wedding ceremonies. As a matter of course, most things that go on in the community are simply not told to outsiders, and they are adept at switching the topic of conversation depending on whether there is someone from outside the village present. This means, for example, that a Sunni person stationed from outside the village, a school teacher or mosque *imam*, may be treated with genuine liking and respect, but even after a number of years have passed, because they have not seen the *cem*, or discussed the *Buyruk*, have almost no idea of the ordering principles of Alevi culture.[29]

Whilst it is impossible to be sure of events that took place so long ago, the villagers tell me that this method of accommodating their private lives with the outside world worked well. The state's administration of the countryside was based on a presumption that communities consisted of settled villages which, as long as they paid their taxes when required and provided conscripts on time, would more or less run their own affairs.[30] The courts also took a long time to have a serious effect on village life.[31] The villagers were in any case used to concealing their religious ceremonies, so that the new ban on *tarikat* activities did not discommode them unduly. It is likely that the distant relations with the larger *tarikat* headquarters were badly disrupted. The Bektashi *tekke* was closed down firmly, and it would have been difficult for their patrilineages, the *efendis*, to operate freely in their relations with the villagers. Whilst this was brought up by some of the people I spoke to at the town of Hacı Bektash itself, it was not mentioned at all by the villagers, who are quite insistent that it was politically the best period of their existence: that they were able to feel part of the new nation, whilst at the same time the community was strong, and the *dedes* respected.

Social Change

In an important article, Stirling notes that many sociological changes in the Anatolian countryside may be linked to the subsequent economic development of rural areas rather than the initial impact of the Republic.[32] Whilst he was referring to the effect of the reforms on the Sunni village communities, this model also appears appropriate to the Alevis. At the time of the declaration of the Republic, physically and economically, the villages I worked with remained undeveloped. The vast proportion of the goods consumed by them was provided through subsistence farming and the exploitation of the immediate environment. The older villagers told me that in their youth there was no tea, now ubiquitous in all parts of the country. Before that they drank soup as a hot drink. Health services were minimal. Almost all energy needs were provided by humans or beasts. Electricity was introduced only in the 1970s, and running water in the 1980s. Even when I was in the village, in the late 1980s, about half the households tilling fields did so with a pair of oxen drawing a single-shoed hoe. For these people life was (and may still be today) harsh, and old age quick to come; men told me that they expected to marry at fifteen or sixteen, to be heads of their own households at thirty, and to die at forty.[33]

It is possible that our estimates of economic change in rural communities in the early part of the Republic will have to be revised. It would certainly be quite wrong to assume stagnation: people were actively attempting to better their lot, and some development is discernible from contemporary reports.[34] Nevertheless, in the area I worked, development seems to have had really striking social effects only in the 1960s and 1970s. One of the first signs of this appears to have been a rapid rise in population. This increased pressure on resources to the point that people found it difficult to produce sufficient food for subsistence from the existing fields. Unless they were very fortunate, they had to walk sometimes two or three hours to gain access to new areas to open fresh fields, making it difficult to maintain or protect crops growing within them. At that time, arguments over land and water allocations were frequent. Nevertheless, outward migration was low. Though villagers did seek seasonal labour further afield, only one or two left permanently.

This difficult, even volatile situation appears to have been resolved by the opportunities offered to go to work in Germany and other European countries, and many villagers went willingly until restrictions began to be placed on their doing so at the end of the 1970s. Later, internal migration, particularly to Istanbul and Ankara, grew from being a trickle to a flood. At the time that I conducted my research, between 1988 and 1990, households were still leaving, and they estimated that two thirds of the village population was living in Europe or in other cities in Turkey. Of those in the village, most supplemented their income with remittances from relatives working elsewhere. A few had retired to live on their pensions, having been out of the village for much of their lives.[35]

The effect of this, and other changes on village life, has been to shake the strength of its traditional religious practice. From the early 1980s onwards, the number of *tarikat* ceremonies dropped appreciably. Even these sometimes did not run smoothly, as if the villagers were beginning to forget the rules by which they were run.[36] Whilst it is easy to notice the empirical fact of this taking place, it is more complicated to tease out the different factors which may have helped bring it about. From a slightly abstract point of view, admittedly, it appeared to me that one of the reasons is the growing rapprochement between the nation-state and village life. As development continues, and villagers are becoming aware of the possibilities of becoming part of the consumer world, their orientation moves from being part of an inner community, with its chain of authority leading through the *dede* to *Hacı Bektaş* and *Ali* on the one hand, and the power of the state on the other. Now that the villagers want to become urban and to develop, the state, vastly more powerful than any means at the villagers' command at achieving this goal, is becoming ever closer, and more relevant. The *muhtar* is seen as representative of this authority, and gains strength accordingly.

The villagers themselves explain frequently that the most important reason for the change is a lack of strong, resourceful leadership from the *dedes*. This is certainly true. In all the communities that I knew, the *dedes* had weakened. Sometimes this was due to specific circumstances, such as an exceptionally strong *muhtar*. Thus, in the village where I lived, the *muhtar* had struggled against the *dedes'* temporal power for much of the previous twenty years. He was a convinced sceptic. He appears to have fought his greatest battles during the 1970s, when the then leading *dede* wanted to stop any of the village women moving to Germany. The *muhtar* won, and grew in strength accordingly. The *muhtar* also demonstrated his opposition by cutting down a tree which was supposed to be a *yatır*, to possess magical properties. Of this, he told me: 'They said that lightning would strike from the sky, but it didn't'. He also, with a group of like-minded friends, uncovered a shrine supposed to be the relics of a holy man at which the villages stopped to pray on their way to the mountain pastures each summer. They claimed only to find horse bones lying within. Buoyed up by these and other successes, during my time in the village, it was the *muhtar* who solved most of the petty quarrels which occurred from day to day, and who was the acknowledged leader of the community.

Even where such forceful opposition has not emerged, the *dedes* appear to have weakened. Traditionally, and still to some extent today, the particular person who comes to lead any *dede* lineage depends partly on seniority and partly on his vocation, skill, experience and intelligence. Yet, in a village, where a large number of the males have migrated, it tends to be those with less initiative who remain, and the remnants of their lineage can no longer easily produce capable people. Also, the experience of life that would enable a *dede* to deal with questions thrown up by the modern world is paradoxically only available to those who have left the village ties and taken up a profession elsewhere. The inherited ties between *dedes* and *talips* are also increasingly affected; when a person may be distant, in Germany, or in Istanbul, it is hardly likely that the *dedes* in the village are able to intervene or help efficiently with the problems that their new environment may bring.

A similar argument can be made in terms of changes in the community. Unlike the Sunni villages, the Alevis are nearly always dispersed among smaller village quarters, *mahalle*, which may be substantially distant from one another. Along with the individual households, these communities are the basic economic unit, with distinctive field, water, pasture and forestry rights. They are also the setting in which *cem* services take place. In order to form a village, a number of these *mahalles* are gathered together by the state. The village, not the *mahalle*, is written in identity cards as a person's address. The village is the unit for which services are awarded, and the *muhtar* likewise is elected on the basis of the village unit. There is, therefore, an inherent contradiction between the sedentary, subsistence economic community, and group identity which is imposed upon them from outside. As the economic base of the village changes, and as people become accustomed to creating more of their identity through their place in the outside world, it is this officially designated village unit which comes to take predominance over the *mahalle* that they may come from. Yet through their reluctance to attend to the village mosque, at the time when I lived in the village there was no easy way that this evolving collective identity could be expressed through religious ceremony.

Belief and culture

Whilst the conventional warning on trying to understand other cultures is never more apposite when looking at questions of belief, it seems that one of the consequences of this social change is that many of the Alevis whom I have met are finding *literal* belief, that is, the absolute conviction in the traditions of Ali, the *Buyruk*, the sanctity of the *dede*s, more difficult to sustain. It is difficult to provide exact proportions, but very roughly the village appears to be composed of cultivated sceptics of the sort exemplified by the *muhtar* (these people are most actively intellectually engaged with the political left), a smaller number of people, particularly the *dede*s who practise firm, unreconstructed belief, and a more quiescent remainder who would like to believe, but note and regret the practical difficulties that have transpired in the practice of their religion. Within this basic pattern, the younger generation is more likely to be sceptical than the older, likewise men more likely than women.[37]

The picture is complicated by a particular nuance in the relationship between faith and expression of 'Aleviness', *Alevilik*. Even those who are most sceptical do not reject the poetry, music, dance and song that is part of their lives in the village. Indeed, this readiness to see *Alevilik* in a secular setting emerges even more strongly among those people who are most against religion and the hierarchical authority of the *dede*s. These people may stress, for example, that the *edep* prescription, 'to be master of thy hand, tongue and loins' is simply a sensible way to lead one's life in the community, and needs no enforcing by an authoritarian figure or sacred creed. These same people often are extremely fond of *muhabbet*, collective drinking sessions that in the village take place most frequently during weddings. They hold these sessions also in the towns, and if there is no minstrel present, they supply the lack through recorded cassettes of Alevi music.

It is worth dwelling on this point. The Alevis enjoy immensely collective dancing, being with their fellows, and playing their music whether or not it takes place in overtly religious ceremonies. Indeed, it is tempting to regard religious and secular occasions in Durkheimian fashion, wherein the profane becomes a ritual opposition to the sacred. Some such contrast might indeed legitimately be drawn. During both, men and women may dance together, but religious gatherings are closed to outsiders, and they are presided over by *dede*s. To be drunk at such a gathering is sinful. Secular celebrations such as may take place at weddings, on the contrary, are merry, liberally supplied with alcohol, and open to all. At weddings, leadership is supplied by lineages specialising in music, the *davul* (drum), *zurna* (a double-reeded instrument, a folk oboe), and *kaval* (shepherd's flute), music that might be considered a counter-point to the minstrel *aşık* in the *cem*.

Yet, to invoke such a straightforward opposition would give a mistaken impression. Rather, the secular dance draws on, and is influenced by the customs in the *cem*. During the drinking gatherings, which they know as *muhabbet*, the Alevis often may call for the same minstrel, *aşık*, who plays in *cem* ceremonies. When called to the table, he may play popular folk songs but also distinctly Alevi pieces, such as *deyiş*, songs mourning Ali that may also be heard in the *cem*. At the end of the *cem* ceremony, after the '*sema* of the forty', which celebrates Ali, they conclude with a quick-stepped fast-moving *sema* known as the *gönüllü sema*, in which women whirl full circle with their arms outstretched, and men also half turn, raising their arms sharply in time to the music. They also dance this *gönüllü sema* during the *muhabbet*. Men, even arch sceptics of religion, may delight in these dances, which last far into the night.

In the traditional setting, there is further ambiguity about these collective-drinking sessions. They are by no means overtly religious, yet they have mystical overtones. To sit, to drink, to share the experience of being with one's colleagues in peace, is in itself an auspicious thing to do, and evocative of divine love (*aşk*). They are often formally conducted. During them, people take their drink together, and one person is denoted the leader of the group, or *saki*. No one may leave the table without permission from the *saki*, or drink out of turn. If they do so, then they are theoretically punishable with a fine of a cockerel and a bottle of *rakı* (a strong drink similar to *pastis*), known as an 'Angel Gabriel'. Some *dede*s may regard the *rakı* drunk during *muhabbet* as having become sacred, in this case renaming it *dolu* (lit. 'filled').[38] Often, they follow a sip of *rakı* with a piece of meat or a grape, sometimes handed ceremoniously from one friend to another. Both of these have explicit symbolic significance: the meat recalls sacrificial morsels (*lokma*), which are handed out at the *cem*, the grape recalls an event when the original forty were at Ali's side during his divine *sema*, when sherbert for all to drink was made from a single grape. There are even distinct ideological parallels: just as during the *cem* there are explicit declarations of mutual peace, during *muhabbet* men may become extremely drunk, and in turn rise to their feet, and declare that all here are *dost*, friends, companions, lovers in the spiritual sense.

During my time in the village, such extrovert ceremonies were far more frequent than the explicitly religious. On the cusp of being sacred though joyful and full of alcohol, they are a way for even the most left-wing of persons to enjoy the experience of being an Alevi without feeling that they are at an ostensibly religious ceremony.[39] Partly also, they are simply easier to stage, and even among the more pious villagers they are a way of celebration that they can enjoy. They also provide a convenient way to celebrate the village community. One of the most frequent melodies, one that they played on almost any instrument, or even sang unaccompanied, on occasion literally repeated dozens of times over the course of a wedding or other gathering, was known as the 'village song'. They were intensely proud that it had been made into an electronically recorded version by musicians who were partly drawn from their émigré community in Germany, and they played this tape also when travelling in their minibuses to and from the local town centre.

Thus, there is a fission within Alevi communities which allows their culture to be celebrated in settings which do not call for *dede*s or strict privacy and which neatly dovetails with the Republican desire to experience community through secular ritual. This parallel may become expressed in formal, as well as informal occasions. One of the key ways that the Republican culture is inculcated is through an insistence that nationhood should be explored and celebrated through the folk dance of Anatolia. This is entirely in accordance with the existing Alevi mode of ritual celebration of their community. When they are requested to provide dancers at nationalist celebrations of the sort which take place at schools and public places across the country on Republic Day, they provide girls and boys to dance the lively dance that ends the *cem* ceremony, the *gönüllü sema*, and feel no incongruity in doing so. In this way, they are able to express their identity with the Turkish nation through a custom which is a quite central part of their religious and cultural tradition.[40] This is in sharp contrast with the Sunni village communities. Whilst similar folkloric dances are found in Sunni villages, they are not part of their religious cosmology. Indeed, they are often disapproved of, even rejected by pious people, who may not feel any particular sympathy for them at all. I have a vivid memory of passing Republican day, 29 October 1989 in a Sunni village, watching such a display outside their village school, and elderly men muttering audibly 'Sinful! Sinful!', '*Günah!, Günah!*'.

As the Alevis move to the cities, and integrate with the Republic more closely, it is this theatrical, open demonstrative aspect of their indigenous culture that has come to dominate over their secret, introverted rituals. Not everyone may concur, particularly the older men or the *dedes* themselves, but they are now a minority within the Alevi movement, and have not been able to prevent it. When in the village, I myself had some experience of this conflict. Whilst in the last ten years, Alevi culture has become much more open, in the late 1980s, many people did not wish me to come to the *cem* ceremonies. Some felt that I was a spy for the Turkish Government, others that I was working for the CIA. Nevertheless, the *muhtar* was able to persuade one of the *dedes* who was visiting his followers in the village that I was a genuine researcher. This *dede* acquiesced saying '*Kendi köyünde muhtar Sultandır*', 'In his village, a *muhtar* is Sultan'. Though I was permitted to enter the ceremony, some of the *dedes* in the village stayed away on the grounds that it was a profound mistake to permit a non-Alevi into a private ritual. Other people did attend. They justified their doing so, and my being there, by saying that their relatives in Germany had begun to show the *cem* in public, in Alevi culture demonstrations at sports stadiums, and that they wished to be as forward looking in their own village.[41]

The same argument at a wider level could be seen at the annual Alevi festival held at the town of Hacı Bektash. This gathering, now even larger, was already a significant event when I went in 1990, with perhaps twenty-five thousand people present from all over Turkey.[42] Politicians came from all parties: notably, the Motherland Party's Minister of Culture at that time, and the head of the Social Democrat Populist Party (*SHP*), Erdal İnönü (İsmet İnönü's son). These politicians made a series of major speeches in an open-air arena. At the same event, there took place a series of exhibition *sema* dances in the closed sports hall. Not only the more usual *sema*, but also the *kırklar sema,* that marks the Alevis learning the secret mysteries of life from Ali. These were often beautifully danced and very divergent from each other in style. Most of the audience were delighted to see them, but a few elderly Alevis were very distressed, saying that the celebration of the *kırklar sema,* the most sacred of the Alevi dances, was not something that could, or should, be performed in front of everybody. Their protests went unheeded. Further, even though the main attractions were very well attended, it was mainly mature men and their families who were present at them. It turned out that an alternative concert, more informal, had taken place a few kilometres away, which had been even better attended. The star attraction at it had been *Arif Sağ,* a famous musician who was also a Member of Parliament for the SHP. Though not himself an Alevi, Arif Sağ is a virtuoso *saz* player, adept at weaving left-wing protest songs and traditional Alevi music together, and tremendously popular among the young.[43]

This pattern can be discerned too in the trusts and associations that the Alevis have opened. The Alevis have long been active in creating their associations, on a local, national and even international scale. Prominent, among these but numerically small is the *Cem Vakfı,* which has its centre in Istanbul. The aim of the *vakıf* is to re-orientate Alevi religion towards the state in such a way that it becomes perceived as a primarily religious tradition, a legitimate, moderate form of Islam that should be recognised by the Republic. To this end they publish a journal, *Cem,* and organise conferences, press releases and so on. The argument that they put forward is that the Alevis represent a substantial proportion of the people of modern Turkey, and pay their taxes just as every one else. In spite of this, they receive no acknowledgement from the Directorate of Religious Affairs. As a solution, the *Cem Vakfı* seeks recognition from the state, and money for the creation of Alevi schools that will permit their traditions to be taught. At their head is an urbane, learned Professor of Law who marshals his arguments carefully. He has achieved a little success. In 1998, President Demirel received him to discuss the Alevi question. In 1997, he had organised a conference on the question of state-led religion in Turkey, which the head of the Directorate of Religious Affairs, after initial hesitation, did attend. Through the press attention that the event attracted, and the *Proceedings* of the conference, which have now been published, he has made a successful small step towards Alevi recognition.[44]

His efforts are highly controversial among the Alevis themselves. Many simply do not like the state at all, and wish to have nothing to do with it in any form. In conversation, they say that they have not forgotten centuries of persecution by the Ottoman State. They may say too that their fears are justified in the contemporary world. Since 1950, when Menderes assumed power, many Alevis say that the Republican heritage has been steadily eroded, so that the state is the instrument of oppressive Sunni Islam as much as it ever was before. As evidence, they point not just to the increased visibility of Islam in the public life of the country, but also to specific cases of assassination or murder as occurred in Çorum, Kahramanmaraş, or Sivas. Indeed, when taken together with the creed of Hüseyin's martyrdom at the Kerbala, they often envisage their history as that of a persecuted minority from the foundation of Islam, through the Ottoman Empire to the present day. This continuous sense of persecution is also one of the most frequent themes of their resurgent literature.[45]

The *Cem Vakfı* movement is also not in tune with the majority of the younger Alevis, who see no reason to subordinate themselves to a religious figure. Sceptics may be polite to the *dede*s but, for them, formal religion has almost totally lost its capacity to act as a system of social control. They do not expect their quarrels to be mediated by the *dede*s, do not wish to bow to them, nor do they regard them as being their confidants in times of difficulty. They anticipate that any legal dispute that they have will be solved through the Republican courts if necessary. They are aware of the moral lesson inculcated by religion, and may refer to the importance of the 'three conditions', of being on good terms with their fellows, of the community acting in concord, but have internalised such precepts in such a way that they no longer refer to a sacred tradition to justify them.

Such people, particularly if they are young, are far more likely to belong to the extensive chain of *Pir Sultan Abdal* associations, which represent a more politicised institutional framework and see *Alevilik* quite explicitly as a culture, *kültür*. Here, once again, though the kernel of the event may still be a *sema* and a *cem*, which for many people will have religious significance, the setting in which it is presented is open and celebratory rather than overtly sacred. A pertinent example is the programme of the public festival that was to be held at Sivas on 2 July 1993, but famously led to the riot, and deaths of many of the visiting speakers.

The Sivas Festival

Organised by the *Pir Sultan* association, the festival was advertised in its magazine on 7 June 1993, as the 'Fourth Traditional Pir Sultan Abdal Cultural Event'.[46] The programme was to last over two days, and take place in several different locations. It was to be joined by representatives from the Ministry of Culture, then in the control of the *SHP*. The bulk of the speakers consisted of leading Alevi musicians and writers, such as Pehlivan, who has written a thoughtful work on the relationship between the Alevis and the official, state support of religion.[47] Also advertised to be present were Aziz Nesin, the prominent and prolific writer of self-acclaimed atheist bent, and the popular *saz* teacher and musician Arif Sağ.

The content of the programme revolved around slide displays, theatre, film shows, panels of speakers and discussions of secularism. It also drew on the different parts of Alevi tradition that are found in the *cem*. In the *cem*, people are welcomed with a song played by a minstrel, '*Hoş Geldiniz!*'. So too, was the event to be opened, in the presence of the Sivas provincial governor, by Arif Sağ and to be followed by a demonstration *sema*. In the afternoon, a discussion of secularism at which members of the *SHP* were billed to speak was scheduled to be followed by a minstrel competition. Then, in the early evening, a communal sacrificial meal was planned to take place. In the programme, all are invited to attend, and have to bring 'nothing but cigarettes', because the meat will be provided and distributed by those who wish to offer a sacrifice. The evening was to be occupied by a *cem*, not now indoors, but in the open air, in the central square of a particular village within the Sivas area.

The previously private, secret inner world of the Alevis could hardly become more openly celebrated, or more openly, publicly politicised. The tragic irony, of course, is that in this public announcement of their opening to the world, rather than their safer worship only within their own communities, they gave warning to the very forces that originally propelled them to remain hidden, and opened the way to the murder of several dozen of their people.

Conclusions

This chapter has been an attempt to illustrate the way a traditional, rural mystical tradition can metamorphose into an urban secular philosophy. In order to clarify any misunderstanding, I should reiterate that my model of the transition is that the Alevi movement has two main strands, which often appear intertwined. There are those who do not see *Alevilik* primarily as a faith, but consider it a rich culture possessing a viable humanist philosophy for life in the modern world. There are those also who whilst retaining their faith have no objection to *Alevilik* being incorporated into this wider movement. A far smaller number do object to this transformation, but they have no practical means to prevent it. Both the dominant currents may come together by celebrating the previous occluded aspects of *Alevilik* as a folkloric, or traditional Anatolian way of life, and this, the public creation of tradition, now dominates the Alevi debate in modern Turkey.

Those who wish to practice *Alevilik* as a living religion have reacted in part against the difficulties that they face. This impulse has resulted in the construction of *cemevleri*, lit. '*cem* houses', across the countryside, which have become small specialised places of worship where people may gather discreetly to pray and hold ceremonies. In the village where I worked, for example, they have since 1995 constructed a village *cemevi* through private subscription. This is, for them, an innovation in that they used always to hold ceremonies in a private, rather than in a communally owned, house. However, in doing so, they have gained in flexibility: they are not tied to a particular lineage or follower inviting a specific *dede*. By widening the potential congregation to the village as a whole rather than to a single *mahalle*, there are more likely to be sufficient people able to attend. Whilst I have not been able to visit the village recently, they inform me that they have relaxed slightly the commitment that a *cem* must always be accompanied by a sacrifice, using a vegetable or fruit substitute for meat if no one has the means or inclination to provide a beast. In the cities too, there has been a movement towards building *cemevleri*. Here, they may become bases for Alevi activity of all kinds, and take on some of the characteristics of a mutual social support organisation. Still in theory illegal, they may be closed down at any time should a municipality decide to do so.

As time passes, and the left wing in Turkey becomes further eroded, it is often asked whether the Alevis' affinity with the left-wing Republican parties will become less prevalent. To some extent this may come about. After the debacle of the *SHP* scandals in the early 1990s, many Alevis were less inclined to feel the old loyalty to their Republican political antecedents. However, there is a question of alternatives. They were not at all inclined to vote for the Welfare (now Virtue) Party, though the Welfare Party did sometimes attempt to claim that the Alevis should vote for them saying, just as the Alevis are defined as being religious group, so the Welfare Party were the only party who placed religious feelings to the fore of their politics. This argument would be more convincing had not the Welfare Party itself acted against a central Alevi *cemevi* in Istanbul whilst Tayyip Erdoğan was mayor by closing it down. Some Alevis may tend very slightly towards the True Path Party (*DYP*) or the Motherland Party (*ANAP*), though this is less likely after the recent scandals affecting them. Further, many Alevis are extremely fond of Ecevit. Ecevit's recent rise again to prominence makes it likely that they will vote for his *DSP*, or the remaining rump of the *CHP*, particularly if they feel that they are the only two parties that can be trusted to act in resolutely secular fashion.

One of the problems that those in authority must face in any attempt at planning for the Alevis is that they appear to be faring less well than their Sunni counterparts in the race to modernise. That is, they may become an economic underclass as development continues. There is no explicit or official discrimination, but there are a number of reasons for thinking that this might be the case. Many of their publications recount the difficulties that they experience in Turkish society. Working almost entirely through the Republican People's Party, they have effectively become a huge patronage group that, because the last time it was in sole power was during the one-party period, has never been part of a modern majority government. Being rural until recently, they have fewer established people working in the towns than the Sunni. This is highly significant in a society where social betterment is substantially channelled through individual families gradually increasing opportunities for one another. There is a danger, therefore, that they may become attracted to exclusionist politics that emphasise their lowly class position, and in some of their literature this tendency can be seen already.[48]

I have discussed the Alevis primarily from the point of view of their religious faith in the modern world. There is also a danger that the cultural revival, which appears to be gaining momentum from day to day, will harden. In previous years, there has been no one form of Aleviness, rather a number of parallel traditions which resemble one another, but with no unifying social order. There is a process of re-evaluation of the Alevi culture and heritage which may lead to the codification of different Alevi schools, each with its own texts and moral codes.[49] The creation of these different areas of thought will inevitably lead to speculation as to which is the true, the final form of the Alevi religion. In practice, however, any claim to be a true form of Aleviness will be empirically incorrect, simply because Aleviness has over the centuries arrived at such complex forms of accommodation. It would be a terrible irony if the Alevis were to have escaped the danger of religious bigotry in their traditional setting, only for intransigent boundaries to develop in the secular Republic.

Whether or not this will happen depends greatly I think on the way that the evolving Sunni orthodoxy develops its policy towards the Alevis. Of course, there is no one Sunni movement, but there is a powerful group of thinkers consisting of the professors in Theological Faculties, senior officials in the Directorate of Religious Affairs and leaders of the some of larger *tarikat*s. The *Nakşibendi*s for example are close to this group, though the *Nurcu*s and Gülen may distance themselves from them. In the winter of 1995, among a group of specialists on the Alevis, I was invited to a conference to address a selection of people drawn from these circles. It was extremely puzzling both to me and to senior Alevis in Turkey that we should have been asked to talk to an invited audience for whom *Alevilik* was a strange and patently not very pleasant phenomenon. As the conference unfolded, I had a strong sense that its purpose was to clarify just where they objected, and where they could find common ground with the Alevi religious position. Indeed, the summing up by a dismayed professor of Islamic Theology explained point by point where the Alevis differed from his conception of correct Islamic practice.

This is only a cameo, but it does indicate how very difficult it is to reach an acceptable compromise at the level of religious teaching between the two positions. The fear that explicit recognition on the level of an alternative version of Islam would provoke, rather than impede, the creation of ethnic boundaries, is I think one of the reasons why the authorities are today slow to recognise the Alevis. The hitherto cautious steps to approach and assimilate the Alevis openly into the Republican state are surely likely to be equally careful in the future. Nevertheless, the sheer religification of so much of Turkish society means that the disastrous scenario, wherein secular and believing Alevis alike combine together under the banner of their culture against Sunni activists in a violent confrontation, is more possible than it has ever been before.

All this means that the Alevis are likely to remain a distinct cultural and political group in the Republic, one that, if the current tendency continues, will find itself on the secular side of the religious divide, although not particularly close to Republican authority. Their clear left-wing tendency, combined with the fact that the military has so clearly plumped for moderate orthodox Islam rather than the original drastic secularism of the Republic's founding period, means that it is likely they will remain out of sympathy with the powers that be. Again, there is an irony here: as they move to become part of urban society, many (though not all) Alevis have gone through a profound inner transformation, whereby they no longer regard the moral conduct of their lives as being one sanctified by divine command. As a result, it appears that among them, religion has assumed a position close to that advocated by Atatürk: a cultural orientation, possibly a private belief, but no longer a fundamental organising principle of self or society. Nevertheless, the secular authorities' increasingly active interpretation of the place of orthodox religion within the modern, reformed, changed Republic means that the potential for future unease remains very great indeed.

| 7 |

Conclusions

In this work, I have argued that the accommodation of Islam into the body politic of the state has been far more subtle than the dominant image of Turkey in the West implies. To conceive of the Islamic resurgence in Turkey purely in terms of a political conflict between the state and the Welfare Party (or its successors) is both fallacious and profoundly misleading. Religious belief plays an enormous part in people's lives outside the overtly Islamic activist sphere, and the Turkish state has not reacted against this religious practice in a blunt or unreflecting manner. Quite the contrary, through the existing institutions of civil society, diverse political parties, and the myriad links between state and citizen, the state has absorbed a great variety of approaches and facilitated a high degree of re-Islamisation. In turn, this flexibility helps to explain why, until now, the religious resurgence has been relatively peaceful.

Whilst without a doubt the rise of political Islam is highly significant, it must be seen also in the context of other movements, such as the emergence of the Alevis, which contribute toward the overall heterogeneity of life in Turkey. These streams of thought are part of a much wider and complex process whereby Turkish society, though remaining tremendously varied, appears to be becoming more overtly and sharply divided between secular and non-secular approaches. The military, led by the army, and senior bureaucracy have responded to the danger by deciding to emphasise and to teach moderate Islam ever more actively. As the measures of 28 February 1997 indicate, they intend to combine this move with increasingly careful regulation of politics, the civil service, and the media.

Not all Turks approve of this decision. Those who do not wish to believe at all, for reasons of inclination (pursuit of consumer pleasures over all else), political motivation deriving from Marxism, philosophical scepticism or various combinations of all three, whether Sunni or Alevi, often deplore fundamentalist Islam. Yet they dislike, too, the mechanisms of ideological control which the state appears to be forced to employ, fearing that these measures may be used against all sorts of groups, not just Islam. They may point, for example, to the tight censorship of the public broadcasting institutions. In the winter of 1988, a highly popular satirist found his programme removed from the air for a tasteless remark about the private life of a leading politician. It was not an attractive joke but suspending his broadcasts appeared to many people in the press an inappropriate way to respond to a personal jibe.[1]

Sceptics of this inclination may also wish that the state would not support religion at all, saying that to do so is by definition anti-secular. Often, they regard the army as an integral part of the increase in Islamic sentiment in the country as a whole.[2] They may also claim that there has been a substantial shift in the public perception of religious sentiment: that until recently, in the cities at least, it has been possible for a person in Turkey to be an atheist and not to fear for his or her life. Even if they are exaggerating the degree of secularism in the past, there is not the slightest doubt that it is now dangerous for a man or woman to deny openly belief in God. To do so invites condemnation from the clerics, accusations of 'provocation' from the courts and violence from those who feel that they have the right to take the law into their own hands, however firm may be the voice of quietism from moderate believers. These last fear that a further conflation of orthodox Islam and the state, motivated by whatever impulse, will force people into a public conformity – for them a religious hypocrisy, that the Kemalist revolution aimed at removing.

If all else fails, then the armed forces will undoubtedly stage a further coup. Yet a coup is no easy answer. As the years go by, it is becoming ever clearer that the 1980 intervention had profound effects on Turkey. A full-scale coup today would have instant repercussions in a country that is vastly more integrated with the international market, with trade, and with tourism than in 1980. The country itself is more difficult to govern, with the rise in electronic media, and complex business holdings making it almost impossible to go back to the straightforward *étatist* teachings of previous years. It hardly seems possible that this diversity can be brought under control without a level of direct coercion that would impede everyday life in an even more serious way than did the events of 1980.

The future

If a coup is not an easy way out, are there other possibilities? One frequently mooted theory is that within a generation or two, such interventions may not be necessary anyway. It relies on what might be called the routinisation of Islam. It holds that the experience of Christianity in Western Europe is generalisable: belief does fade in the face of affluence. By analogy, therefore, as she grows steadily richer, Turkey will also experience a similar decline of active Islamism. Secular intellectuals gain enormous solace from this thought. It means, in effect, that the status quo is the right way forward: that if governments behave sensibly in the economic field, if everyone's lot continues to improve, if wars are avoided, then everything will be fine. Religious passions will be blunted by comfort.

Islamic thinkers, such as Bulaç, take this theory seriously also, though in this case they are equally worried lest it be true. Indeed, they sometimes extend this train of thought by remarking that there is a further relevant element. In the modern world, the economic development that has secularised religion has invariably taken place within the framework of the nation-state. Given that believers wish to live in affluence and to retain their faith, it might be that they have to find something other than the Turkish nation in which to achieve it. They sometimes regard Iran as a possible alternative model, or may turn to creating a unified Islamic world.[3]

Whilst interesting, the pan-nationalist Islam option appears impracticable. Turkish nationalism has been widely, even wildly, successful in the Republic among the majority of the people. The willingness with which youths go to conscription, singing songs and playing drums in the bus stations, the enthusiasm that the deployment of Turkish soldiers gives rise to among the mass, the reverence that many Turks feel for Atatürk even though they may dislike the religious reforms and the rise of the nationalist *MHP*, all testify to this. A faith *sans frontières* is unlikely to make headway against such commitment in the foreseeable future.

The relationship between economic development and secularism is less clear. Different spheres of Turkish urban life appear secularised. The burgeoning industrial, tourist, leisure and service industries have all contributed towards an ethos of consumer internationalism that owes little or nothing to religious sentiment. Large companies, too, often have an overtly secular ethos. The powerful businessmen's confederation, *TÜSİAD*, has acted as a steady and clear force in favour of greater unification with Europe, and periodically warns against the dangers of Islamism. There is direct evidence also that religion may give way in the face of the temptation of affluence in the rural areas. A recent doctoral dissertation by Cemil Bezmen, for example, has illustrated that in Capadoccia, one of the most popular tourist destinations, the resurgent Islamic movement has been unable to take political control in the local towns because of the locals' fears that it will damage the tourist industry. Meanwhile, the great number of visitors to the area supports a network of clubs, bars and restaurants in which local men interact with tourists and appear to embrace some of their *laisser faire* attitude to religious commitment.[4]

In spite of all this, there are signs that the relationship between secularism and an increasingly affluent economy is not straightforward. The *Nurcu*s, who claim to overcome the schism between technology and faith are hugely popular. Newly created urban settlements invariably are still formed around mosques, and religious activity appears to be as active within these new urban communities as in village life. There is also a growing sector of Islamic-oriented business, combined under the name *MÜSİAD*, estimated to control about ten per cent of Turkey's trade.[5] The Islamic banking and investment sector is also growing quickly, supported earlier by Özal, and then by Fethullah Gülen. The Islamic trade sector is dwarfed by the size, extent and scope of Western-oriented business activity, much of which has little sympathy with the Islamic movement, but its existence indicates that faith and business are not incompatible. Above all, it appears that for many people to be modern and religious is achievable. Even if part of Turkey's society is irrevocably secular, other parts simply do not appear as susceptible as the secularisation-through-affluence theory predicts.

Political Islam

It is sometimes argued that the political Islamic movement has now peaked. This argument was made after every single instance of the Welfare Party's advance during the 1980s and 1990s. Nevertheless, after the comparative decline of the Virtue Party in the 1999 elections, it may at last have some evidence in its favour. Does this mean that their strength is broken forever? I do not think so. Whether Virtue will in the future gain a majority is difficult to predict. If all things remain constant they are certainly capable of doing so. To gain 111 seats, after all, within a few months of being closed down and having their assets confiscated, is still a major achievement, and their strength in the municipalities is still notable.

The Islamic movement, is therefore in a position to play a major role in government in the coming decades. It may even become stronger. The tendency of Turkish political parties to fracture, even when ideologically compatible, weakens any collective front that it might otherwise put forward, as the split between *DYP* and *ANAP* on the right illustrates. The left has its problems too. Ecevit, though now riding high, at seventy-three is the oldest representative in the Assembly, and may find it difficult to stand again. The *CHP*, in failing to pass the electoral barrier in April 1999, have weakened the left still more. It is perfectly possible, even likely, that some future government will contain a large component of *FP* deputies, allied perhaps with one of the splintered right parties, or perhaps with the *MHP*, the new party in the equation.

This in turn might potentially create a re-run of the scenario that created such instability during Erbakan's period in office. It should be recalled that the key question in Turkey is not whether fundamentalists will take absolute power through a revolution. There is no foreseeable chance that they will do so: the army, and other secular elements are simply too strong, and too aware, for them to confront head-on with any chance of success. The issue is rather whether they may strengthen sufficiently to render explicit, and violent, a division between secular and actively religious sectors of the population. This they may indeed succeed in doing. Many of the factors that permitted Welfare to gain such initial success remain: the urban poor, the skewed income distribution, and inflation. As the effects of the youthful population hit the job market, it can hardly be doubted that social control in poor city areas will remain of pressing concern.

Moderating Islam

A related, and frequently employed, argument is that rather than continue on such an open collision course, political Islamic groups will moderate their approach, and therefore any designs they may have on the secular system will quietly fade. In part, this contention has been addressed already. It overlooks the fact that the party in power, or sharing power, has a myriad of ways at its command to achieve social change. The aggressive rhetoric of religious revolution was only a small part of the Welfare Party's activity, and by far the least effective. Their long-term programme was quite clear. It was a gradual endeavour: changes in civil service personnel, control over art and other activities of which they disapprove on the grounds that they are immoral, support for orthodox religion leading to a greater control over the public spaces of the community, a shift away from the European orientation that has characterised the Republic until now, and the creation of a parallel judiciary through the re-introduction of *şeriat* family law. If in the future the Virtue Party (or whatever replacement may emerge) does refrain from explicit calls to religious violence, it can obviously only be a good thing. However, this does not imply any necessary lessening of their goals. It is naïve to believe that a political programme driven by those who have spent their lives in the pursuit of achieving the slow accumulation of Islamic change is going to be abandoned simply because they encounter opposition, particularly if its supporters feel that they have a mandate from the people to continue the struggle.

Does this mean, then, that there is no alternative but for the army to intervene once again as violent clashes between non-secular and secular groups lead the country into internal chaos? No. Such a violent confrontation may happen, but it is not inevitable. The transfer of votes to the far-right but secular Nationalist Action Party from the Welfare/Virtue spectrum is held by many people to indicate that, on this occasion at least, the actions of the National Security Council and the Constitutional Court have been respected. Further, the Republican system is well established. It has shown itself very flexible to change. To many, even if not all, it is an acceptable package. In addition, whilst the trends we have discussed appear to be indelible ideological positions within Turkish society, in practice how much political and active commitment they will gain from their respective supporters is subject to a fine balancing of variables, and is capable of change depending on economic and other factors.

Turkey and the external world
The direction that Turkey will take partly depends on the actions of the international community. Even if we have no ready desire to address Turkey's internal situation, we are already indirectly part of the conflicts within Turkey in many different ways. There are the formal links with NATO, with the European Union, and the Council of Europe. Globalisation itself, which receives so much of its stimulus from the developed countries, is partly responsible for developments in Turkey and for the positions that Turks have adopted. Having encouraged her involvement with the European Union, cultivated her as a trading partner, and established the Customs Union, all in the interests of universal affluence and sociability, it hardly seems appropriate for the international community to deny any responsibility for the internal divisions that are in part a response to this close engagement. Further, and by no means least, whilst surprising, it is hardly possible to exaggerate the level to which Turkey's internal affairs are linked to their perception of how they are treated in Europe, America, and the rest of the world.

Take once more the controversy over Turkey's possible accession to the European Union. Some European Union officials undoubtedly believe that they were not actually snubbing Turkey in December 1997. Nevertheless, soon afterwards there emerged a rise in bellicose nationalism in Turkey whose consequences are still becoming apparent. The ultimatum that the generals presented to Syria very nearly led to open warfare. Whilst their aim, to dislodge the PKK leader, Öcalan, has been a longstanding one, it is no coincidence that their temper snapped just at a point when relations seemed at a low time with the European Union. Further, whilst no doubt unintentionally, to the Turkish people it has looked increasingly as if the European Union is combining with Greece to form common cause with that country in its quarrels with Turkey, particularly in that it permits a veto to be imposed freezing EU financial support. That Greece was attempting to shelter Öcalan when Turkey finally apprehended him simply serves to reinforce these fears.

Such mistrust serves to increase tension in the region, and has further quite unpredictable effects on Turkey itself. Indeed, one possible scenario which has been mooted among intellectual circles in Istanbul would be a sharp conflict in the Aegean leading to an unforeseen military reverse. The army could then loose prestige, resulting in a catastrophic loss of popular support for its secularist measures, a sweeping election victory for an Islamic nationalist party, and a coup that, unlike the last intervention in 1980, would not have mass support. The resulting civil upheaval in Turkey would hardly be favourable to Europe.

Given then, that there is a complex, and profound interconnection (though not always in a predictable way) between our activities in Europe and the religious situation in Turkey, what measures might be suggested? Obviously, we cannot take a position on telling people how to believe. However, one clear, unmistakable message would be to indicate to Turkey that she is not being frozen out of the European system. This would help immensely in breaking a reorientation that leads towards extremism of various sorts, including political Islam. This does not have to be instant membership, or anything like it, but it should be a number of planned measures that will indicate that we are not creating a cultural barrier between our two worlds. A beginning certainly might be to release aid money that was earmarked, but not awarded, on Turkey's accession to the Customs Union. Even such comparatively small measures help enormously in drawing votes towards moderate parties by indicating that the western-oriented premise upon which the Republic was founded is not moribund.

It is interesting to conclude by speculating on why this *rapprochement* has not happened, indeed on why the situation has worsened so markedly during recent years. Partly, decision-makers in Turkey do not always realise how their actions may be interpreted in Europe, nor do they trust Europe to react in the appropriate way when they feel there has been progress. The European Union itself, whilst right to place importance on the Cyprus and the Kurdish issues, has undoubtedly permitted an international organisation based on creating economic and social links to be appropriated for specifically political agendas. The result of this collective, and accelerating series of misunderstandings may, in the end be an increasingly isolated Turkey in which armed conflict between those for and against secularism can only be suppressed by an authoritarian regime of unprecedented rigidity. Such internal unrest would only help to provoke economic crisis, resulting in an even more difficult and precarious life for the mass of urban poor, and indeed would damage an already highly significant market, and one with a great potential for expansion. This may not happen, these are after all, concluding speculations. If it does, however, lack of engagement, prejudice or even indifference by politicians and officials in Europe will have played a very substantial part in creating a catastrophe that they can still act to prevent.

Notes

Introduction

1. Cf. *The Economist,* editorial, 17 April 1999, also the Article 19 report published on 24 July 1998.
2. Cf. B. Lewis (1997).
3. See, for example, the *Catalogue* (1993) published by the General Directorate of Museums and Antiquities celebrating the national exhibition on women in Anatolia, also the many official or semi-official publications on folklore eg. Uysal (1989).
4. On the *imam-hatip* schools see Akşit (1991).
5. See the comment by Mortimer 'It suddenly became clear that what had seemed the strongest as well as the most pro-Western regime in the Muslim world "was being brought to its knees by crowds of people"'(1982: 15).
6. This variety of religious styles comes out extremely strongly in the essays edited by R. Tapper (1991).
7. Summaries of these basic principles of Turkish Islam may be found in various publications, some in English, eg the *Concise Islamic Catechism* compiled by Soymen (1979: many reprints).
8. On the daily practice of Islam in Turkey, see the work of Richard and Nancy Tapper, eg. Tapper, N. (1985), Tapper and Tapper (1987).
9. The *tarikats*, described in Chapter 3, may vary greatly from each other but, simply put, are hierarchical organisations of followers who respect a leader privileged before other men in the eyes of God. See Norton (1994) for a clear introductory comment on Turkish brotherhoods, also De Jong and Radtke (eds. 1999).

10. On the early Republican approach to Islam, see the essay by Reed, and that by Rustow, in Frye (1957).
11. See also Lewis (1988) in the preface written for the French edition of his *Emergence*.
12. On the rise of the Islamic private sector see Bulut (1995).
13. Lewis (1961) suggests that use of the headscarf in villages even increased after the founding of the Republic, partly perhaps as a function of the increasing codification of religion.
14. It is interesting to note that this last has been a long-running phenomenon: *Cumhuriyet*, 18 January 1975 reports that University lodgings coming under the influence of the MSP (Erbakan's second political party, with which he shared power in a coalition government at that time) insisted that female students should perform their prayers and cover their heads.
15. For a discussion of the headscarf issue see Özdalga (1998). Tekeli (1995) provides a comprehensive and varied reader on women's affairs in Turkey.
16. See the pamphlet by Browning (1985).
17. The influence of the Alevis outside their own community has hardly been studied, but see Dumont (1991).
18. See Barchard (1998).
19. See, for example, an article by the journalist Hugh Pope (a prominent proponent of this position) in *The Wall Street Journal*, Tuesday, 4 May 1999 when discussing a row over women deputies wearing headscarfs in the Assembly, 'Turkish authorities risk appearing backward when it comes to issues of democratic rights like freedom of expression. Incidents like this one are a big part of the reason the European Union, for example, holds Turkey at arms length. Meanwhile, the Virtue Party seems less of a threat these days'.

Chapter 1

1. Among many others, see Orga (1958).
2. Notices of this frequently appear in the press, eg. *Cumhuriyet*, 12 January 1996: 'for renting his house to the three members of the Aczmendi *tarikat*, (xxx) has been sent to prison by the Rize

prosecutor'.

3. On the state's role in the development of Anatolia see Wagstaff (1989).

4. Of the many accounts of this period, the best are still perhaps Lewis (1961), and Balfour [Kinross] (1964). Dr Andrew Mango, who has very kindly shared his insights with me, has written a new biography of Atatürk, published as this work was going to press.

5. There are numerous partial chronologies, but the most complete seems to be Robinson (1963).

6. These areas are covered more fully in the essays edited by Özbudun, and Kazancıgil (1992).

7. Makal (1954).

8. See Andrews (1989).

9. See, for example, Berzeg (1990), a work devoted to demonstrating the important contribution played by the Circassians (*Çerkez*) in the founding of the Republic.

10. Cf. Tunaya (1962). One of the most famous of these early interpretations is that by Ziya Gökalp, who influenced by Durkheim, recognised, and attempted to retain the collective solidarity that could come from religious ritual. For an English translation of his writings, see Gökalp, Z. (1959). Cf. also Stirling (1958), or Lewis (1961).

11. The Turkish replacement for the Arabic *ezan* is as follows 'Tanrı uludur/şüphesiz bilirim bildirim Tanrı'dan başka yoktur tapacak/ şüphesiz bilirim bildirim Tanrı'nın elçisidir Muhammed/Haydi namaza/Haydi felaha/(morning only) Namaz uykudan hayırlıdır/Tanrı uludır/ Tanrı'dan başka yoktur tapacak.' (Given by Halil Nebiler, in *Cumhuriyet, Şeriatın Kilometre Taşları*, page 12). It was first read in 1932. The Koran in Turkish appears to have been read at about this time also, though Lewis (1961), notes that the translation was not, at that time, concluded.

12. Gündüz, Gül and Kaya ([1992]: 18).

13. Fığlalı (1988: 52, 58 and 56 respectively).

14. A third institution, the *Vakıflar Genel Müdürlüğü*, the General Directorate of Pious Trusts, has had the function of maintaining and administering an important part of the Ottoman religious and architectural heritage. See Chapter 2.

15. See Appendix 3, and Chapter 5.

16. I am most grateful to Dr Andrew Mango for bringing this point to my attention.

17. Delaney notes in her fine ethnography of a village near Ankara that a local *imam* was reported, and removed, for making too-fiery sermons in the mosque (Delaney 1991).

18. *Diyanet İşleri Başkanlığı* (1993) Ankara. (Brochure published under the auspices of the Research, Planning and Co-ordination Department of the Directorate of Religious Affairs).

19. See the description by Çakır (1993: 130-138) where he outlines the attempts made by the *Süleymancı* group to increase their number in the Directorate of Religious Affairs.

20. Cf. Tapper (1990: Intro).

21. Gözaydın-Tarhanlı (1993, 1995). To my knowledge, her detailed and interesting study is still the only extended treatment of the Directorate.

22. Yurtdışı raporu (1993: 1,2, and 3 respectively) Some specific figures: the report also notes that the Directorate has 393 religious teachers in Germany, 84 in Holland and 66 in France. It has also 5 in Azerbaijan, 6 in Kazakhstan and a lesser number in the other Turkic states. It also takes on the lesser duty of supplying religious personnel to the Republic of Northern Cyprus, which is greatly dependent on Turkish aid overall.

23. See particularly Tapper and Tapper (1991).

24. Cf. Stirling (1983).

25. Gellner was fond of pointing this out in his works, eg. (1981).

26. These incidents have been documented afresh by Brockett (1998).

27. See Gellner (1981: Chapter 1), Van Bruinessen (1992).

28. For a monograph on political opposition in this period see Zürcher (1991).

29. The political development of the Republic has been described in many publications, see for example, Ahmad (1977), Zürcher (1994), Shaw (1977), also there are a large number of edited volumes covering more specific aspects, such as Hale (ed. 1976), Schick and Tonak (eds. 1987), or Kedourie (ed. 1998), Toprak (1981) covers religion in the early Republic.

30. Zürcher (1994: 227).

31. See also Vahide's biography (1993) of Nursi which, written as a

follower, gives an excellent perspective on how strongly this early period is still resented.

32. Shankland (1999b).
33. Tunaya (1962) for a general account of this period, including re-opening the *Eyüp Sultan* tomb (page 224).
34. As well as the Stirling comment quoted above, see Toprak (1988: 123).
35. Cf. Robinson's account of the Menderes decade (1963).
36. Lewis (1974).
37. For a detailed discussion of the lead up to the *coup*, see Hale (1994).
38. Quoted in Bulut (1995b).
39. See Baldwin (1990) for a description of the introduction of Islamic banking.
40. Pope and Pope (1997).
41. The repeal of Article 163 has given rise to continuing disquiet in the State Security Council. In fact, it was passed through the Assembly as part of law 3713 which at the same time as tightening up on anti-terrorist activity, also included two liberal measures, the annulment of Articles 143 and 144, and the legalization of the use of Kurdish. Articles 143 and 144 were derived from the Italian penal code of Mussolini's day, and banned the use of class distinctions in political activity. The left wing, felt, rightly, that even a faint touch of Marxism might make them in breach of the law, and for long had wished for its removal. The package overall might therefore be seen as a quid pro quo, with something for both rightist and leftist political spectrums. For a contemporary discussion of this fascinating episode see Mango (1991: 14-15).
42. Birand (1984).
43. For a recent appraisal of the coup see Dağı (1998). Birand (1987) offers a good insight into the lead up and its immediate aftermath.
44. Yavuz (1993: 80).

Chapter Two

1. That ideologies are often imposed *in toto* is a point made by Gellner in various writings (eg. Gellner 1973).

2. On complex cause and effect at a macro level see the recent work of Macfarlane (1998) on population change. For a micro-analysis in the Turkish context, see Stirling (1973).
3. See, for example, Pope and Pope (1997). A similar approach underlies Göle (English translation 1997). For a review comment on this last work see Ayata (1993).
4. Warkworth, Lord (1898).
5. Among the many works on the role of the state in Turkey, Sirman and Finkel (eds) (1990) gives a good varied overview.
6. Buğra (1994).
7. A little example: Brockett (1998) notes that after the introduction of the hat-law, some people concealed a *turban* beneath the more Western-style hat, outwardly at least conforming to the change. More recently, as the newly formed Virtue Party *(FP)* were going through their swearing-in ceremony in the Grand National Assembly for the first time, one of their deputies, Merve Kavakçi, refused to remove her headscarf. This blunt defiance of authority was reported widely, and shortly afterwards the Public Prosecutor applied to have the Virtue Party closed down. Part of the anger against her stemmed from the fact that she had acted in a way that simply could not be ignored, and therefore deprived the Republican authorities of the chance to show that they were prepared to offer a period of *laisser faire* to the newly-founded Islamic party.
8. Cf. Mardin 'Hints, admonishments, mild remonstrances, repeated entreaties are part of the Turkish way of doing things before we reach the drop that makes the glass spill over'. (1969: 383-384).
9. See the essay by Sirman (1990).
10. Again, Mardin's very erudite article is apposite: 'diffuseness of control seems to be characteristic of Turkish society, harsh orders to comply with norms or uncompromising directives are not part of the Turkish administrative style, neither are they a characteristic of the Turkish way of life.' (1969: 383).
11. For a comment on this type of activity within the education system see, Stirling (1975).
12. Cf. Stirling (1965: 284) 'Turkish society is almost military in its hierarchy'. An example of how important this ranking in everyday life can be: a friend of mine in the Turkish bureaucracy was most put out

when a British academic moved from being 'Dr' to 'Professor' from one year to the next. His complaint was that if he had known that the now professor had been already a 'Reader' (*doçent*) and therefore on the path to promotion, he would have behaved towards him accordingly. He felt that the custom of not using the title 'Reader' in conversation was therefore misleading and could lead to serious misunderstandings.

13. There are hundreds of examples of this in the press. See, for example, a report in the Turkish *Probe* from 17.01.97 'that Islamists took the lion's share in the division of key security posts in a recent reshuffle of the police network, bagging 21 posts to the DYP's 13. [This was] not seen as particularly pleasing to secularist opponents of the coalition.'

14. Yalçın (1994) for the early, MSP, influence on the Ministry of Education, Toprak (1988: 131) for a comment on Dinçerler.

15. See, for example, a recent newspaper headline '*Aleviler artık örgütleniyorlar*' ('The Alevi begin to organise themselves').

16. See Shaw (1995: 74-75). See also Barnes (1992).

17. Whilst initially controversial (because revenue from the Trusts was sent directly to the Finance Ministry), the *Vakıflar Genel Müdürlüğü* has not been overtly politicised nor (as yet) at least become greatly influential. For its role in the early part of the Republic see Reed (1957).

18. Lewis (1961: 407), Gözaydın-Tarhanlı (1995: 42).

19. Gözaydın-Tarhanlı (1995: 43).

20. Stokes (1992).

21. Gözaydın-Tarhanlı (1995: 43) notes that this power has caused at least one prominent Turkish academic to worry about the power that such associations may wield over state institutions.

22. Yücekök (1971).

23. Yücekök's statistics are also useful in showing the equally astonishing success of Menderes' decision to permit Koran courses after he came to power. Some of these were in part administered by the Directorate of Religious Affairs, but it was also possible to apply simply for recognition (and thereby permission) to run them openly. This resulted in a very rapid increase in numbers, from 237 in 1951 to 2,510 by 1968.

24. Reed (1956: 158, 157).

25. For example, the claim that *imam-hatip* schools that have been fully

paid for by private citizens should receive immediate state recognition and support was demanded by the National Salvation Party under Erbakan when in a coalition with Ecevit in 1974 (Yalçın 1994).

26. This device of funding state institutions by public subscription has even influenced international relations. That the British decision to confiscate two battleships ordered by the Ottoman Empire eased Enver's decision to ally with Germany is widely known, but it is less well remembered that the fury in Turkey was vastly exacerbated by their being paid for by donation rather than from the treasury. On this point see Lewis (1961).

27. See Tunaya (1962), who quotes verbatim from the Assembly records, *tutanak*.

28. I hasten to add that I am very well aware that *dernek*s are regularly closed down for anti-secular activities. However, the point remains that if such associations remain within the clearly prescribed law which forbids using associations for anti-constitutional activities, they are permitted room to manoeuvre and to flourish. A useful article on the expanding role of religion in the civil process, and on the question of civil society in Turkey is Toprak (1996).

29. Hann (1996: intro).

30. Gellner (1995).

31. Thus, the *Diyanet İşleri Bakanlığı* used money raised through private donations to the *Diyanet İşleri Vakfı*, often from workers in Germany, to send students abroad to study religious subjects. The availability of the money from the *Diyanet İşleri Vakfı* meant that they were able to do this far more easily than they would have been had this money been requested through the usual state channels. These actions, whilst not official state policy, were nevertheless perfectly legal. I am obliged to Mr John Norton for bringing this example to my attention.

32. Hann (1990) notes this possibility in his monograph suggestively sub-titled *The Domestication of the Turkish State*.

33. Yücekök (1971: 133).

Chapter Three

1. Gellner (1981). For a general introduction to the brotherhoods in Islam see Trimingham (1971).
2. For a contemporary traveller's account on their activity in Anatolia, see Morier's *Journey* (1812); for a study of a major revolt, Ocak (1989).
3. On the role of the *tarikats* among the Kurds, see Van Bruinessen (1992), who notes that the degree of local influence exerted by the sheikh may vary according to the level of central control at any particular time. Disputes, and their mediation, among the Alevis are discussed in Chapter Six.
4. Çakır (1993) gives a good impression. For a brief comment in English, see Norton (1994).
5. See, for example, the volume by Arberry (1961), which followed the monumental translation by Nicholson, his teacher.
6. Lewis (1961: 403).
7. I use 'appear' advisedly. It may be that there is a greater role than I have perceived, perhaps among the small traders which still dominate the town centre. There are also signs of resurgent popularity in Istanbul, particularly among middle-class women. However, this rather reinforces my point: in the spheres where *Mevlevi* ideas are most popular they are celebrated as a cultural philosophy, as an attractive vision of peace, available to all, rather than being confined to a discrete organisation of believers with a clear political and financial dimension.
8. Algar (1997: 51 and 62).
9. See Şahiner (1976: xiii).
10. Mardin (1989).
11. For a discussion of the later splinter groups see Beki (1995b).
12. Mardin (1989: 99-100).
13. Beki (1995b).
14. See, for example, Tunaya (1962: 239).
15. Broadly speaking, this does appear to be an accurate representation of Said-i Nursi's position. See the account in Vahide (1992), and his own writings, many of which are now also in English, eg. Nursi (1992, 1994).
16. Bulut (1995a: 233-262).

17. For detailed reports see again Bulut's (1995a) very useful transcription of the relevant documentation.
18. Yorukan (1993).
19. General Turhan Olçaytu, quoted in Bulut (1995a: 72-73).
20. For recent instance of this approach see the entry 'Religion' in Heper (1994).
21. Cf. Stirling (1983). Robinson makes a similar observation (1964).
22. Nancy and Richard Tapper (1987), who found that in Eğridir, the townspeople were able to conceptualise their religious lives in complex, but avowedly satisfactory, ways around the secular state.
23. Meeker (1991), Mardin (1989) and Delaney (1991) respectively.
24. Ataseven (1985), Balaban (1986), Bayrakdar (1989), Keşkioğlu (nd), Nurbakı (nd).
25. Stirling in Shankland (1999b).
26. Cf. Mardin (1989: Chapter VI).
27. Nursi is very difficult to translate. This passage is taken from an anonymous translation from the *Risale-i Nur* (Nursi 1994: 252-253, orig. emphasis), and is comparable though different in style from Vahide's 1992 version (Nursi 1992: 251-252).
28. It is important to be quite clear here, in that as recently as 1993 Toprak felt that the core intellectual Islamist position was anti-scientific (Cf. Toprak 1993). Partly, the difference between her and my views is terminological. I assert that, given the desire to attain affluence and to develop, orthodox believers are faced with a choice: to integrate their faith with science or to reject faith in favour of science. Most wish for, and attain, the former. In thus rejecting a materialist perspective, Islamic intellectuals' positions may be regarded as 'anti' science. Nevertheless, this does not preclude their embracing knowledge of the physical world or their availing themselves of its technological benefits.
29. This was reinforced by a speech made by Deniz Baykal to the National Assembly on 13 October 1998. In it, he criticises the state for not acting incisively enough against pro-headscarf demonstrations that had happened that previous weekend. He blames 'the government for underestimating the importance of the event' and refers to their actions as being 'hesitant and indecisive' (*Turkish Daily News*, 14 October 1998).

30. This pattern was illustrated afresh in June 1999, when tapes recorded by *Fetullah Hoca* were released showing that he advocated slow infiltration of the state by Islamic sympathisers. Whilst the Prime Minister of the day, Bülent Ecevit, was anxious to support him, the public prosecutor was much clearer that *Fetullah Hoca* lay in breach of the law, and announced an investigation.

31. Cf. Bulut (1993a) for the trials, Norton (1994) for a brief comment on their organisation, Çakır (1993) covers them in more detail.

32. *'Kilometre taşları'*, This meeting is also mentioned by Çakır (1993).

33. See Bulut (1995a).

34. This is a crucial point. People being tried on suspicion of anti-secular activities do sometimes make the claim that their offence is purely political, and therefore their appearance in court at all, merely a case of misplaced authority. Again, whilst one sometimes suspects that this is the case when nationalism comes into question, this accusation is less apposite in religious prosecutions, where cases seem to be characterised by scrupulous and careful, even overwhelming evidence. The recent Welfare Party trial exemplifies this.

Chapter Four

1. Rustow (1957: 101-107).

2. See notably the work of Toprak (1988) who uses almost exactly the same categorisation nearly thirty years later. See also Çakır (1993: 222-225).

3. Eg. See Hale and Finkel (1990: 135) 'the centre of gravity of Turkish politics seems to have lain permanently on the right of centre'.

4. From the one-party period, Yalçın (1994: 56) notes the *İslami Koruma Partisi* (Islam Protection Party) founded in 1946, and immediately closed by the authorities, the *Muhafazakar Parti* (Conservative Party), opened in 1947 but unsuccessful at attracting support, and the *İslami Demokrat Partisi* (Democratic Islam Party) founded in 1951 and closed down soon afterwards. The *Millet Partisi* (Nation Party), which had formed by separating from the Democrat Party in 1948, was closed in 1954, and its successor in 1955.

5. 'Senators' refers to an experiment in creating an upper house which

lasted only from 1961 until 1980. Almost the only trace of this now lies in the large chamber at the present-day Assembly, originally built to take both houses at the same time for special gatherings.

6. It appears that a fall in the *MSP*'s support in local elections held earlier in January had persuaded them to take their place in government.

7. Cf. Çakır (1993), Yalçın (1994).

8. Yalçın (1994: 67) 'It is said that Air Force General Muhsin Batur and General Turgut Sunalp went to Switzerland, and offered every assurance to Erbakan for his return to Turkey to found a party'. This visit is also mentioned by Bulut in his *Ordu ve Din* (1995a: 71-72). Both the authors also mention that, although Erbakan's first party was closed down by the Constitutional Court, no further charges were made against him, and so he escaped the mandatory five-year ban on political activity that would have followed. It should be noted that Toprak (1988: 124) suggests, alternatively, that Erbakan's being permitted to function was due to 'the liberal atmosphere' that developed during the 1970s.

9. Alkan (1984) even suggests that the closeness of the Democrat Party and National Salvation Party's positions might have been a reason for Demirel to encourage their closure.

10. Cf. a pamphlet in which Welfare proclaim their predecessor's success in stimulating heavy industrial investment projects during the 1970s (*Milli Görüş* [1994]).

11. See Hale and Finkel (1994) for a quite outstanding article on this period.

12. The quotation is from the text given in Çakır (1993: 54), as is the description of Coşan's article in *İslam*.

13. These suspicions appeared to be justified when a commission of deputies in January 1997 voted by 8 votes to 7 to clear Çiller of any further investigation, the 8 votes being supplied by a combination of the Welfare Party and Truth Path Party. Cf. *Turkish Probe* 17.01.97.

14. An Islamist/nationalist breakaway party from *ANAP* led by Muhsin Yazıcıoğlu.

15. Birand (1983) gives a vivid picture of the way enmity between political groups helped to render the government impotent in the lead up to the 1980 crisis.

16. The fascinating question of why the Kemalist reforms seemed to be so little resisted is discussed in Stirling (1982).
17. See the essays on social change in Anatolia in Stirling (ed. 1993).
18. For an interesting study of the place of Kemalism in education in the early Republican era see Kazamias (1966).
19. Cf. Stokes (1992) for an ethno-musicological exploration of this theme based on the *Arabesk* music phenomenon.
20. Eg. Alkan (1984: 84) describing their second, less successful general election results writes: 'numerically stable support may indicate that the *MSP* was not a dynamic force that could cope with social changes, hence the proportional decline'. Cf. also Çakır (1993, 1994) who notes *inter alia* that the creation of a movement with an appeal outside their immediate constituency has been one of the most difficult problems all Islamic movements (including Welfare) have had to face. On the Welfare's own claim to mass appeal see comments by one of their leading spokesmen Gül (1996).
21. Ironically, this appears to have been at the suggestion of the *CHP* during the coalition protocol preparations (Cf. Yalçın 1994). On the question of Islamic movements in Europe, Gerholm and Lithman (1988) offers a good introduction.
22. This point was first made, I believe by Hale (1976).
23. Finkel and Hale (1990), Çakır (1993).
24. Passages are translated from Erbakan nd. [1994], and given rather more in full in Appendix 4.
25. Cf. also Çakır (1994). Interestingly, Yalçın (1994) provides the text of a memorandum written by Erbakan in the last months of the *MSP* suggesting that just such a radical reform should be undertaken.
26. This feature was noted already by Finkel and Hale (1990) with regard to the 1987 elections.
27. Cf. Gül (1996) for an interview which illustrates his conciliatory approach 'Welfare is not a religious party, we do not call ourselves an Islamic Party: it wants to represent and to serve everyone in Turkey'.
28. See Table 1 also the comments of the National Security Council (Appendix 3).
29. The use of the English 'establishment' in the left-wing sense of a conflation of reactionary tendencies and authority has been taken into the political/religious debate by the *Turkish Daily News*, which even

though (and partially because) it is an English language newspaper has become a powerful voice in defence of the Welfare/Virtue Party.

30. http://www.refah.org/ingilizce/basinda-kapatilma-eng.html

Chapter Five

1. Held at the Naval base at Gölcük between 21-23 January 1997.
2. See the contemporary press reports, eg. *Milliyet* 28 February, 1 and 2 March 1997.
3. For an example of this type of approach, see Göle (1996).
4. As well as many popular secular publications (eg. Turan 1994), see the newspaper *Cumhuriyet*, which throughout the 1990s has gradually evolved to become the mouthpiece of the Republican/secularist movement.
5. Çakır (1994: 181-185) including photograph.
6. On changing marriage ceremonies, see the very suggestive article by Nancy Tapper (1985).
7. The place of ritual in Kemalism and religion is discussed in Mardin (1989).
8. A similar line was taken by the *Independent on Sunday* 30 March 1994 which refers to: 'much-exaggerated reports of harassment by men in Islamic fundamentalist garb, who have, in isolated incidents, forced women off mixed buses and attacked unveiled women in the street.'
9. Roy (1993).
10. For similar examples see Mango (1990).
11. Violence during the *Ramazan* against those who are not fasting is reported in the press regularly. This point is also strongly made by contemporary critics of the political Islamic movement, for example, a *samizdat* publication, *Turkeys* [sic] *Unveiled* (c. 1997), circulated among intellectuals in Istanbul.
12. See the documentary account *Refah Partisi Kapatma Davası* [The Court-Case Closing the Welfare Party] (1998).
13. There are many accounts of the Sivas massacres, which have themselves given rise to extended comment and interpretation. See for example *Sivasu.* (1994).
14. See, for example, the work of Binnaz Toprak. Whilst it is remarkable

for its erudition, as she is an American trained liberal academic of the sort that the early Kemalists would have lauded, she appears to be busy sawing off the branch she is sitting on. In a scholarly and detailed article published in 1988 she writes of Republican 'sensitivity' and 'an exaggerated vigil over secularism and a disposition to interpret any display of religiousness as an example of obscurantist advance.' (1988: 134). Given that this marked the point just before the Welfare Party's enormous gains, a certain sensitivity as to their aims seems to have been prescient rather than otherwise.

15. Cf. the essays in Hale (1976).

16. Sociologically, one might explain this fractured political environment by pointing out that if patronage spreads down through society very extensively, then even a small group may find it worthwhile to take even a tiny part of the governing of the country: one member of the assembly is in itself an important goal, a way that a group may gain a significant and perhaps distinct voice. In this way, politics reflects a diverse society closely, more so than Britain with its 'winner takes all' political organisation.

17. The spirit of this approach is caught well by Tapper and Tapper (1987).

18. Turgut Özal himself is sometimes said to have been influenced by the Mormons' attaining affluence whilst retaining belief, and therefore was attempting to create a similar model for Turkey. I am indebted to Dr Andrew Mango for pointing this out to me.

19. I should make it clear that I am aware that there are many different currents of music in Turkey, such as the *Arabesk* described by Stokes (1993), or the Alevi, left-wing rebellious music described in Chapter 6. I am particularly interested here in pop music as an unlikely field for religious fundamentalism.

20. On the effect of Atatürk's reforms on women see the suggestive pamphlet by Browning (1985).

21. Cf. a similar observation by Sirman (1996).

22. Among many accounts, see Ahmad (1993).

23. Yalman (1969), mentioned in Gellner.

24. Birand (1987).

25. I am deeply indebted to Professor Sina Akşin for his cordial help in

providing the statistics above, and for his illuminating paper on these issues (Akşin 1998).

Chapter Six

1. Out of many, see Şener (1982) for a very popular summary of Alevi religious history; Şener (1994) for commentaries on contemporary Alevi problems; Bozkurt (1990) for a discussion of different Alevi customs; Birdoğan (1990) for a similar and even more extensive description of Alevi traditions; Pehlivan (1993) for a discussion of the Alevis' links with the Directorate of Religious Affairs and state-led religion; Öz. (1995) for an examination of Alevi history, and Kaygusuz (1991) for a novel conveying some of the difficulties facing Alevi villages in Anatolia as they modernise.

2. Two recent volumes of essays, Olsson, Özdalga and Raudvere (1998), and Kehl-Bodrogi, Kellner-Heinkele, Otter-Beaujean (1997) touch upon these issues, eg. Çamuroğlu (1997).

3. Whilst there are many articles, the only sustained treatment based on field research among the Alevis remains Gökalp's pioneering monograph (1980). Comparative research is, as yet, even less developed. The vernacular publications have begun to fill this gap very substantially at a macro level, but have not yet turned to co-ordinated ethnographic work.

4. B. Lewis (1961), G. Lewis (1974), Zürcher (1994). Shaw's (1977) two-volume history is also lacking. He confines himself largely to the documentary evidence, something that the Alevis have tended not to produce until recently. In the future, the situation should improve. As well as the purely indigenous research, the first two collaborative efforts between academic and independent Alevi researchers have now been published (Kehl-Bodrogi, Kellner-Heinkele, Otter-Beaujean (1997), Olsson, Özdalga and Raudvere (1998), and more are being planned.

5. I hope to explore this argument in more detail, though a comparison with the Stirling's Sunni village ethnography has appeared Shankland (1994). See also Shankland (1993).

6. For Alevi village ethnography see Gökalp (1980) or Naess (1989).

7.   See, however, a recent appraisal by Van Bruinessen (1997).
8.   Andrews (1989), new edition forthcoming.
9.   On this topic see Gökalp (1984) and also the famous researches of Mélikoff (1993).
10. Cf. Birge (1937: 211).
11. Hasluck (1929).
12. Moosa (1988). Kehl-Bodrogi (1988) gives an insightful overview of Alevi society and its relationship with Islam as a whole. Petrushevsky (1985) is also very helpful. The rather uncertain term 'syncretistic' is also used to describe the Alevi form of Islam, as in the collected essays edited by Kehl-Bodrogi *et al* (1997).
13. Cf. Mélikoff (1975), who attests to its importance and the article by Otter-Beaujean (1997). There is more than one text known as *Buyruk*, and these may have varying degrees of overlap.
14. See also Moosa (1988: 117-119).
15. See Schimmel (1975).
16. For a note on Ahmet Yesevi and Turkic mysticism see Barnes (1992).
17. Turkish personal pronouns do not possess gender.
18. On the potential connection with Christianity, see Kehl-Bodrogi's monograph (1988). Malcolm (1998) gives an interesting perspective on how Muslim and Christian communities living side by side may adopt such 'crypto' practices.
19. I am grateful to Professor Altan Gökalp for pointing out that the *dar çekme* ceremony described above is extremely close to a ceremony of mourning which is practised by villages in Greece today.
20. Cf. Gilsenan (1973) for a sustained discussion.
21. This is often overlooked in works about the Alevis, but see the work by Metin (1994) entitled 'Folk Courts Among the Alevi', which stresses the Alevis' dislike of *'şeriat'* courts, and the substitution of their own way of doing things.
22. See also Gökalp (1980).
23. Cf. Gellner's description (1969) of the way that the Ahansal Saints in Morocco may build their reputation.
24. For example, see the work by Evans-Pritchard among the Sanusi (1949), and the later rebuttals by Peters (1990).
25. See, for example, Şener (1991). See also the little pamphlet *Alevilik nedir?*, 'What is Aleviness?' (1993).

26. Unfortunately, I have not researched among the Alevi Kurds. My impression is that lacking both a Sunni Islam background and an existing Turkish ethnic identity, they find it particularly difficult to integrate culturally with the Republic. It might be for this reason that so many appear to become very left wing, even Marxist, in orientation. I regret deeply my lack of experience in this area.

27. In parallel fashion, there is a work written by a Kurdish Alevi, which suggests that the Kurdish Alevi movement derives from Zoroastrianism rather than Islam brought by the Arabs (Bender 1993).

28. In his account, Gökalp (1980) also stresses the importance of this distinction, though the terminology is slightly different.

29. In North African Islamic societies, a similar contrast may be made between *makhzen* and *siba* (within and outside the rule of state), cf. Gellner (1981).

30. Cf. Stirling (1983).

31. Personal communication Stirling. See also the work of Starr on the gradual rapprochement of the villagers with the state (1992).

32. Stirling (1983).

33. On the introduction of tea, see Hann (1990). On rapid development within the village, see Shankland (1994).

34. See, for example, the assessment of the Republican efforts in rural areas in Robinson (1964).

35. For a comparative account of migration in a Sunni village see Stirling (1988).

36. Other researchers confirm this impression. See Naess' (1988) account, also the novel by Kaygusuz (1991). Bumke (1989) gives a brief but illuminating account of changes in Alevi Kurdish villages.

37. On gender relations within the Alevis cf. Shankland (1996b).

38. These terms are familiar in Persian Sufi poetry. eg. *Rubaiyat* (1898), or Rice (1965). Interestingly, that same Hafız tradition also demonstrates a connection between collective worship and the secular revelry, whereby people who look askance at a feast are accused of not understanding its mystical meanings (eg., wherein being drunk can be both drunk in the worldly sense and also drunk with love for God). The same ambiguity can be seen in the joyful poetry of Rumi.

39. A roughly parallel instance would be the habit of Royal Naval officers singing 'Old Hundredth' (the navy hymn) both at prayers, and in the

mess whilst drinking, though the words in the evening are rather more ribald. Both are collective celebrations, very similar in content, though only one is ostensibly religious. From a functional point of view this might be seen as a neat way of invoking a common group solidarity in people who otherwise might not come together in the same ritual setting.

40. On the importance of folklore displays in the inculcation of nationalism see Gellner (1984).

41. I hasten to add that I regret profoundly if this intrusion caused any embarrassment. Later, the *dede* lineage whom I had offended showed me enormous warmth. Whatever their inner thoughts may have been, and however appalling this behaviour on my part seems to me now, the village as a whole were always universally friendly and hospitable.

42. I am grateful to the William Wyse fund, Trinity College, for a generous grant to attend the festival.

43. See Stokes (1993).

44. *Din-Devlet* (1998).

45. See, for example, Eral (1993). The best scholarly studies of Alevi history remain Birge (1937), and Mélikoff (1992). Professor Mélikoff's highly distinguished pupil, Professor Ahmet Ocak, also works in this area (Ocak 1989).

46. *Geleneksel* (1993).

47. Pehlivan (1993).

48. See the pamphlet *Alevi community* (1989).

49. See, for example, the little pamphlet *Alevilik Nedir* (What is Alevilik?) that has been produced by committee by one of the religious and cultural centres of Alevi activity in Istanbul.

Conclusions

1. This censorious attitude towards broadcasting is quite regular: on April 27 and 28 1999, the Radio and Television High Council announced diverse penalties, including removal from the air, for Channel E, Interstar, Channel 7, Flash TV, BTV and ETV, as well as for various radio stations.

2. Such an attitude can be seen clearly in the work of Bulut, whose

approach appears to be 'A plague on both your houses!'. (Bulut 1995a: 81).

3. On recent Islamic intellectual thought, see Meeker (1989), Toprak (1987).
4. Bezmen (1996).
5. On the development of small business enterprises cf. Özcan (1995). Bulut (1995b) concentrates specifically on the relationship between religion and business.

Appendices

Appendix 1

Glossary of Turkish Words

Adak - vow, often made at a *türbe* (q.v.).

Ahlak - morals.

Alevi - Islamic minority consisting of perhaps 20 per cent of Turkey's population.

Ali - nephew of the Prophet *Muhammed*, is revered by all Muslim communities, but held in special regard by *Şi'i* (q.v.).

Aptes - ritual cleansing, mandatory before prayers.

Arabesk - popular musical movement.

Aşık - minstrel, folk musician or poet, also has connotations of love, particularly esoteric or mystical love.

Bayram - (religious) holiday.

Bektaşi - famous Anatolian *tarikat* founded by *Haci Bektaş* (q.v.), emphasises mystical understanding.

Buyruk - Alevi sacred text, said to be written by *İmam Cafer*.

Cami - mosque.

Cehennem - hell.

Cem - collective prayer meeting (Alevi).

Cennet - heaven.

Dayanışma - solidarity; reacting or behaving in concerted fashion.

Dede - lit. 'grandfather', respectful name for a man descended from a holy lineage esp. Alevi.

Dernek - society or association.

Devlet - the state.

Din - religion.

Diyanet İşleri Başkanlığı - Directorate of Religious Affairs.

Ezan - call to prayer from mosque.

Farz - obligatory religious duty.

Günah - sin.

Hac - pilgrimage to Mecca.

Hacı Bektaş - Anatolian saint, founder of *tarikat* of that name, held by many Alevi communities to be their leader, also name of Anatolian town where lies his *tekke* (q.v.), now a museum and tomb.

Hadis - sayings attributable to the Prophet *Muhammed.*

Hayırlı - holy or auspicious, also used to describe an act of magnaminity.

Hoca - teacher.

Hükümet - government.

İftar - repast at the end of a day of fasting

İkinci Cumhuriyetçiler - a loose group of largely Istanbul-based intellectuals who sympathise with political Islam.

İmam - mosque prayer leader.

İmam-hatip [school] - schools founded during the Republic in order to train mosque prayer leaders and preachers, though still within the framework of the secular education system.

Jandarma - semi-military, mostly conscript force largely used to keep the civil order in the countryside.

Kadro - post or situation in the civil service.

Kaymakam - sub-province governor.

Kokteyl - (formal) drinks party.

Kurban - sacrifice.

Kuran - sacred book of Muslims.

Kürt - diverse ethnic group traditionally inhabiting the east of Turkey, consisting of about 18 per cent of Turkey's population.

Mahalle - village quarter or, in a town, district.

Medrese - Ottoman (religious) school.

Memur - civil servant.

Mescit - prayer niche.

Mevlana - the monastery complex formerly possessed by the *Mevlevi* (q.v.) brotherhood in Konya, now a state museum.

Mevlevi - The name given to followers of *Celaletin Rumi*, whose tomb is now part of the *Mevlana* museum, known in the West as the 'whirling dervishes'.

Muhammed - the last Prophet, favoured by God to receive the word of the *Kuran*.

Muhabbet - drinking session with both secular and sometimes sacred (esp. mystical) connotations.

Muhtar - elected village (or district in town) head.

Müezzin - caller to prayer from the mosque.

Müftülük - local religious office, part of the *Diyanet İşleri Başkanlığı* administration.

Nakşibendi - a large *tarikat* which insists on the importance of orthodox doctrine.

Nurcu - follower of *Said Nursi*, religious leader who stressed the importance of scientific learning in conjunction with belief.

Namaz - ritual prayer.

Örgütlenmiş - organised.

Protokol - [official] ceremony or ceremonial activity.

Ramazan - month of the Islamic calandar during which believers are called to fast during the hours of daylight.

Sema - traditional dance, esp. Alevi.

Süleymancılar - popular activist Islamic group organised through study hostels which stresses the authority of the *Kuran* and the importance of discipline.

Sünnet - corpus of Islamic lore built on the actions and example of the Prophet Muhammed.

Sünni - the orthodox Islamic majority, consisting of about 80 per cent of Turkey's population.

Şi'i - Shi'ite, a faction within Islam which broke from the followers of *Muhammed* after his death, claiming that the legitimate succession of the Islamic community was through *Ali* (q.v.).

Şirk - assuming that God may have equal partners, a heresy of which members of *tarikat*s are often accused by orthodox clerics.

Tarikat - Islamic brotherhood.

Tasavvuf - mysticism.

Tekke - place of worship of a brotherhood, often centred on the grave of a holy man.

Torpil - the specific use of influence in order to obtain a position or favour.

Türbe - tomb.

Türk - the ethnic majority of modern Turkey, consisting of about 80 per cent of her population, also used to imply allegiance to modern Turkey and the Republic.

Türk Devletleri - Muslim states of the former Soviet Union.

Ulema (pl.) - clerical officials in the Ottoman Empire.

Vakıf - pious foundation, charitable trust.

Vakıflar Müdürlüğü - Directorate of Pious Foundations.

Vali - provincial governor.

Yezidi - small, very unorthodox religious minority mostly found in the east of Turkey.

Zabıta - law and order force employed by municipalities.

Zaviye - brotherhood lodgings.

Zekat - alms.

Appendix 2

List of Political Parties Mentioned

AP - *Adalet Partisi*, Justice Party. Active from 1960 until 1980, led by Süleyman Demirel after the closure of the DP.

ANAP - *Anavatan Partisi*, Motherland Party. Founded in 1983 by Turgut Özal, markedly right of centre, favourable towards orthodox religion.

BBP - *Büyük Birlik Partisi*, Great Unity Party. Small breakaway party from *ANAP* led by Muhsin Yazıcıoğlu, draws also on the *MHP*. Extreme right-wing Islamist.

CHP - *Cumhuriyet Halk Partisi* - Republican People's Party. Oldest extant political party, derived from the original *Halk Partisi* (People's Party). Closed down in 1980, re-opened again in 1990). Markedly secular.

DP - *Demokrat Parti*, Democrat Party. Moderately right-wing party, favourable to religion. Led by Adnan Menderes until its closure in 1960.

DSP - *Demokrat Sol Partisi* - Democratic Left Party. Founded by Bülent Ecevit in 1983. Nationalist and secular, rather suspicious of Western influence in Turkish affairs.

DYP - *Doğru Yol Partisi*, True Path Party. Founded and led by Süleyman Demirel after the closure of the AP. Led by Tansu Çiller, Turkey's first woman Prime Minister, after Demirel became president in 1993.

FP - *Fazilet Partisi*, Virtue Party. Founded after the Welfare Party's closure in 1998. Came third in the April 1999 elections.

MÇP - *Milli Çalışma Partisi*. Nationalist Work Party. Far-right wing, led by Alparslan Türkeş until closed by the *coup* in 1980. Re-opened as the *MHP*.

MHP - Milli Hareket Partisi, Nationalist Action Party. Far-right wing. Led for many years by the late Alparlsan Türkeş. First great success in the April1999 elections, led by then new leader, Devlet Bahçeli.

MNP - Milli Nizam Partisi, National Order Party. Erbakan's first political party. Active for a brief period between 1969-1970.

MSP - Milli Selamet Partisi, National Salvation Party. Necmettin Erbakan's second political party, active from 1972 until 1980.

RP - Refah Partisi, Welfare Party. Founded in 1983. Led by Erbakan from just after its foundation. Explicitly religious in orientation, closed by Constitutional Court in 1998.

SHP - Sosyal Demokrat Halkçı Parti, Social Democrat Populist Party. Active after 1983, moderate left-wing secular, shaken by scandal, merged with the re-opened *CHP* in 1993.

Appendix 3

National Security Council Recommendations, 28 February 1997

Introduction

The Security Council is a select group, consisting largely of the President of the Republic, the Prime Minister, Heads of the Armed Services, and Foreign, Interior and Defence Ministers, though other figures may also take part in their deliberations. On the occasion of the regular monthly meeting whose decisions are quoted from here, President Demirel was in the chair. Erbakan was present as Prime Minister, and Çiller as Foreign Minister. The clear and succinct resolutions that the Security Council adopts are remarkable in themselves, and all the more so because, though openly aimed at the political Islamist movement, they were adopted in Erbakan's presence. It is hardly surprising that he resisted signing them for a week after the Council meeting was held.

The decisions are prefaced by a conventional but important preamble that reports the meeting's affirmation of the secular basis of the Republic, the desire that Turkey shall join the European Union as soon as possible, its readiness to support the Turkish Republic of North Cyprus when evaluating the Cyprus question, and its commitment to the indivisible basis of the nation. It notes also a decision to extend the period of martial law in the east for a further four months. The preamble moves on to say that the tension and uncertainty in the country as a whole are causing needless speculation both in foreign eyes, and within Turkish society, and that the meeting therefore decided to take certain precautions, and to inform the Council of Ministers accordingly.

Though terse, the measures are largely self-explanatory. They reflect a preoccupation with safeguarding secularism and preventing divisions in the body politic. They are aimed at perceived attempts by the brotherhoods and other 'extreme' religious groups to operate through the wider civil and state institutions of Turkish society to increase their influence. It is for this reason, that the measures include such diverse subjects (hostels, trusts, local government, the courts, education, bureaucracy, religious foundations) among the areas where they feel religious activity needs to be impeded. Several of the measures refer obliquely to contemporary events. It is perhaps worth noting briefly that measure 5 is provoked by Erbakan's public reaffirmation of his intention to build mosques in overtly secular environments, such as in Taksim Square, Istanbul. Measure 12 in part refers to anti-secular activities within municipalities, such as speeches by religiously-inclined mayors (eg. Tayyip Erdoğan) against the Republican legacy. Measure 13, governing clothing, refers mostly to the headscarf debate. Measure 16 is designed to impede the formation of private, semi-uniformed protection squads, particularly such a group employed by Erbakan. During his time as Prime Minister this squad used to come into conflict with the state-supplied security men, and the army notably refused them entry into military ceremonies. Measure 17 refers to attempts by the Welfare Party to approach the Kurdish rebels, claiming that the overarching community of believers (*ümmet*) is more important than national interests.

The translation below is from the official Turkish version disseminated by the Secretariat of the National Security Council after the meeting.

The 28 February Decisions

1. Secularism is a founding principle of the Republic's Constitution, the fourth of its irrevocable articles. It must be protected scrupulously and with great care. In order to do so, the existing laws of the Republic must be applied without exception. If the present laws are inadequate, they must be revised.

2. As is required by the [original Republican] law for the unification of education [Tevhid-i Tedrisat], private hostels, trusts and schools with links to *tarikat*s must be transferred to the control of state organs acting under the supervision of the National Education Ministry.

3. The still-forming minds of younger generations must be made aware of the Republic, of Atatürk, of love for country and nation, and of the aim of the Turkish nation to rise to the level of contemporary civilisation. They must be protected from the [nefarious] influence of various centres of activity. Accordingly, (a) Eight years' continuous education must be instituted throughout the whole country. (b) If a family so decides, children who have

completed this education may attend Koran courses. The necessary administrative and legislative changes must be made for these courses' activities so that they [are removed from the responsibility of the Directorate of Religious Affairs and] come under the responsibility and control of the Ministry of Education.

4. Those of our national educational institutions charged with the responsibility to produce enlightened men of religion loyal to Atatürk's principles, to the revolution and to the Republic, must maintain an ethos appropriate to the [secular] essence of the law for the unification of education [Tevhid-i Tedrisat].

5. Religious foundations under construction in various parts of the country must not be made the subject of political exploitation and kept on the agenda in order to present and reinforce a message to certain groups. If there is a [genuine] need for these foundations, they must be realised by the Directorate of Religious Affairs, who will examine the situation and co-ordinate with the relevant authorities and local administrators.

6. The *tarikats* prohibited by existing law number 677, and all the activities declared proscribed in that law must be brought to an end. Their threat to democratic society, and the political and social laws governing the social order, must be impeded.

7. Some media groups have been exploiting the fact that personnel are being ejected from the Turkish Armed Forces by the order of the High Military Council because of fundamentalist activities, attempting to show the armed forces as thereby an enemy of religion. Such media groups, and their broadcasts against the Armed Forces and their members, must be brought under control.

8. Personnel who have been ejected from the Turkish Armed Forces because of links with illegal fundamentalist activities or for contravening discipline must not be given employment opportunities in other public bodies and institutions.

9. Public bodies and institutions, particularly the universities, other educational bodies and every level of the bureaucracy and the courts, must apply similar precautions to those taken by the Turkish Armed Forces in order to restrict the activities of extremist religious groups.

10. In order to protect the contemporary basis of Turkish society from possible clashes provoked by religious exploitation, all activities in our country directed against the regime by the Islamic Republic of Iran must be stopped. Whilst so minded, neighbourly relations with Iran and our economic ties will not be broken, but a packet of measures must be prepared and put into action in order to impede these destructive and harmful activities.

11. The extremist religious movement is provoking a separation between sects in Turkey that is leading to a polarisation within society. These highly dangerous activities will encourage a division into enemy camps. They must absolutely and without fail be prevented, by both legal and administrative means.

12. The legal and administrative procedures pertaining to those responsible for events contrary to the Constitution of the Turkish Republic, Political Party Law, Turkish Penal Code, and especially Municipality Law must be concluded expeditiously, and measures taken to ensure that they do not occur again.

13. Actions contrary to the law relating to clothing and thereby leading Turkey to assume an anachronistic appearance, must be stopped. Above all, and particularly, in public bodies and institutions, the law and the decisions of the constitutional courts pertaining to this subject must be applied scrupulously, and without any exception.

14. The procedures governing the various licences given for short and long barrelled weapons must be reorganised by making this the responsibility of the appropriate regional police and gendarmes. They must be tightened up. In particular, applications to obtain pump-action weapons must be carefully evaluated.

15.   The collection of sacrificial pelts for financial gain by unauthorised organisations opposed to the present order must be stopped. Those not empowered by the law must not be permitted to collect these pelts.

16.   Legal procedures begun against those responsible for security guards dressed in private uniforms must be brought to a swift conclusion. This form of illegal activity may reach extremely grave proportions and therefore all those private security organisations that fall outside the law must be closed and disbanded.

17.   Those who adopt the position that the nation's problems may be solved through placing the community of believers [*ümmet*] above that of the nation [*millet*], and who encourage the idea of approaching separatist terrorist organisations with this slogan, must be impeded by legal and administrative means.

18.   Those who are guilty of acting with disrespect towards great Atatürk, or conducting crimes against him, must not escape prosecution by exploiting law number 5816.

Appendix 4

Extracts from *The Just Economic Order*

By Necmettin Erbakan

Introduction

The Just Economic Order is a booklet of ninety-eight pages in which Erbakan outlines his political philosophy. Broadly, Erbakan accuses the West and the financial system that it upholds of wholesale exploitation. Part of this exploitation is by economic means, including the manipulation of interest, exchange rates, money supply, taxation and inflation. He maintains that this exploitation reduces poor countries, and the workers who struggle to make ends meet within them, to a state of dependent slavery. The other political parties in Turkey are accused of colluding with this exploitation and therefore failing utterly in their duty to the electorate and to the nation.

His solution is radical. He suggests banning interest entirely, and handing over much of the means of production to the state. Indeed, in his vision, the state takes the place of the market in regulating supply and demand. If thus regulated, he suggests that wasteful imbalances between production and investment inherent within the capitalist system will be avoided. This overall message is reinforced by a contrast between what he refers to as *Batıl* (false) civilisations, which include the West, and *Hak* (true) civilisations, of which his proposed 'Economic Order' would be one. He also supports his position by making analogies to geometry, and uses extensive graphs, and illustrative technical drawings.

The text itself is divided into four parts: 1. The Slave Order, 2. The Just Economic Order, 3. Economic and Social Development by Means of the Just Economic Order, and 4. Solving the Problems of Capitalism by Means of the Just Economic Order. The translation here is mine, though I have benefited from an English version also published by the Welfare Party. The full work is perhaps 30,000 words long, thus the extracts below can inevitably only give an illustration of his argument.

THE JUST ECONOMIC ORDER

Imperialism, Zionism and Modern Colonialism

The Slave Order that is part and parcel of the economic system in Turkey did not come about of its own accord. It is a consequence of systematic, planned and deliberate modern colonial initiatives stemming from the imperialist and Zionist forces of this earth.

Zionism is a belief, an ideological force whose headquarters are found in America, in the Wall Street Banks of New York. Zionists believe that they are God's true servants; they are convinced that other peoples have been created as their slaves.

The Zionists have taken control of world imperialism. Using the vehicle of interest-bearing capital, they have colonised the whole of humanity. Through the imperialist states, they control the world's governments.

Imperialism and Zionism support Turkey's counterfeit parties. They work to bring them to their bidding with all the opportunities at their command. As a result, for forty years essentially identical counterfeit, Western parties have been at the forefront. To gain foreign credit, these counterfeit parties have surrendered to the committees of the International Monetary Fund. The slave order has been formed step by step with the promissory notes that they have given.

World imperialism is not just colonising Turkey, but the whole of the Islamic world. The Islamic world's natural resources of all kinds, and above all petrol, are under imperialism's control. The amount of petrol that the Islamic world will produce, the price at which they will sell it, what proportion of the money that comes from the petrol will be kept in the Zionist banks, how much they will be given permission to use, and how they will use it are all proscribed. Accordingly, the Zionists keep a large proportion of the petrol money, 700 billion dollars, derived from Muslim countries in their own banks. They lend part of this money to other Muslim countries as external debt at high interest. In this way, they come between the Islamic nations and are making them pay interest to one another. For example, they have given Turkey 50 billion dollars external credit, in return they make us pay 8.5 billion dollars. In the same way, they have given Egypt 50 billion dollars, in return for which they extract payment of 7.5 billion.

Imperialism and Zionism colonise the Islamic world and the whole of Humanity
This colonialism operates not just through giving loans but in just about every area of life. Imperialism and Zionism colonise humanity through the world's transport system, communications, arms manufacturing, essential strategic industries, trade, banking, the money transfer and credit system, news agencies, and the press. Thus, the slave order established through the counterfeit parties is only part of this wider world-wide scheme.

How the Slave Order Exploits Us
The interest-bearing capitalist system exploits and crushes us through five mechanisms:
1. Interest
2. Unfair taxation
3. The money supply
4. The exchange rate
5. The banking and credit system

These prices have risen continuously, and expense and inflation have grown out of hand. By using these five mechanisms of the capitalist system, World Imperialism, Zionism, Israel and a handful of their corporations oppress large parts of the population.

The True Cost of the Present Economic Order
A worker receives only 8 per cent of the income to which he or she is entitled. The remaining 92 per cent is taken from them. That is, a person who will be earning 100 when the Welfare Party comes to power, is at the moment only earning 8. A person working in today's slave order receives only a twelfth of their entitlement.

Many people today are working for 800,000 Turkish liras gross wage a month. 14 per cent of this is deducted as insurance. This leaves 688,860 TL. Of this, 54,000 is tax-exempt, but of the remaining sum at least 25 per cent, i.e. 158,715 TL, is deducted as income tax. Further, 6 per cent of the gross wage, or 48,060 TL, is taken as a compulsory savings in all firms that employ more than ten people...These deductions already constitute a third of a workers' wages.

Taking the net amount that remains, this person goes shopping. However, within the price that he or she is forced to pay for the goods, a third constitutes interest payments and another third tax. In this way, by the time that they leave the shop their notional 100 units have fallen to 30.

The slave order, not content with this, takes another quarter of the remaining sum through manipulating the money supply, because in recent years the amount of promissory notes and money orders have exceeded the actual cash in circulation by a third.

In addition, exchange rate manipulation takes another quarter of the remaining sum. As is known, the Turkish Lira continuously is falling in value against the dollar. Of the citizen's remaining 22, another quarter is taken so that of the original 100 only 16 now remains.

But the cruelty does not end there. The present slave order takes five hammers out of every six, but after allowing for Turkey's [skewed] income distribution, even that remaining one hammer receives only half of its true price, so we divide 16 by 2 and only 8 remain.

Batıl and *Hak*

According to the mistaken [*Batıl*] approach, rights stem from the following:
1. Power [or force]
2. Majority [rule]
3. Privilege
4. Profit, interest

Without the shadow of a doubt, not one of these motives is justified. The correct and true [*Hak*] justification stems from the following:
1. The rights given to all people by the word of God viz: existence, the right to protect honour, dignity and family, the right to own property, the right to free thought and opinion, the right to freedom of belief.
2. Freedom of Labour.
3. Freedom of contract.
4. Justice.

Communism was destroyed after 70 years of cruelty to humanity. Capitalism continues its cruelty: this will too be destroyed and pass. The only reason that it remains on its feet is that it is artificially maintained as a vehicle of colonialism by Zionism and imperialism. Both these systems are *Batıl* and cannot bring contentment to humanity.

Founding principles of the Just Economic Order
In the *Just Economic Order*, the state manages macro and regional planning, and establishes appropriate investment projects. Accordingly individuals, businesses or charities [*vakıfs*] will be able to choose those projects they wish from these and operate them. The state will support these projects from every point of view.

In the *Just Economic Order*, the state contributes towards economic activities in two ways: general duties and regulatory duties. The general duties are security, management, justice, energy supplies, water, roads, infrastructure, health, education, transport, communications and so on... In addition, the state, regulates production of basic goods. For instance, in the Just Economic Order, today's 'Department of Agricultural Products' would become a 'Wheat Trust' [*Buğday Vakfı*]. Calling this institution a 'trust' signifies that it will make no profit, and is founded only to serve fellow citizens. This trust will be operative throughout the whole country to the limits of its borders. Those who wish to sell wheat will do so to this trust, and receive the market price at that time. Those who wish to buy wheat will also do so according to that day's price, and obtain as much as they wish.

The Principle 'No interest'
In the *Just Economic Order* there is no interest, because interest is wrong, it is cruel. What is interest in the capitalist system? You produce a good and offer it to the market. In return you receive a sum of money equivalent to its value. In the capitalist order, you put this money in a bank. A year later, the money is returned along with interest. You have not produced anything new in this year. Yet a productive equivalent is returned to you in the form of interest. Where has this come from? It may simply be printed. In this case, the rights of everyone are taken and given to you through the inflation that it generates. Or, prices may be put up. In this case, you are taking the rights of the producer, the worker, the poor, impoverished. Both are wrong. For this reason, the person who accepts interest may be likened to someone who drinks the tears of the poor, and eats their flesh and blood – a blood-sucking vampire.

What is tax?
The *Just Economic Order* is based on 'Rights above all'. For this reason, it means that the state only takes that proportion of tax that it is entitled to by

virtue of the contribution that it has made to production and the duties that it fulfils. In the present interest-imposing capitalist order the state crushes citizens, impedes production, distorts income distribution, colonises and imposes cruelty. Accordingly, the taxes and deductions trumped up under various different names are entirely wrong and all must be abolished.

With the foundation of the Just Economic Order, which approximates to an 'Islamic Common Market', development will be much greater, and much quicker
The 'European Common Market' really means a 'European Union State'. Accordingly, the Treaty of Rome is by way of being its constitution. There are two great mistakes within the Treaty of Rome. The first of these is that it has taken Roman civilisation as its cultural root, that is the mentality of 'Power above all'. With this mentality, there can be nothing but cruelty. Prosperity cannot be attained. Its second mistake is to take capitalism as its economic order. This foundation too can never create prosperity, but only cruelty, crisis and social unrest. For these two reasons, in fact the European Union resembles a bus with two time bombs on board that is rolling to the bottom of a precipice.

Conclusion
The Just Economic Order, will save the nation from being the slave of imperialism and Zionism, rescue its riches from the Zionists and those who work with them. In its place, it will bring a wealthy state and wealthy citizens. In place of being crushed by foreign debt and interest, we will be in a position to help brother Muslim states, offering them every form of product and defence supply.

When this is achieved, the children of those three million workers who are even today forced to leave the country, will all wish to return. Working in factories in this country will provide the opportunity to earn greater wages, and result in a better life.

In short, Turkey will become a country that sends not workers to the West, but tourists.

References

Ağaoğulları, M. 1979 *L'Islam dans la vie politique de la Turquie*, Ankara: Faculté des Sciences Politiques, Publication 517.

1987 'The Ultranationalist Right' in I. Schick and E. Tonak (eds.), pp. 177-217.

Ahmad, F. 1977 *The Turkish Experience in Democracy*, London: Hurst (for the Royal Institute of International Affairs).

1993 *The Making of Modern Turkey*, London: Routledge.

Akarlı, E. and Ben-Dor, G. (eds.) 1975 *Political Participation in Turkey*, Istanbul: Boğaziçi Publications.

Akşin, S. 1999 'The Nature of the Kemalist Revolution' in Shankland, D. (ed.), pp.14-28.

Akşit, B. 1991 'Islamic Education in Turkey: *medrese* reform in Late Ottoman Times and İmam-Hatip Schools in the Republic' in Tapper, R. (ed.), pp. 145-70.

Alevi Community Under Attack in Turkey, The nd. [1989] Briefing Paper No. 5, London: Committee for Defence of Democratic Rights in Turkey.

Alevilik Nedir (What is Aleviness?), 1993 Istanbul: Şahkulu Sultan Dergahı.

Algar, H. 1997 'The Naqshibendi Order in Republican Turkey' in *Islamic World Report*, Volume 2, pp. 51-67.

Alkan, T. 1984 'The National Salvation Party in Turkey' in Heper M. and Israeli, R. (eds.), pp. 79-102.

Andrews, P. (ed.) 1989 *Ethnic Groups in the Republic of Turkey*, Wiesbaden: Dr Ludwig Reichart Verlag.

Arberry, A. 1975 (1961) *Discourses of Rumi*, London : J. Murray.

Arjomand, S. (ed.) 1984 *From Nationalism to Revolutionary Islam*, London: Macmillan Press.

Ataseven, A. 1985 *Domuz Eti* (Pig Meat). Ankara: Türkiye Diyanet Vakfı Yayınları, No. 25.

Ayata, S. 1993 'Continuity and Change in Turkish Culture: some critical remarks on *Modern Mahrem*' in *New Perspectives on Turkey*, Vol. 9, 137-148.

Aydın, E. 1994 *Nasıl Müslüman Olduk*, (How We Became Muslim), 4th edn., Ankara: Başak Yayınları.

Balaban, R. 1986 *İlim - Ahlak - İman* (Science - Morality - Faith), Directorate of Religious Affairs publication no. 128, Ankara.

Baldwin, D. 1990 'Islamic Banking in a Secularist Context' in Wagstaff (ed.), pp. 22-38.

Balfour, J. (Baron Kinross) 1964 *Atatürk: the Rebirth of a Nation*, London: Weidenfeld and Nicholson.

Baqer M. 1999 *Khomeini: life of the Ayatollah*, London: I.B Tauris.

Barchard, D. 1985 *Turkey and the West*, London: Royal Institute of International Affairs.

1998 *Turkey and the European Union*, London: Centre for European Reform.

Barnes, J. 1992 'The Dervish Orders in the Ottoman Empire' in Lifchez (ed.), pp. 33-48.

Bayrakdar, N. 1989 *İslam'da Bilim ve Teknoloji Tarihi* (The History of Science and Technology in Islam), Ankara; Türkiye Diyanet Vakfı Yayınları, No. 30.

Beeley, B. 1983 *Migration, the Turkish Case*, Milton Keynes: Open University Press.

Beki, M. nd. [1995a] *Türkiye'de Nakşiler* (The Nakshibendis in Turkey), Istanbul: Yeni Yüzyıl Kitaplığı.

nd. [1995b] *Türkiye'de Nurculuk* (The Nurcu Movement in Turkey), Istanbul: Yeni Yüzyıl Kitaplığı.

Bender, C. 1993 *12 İmam ve Alevilik* (The 12 Imam and the Alevi), Istanbul: Berfin Yayınları.

Benedict, P., Tümertekin, E. and Mansur, F. (eds.) 1974 *Turkey: Geographic and Social Perspectives*, Leiden: Brill.

Berzeg, S. 1990 *Türkiye Kurtuluş Savaşında Çerkez Göçmenleri*, (Circassian Immigrants in the War of Independence), Istanbul: Nart

Yayıncılık.

Bezmen, C. 1996 'Islam and Tourism in Capadoccia', University of Cambridge, unpublished PhD dissertation.

Birand, M. Ali. nd. [1987] *The Generals' Coup in Turkey: an Inside Story of 12 September 1980*, translated by M.A. Dikerdem. London: Brassey's Defence.

1991 *Shirts of Steel: an Anatomy of the Turkish Armed Forces*, London: Tauris.

Birdoğan, N. 1992 *Anadolu ve Balkanlarda Alevi Yerleşmesi* (Alevi Settlement in Anatolia and the Balkans) Istanbul: Alev Yayınları.

1994 (1990) *Anadolu'nun Gizli Kültürü Alevilik* (The Alevi: Anatolia's Secret Culture) Istanbul, Berfin Yayınları.

Birge, J. 1937 *The Bektashi Order of Dervishes*, London: Luzac & Co.

Bowie, F. (ed.) 1997 *The Coming Deliverer*, Cardiff: University of Wales Press.

Bozkurt, C. 1990 *Aleviliğin Toplumsal Boyutları* (Social Dimensions of the Alevi Movement) Istanbul, Tekin Yayınevi.

Brockett, G. 1998 Collective Action and the Turkish Revolution: Towards a Framework for the Social History of the Atatürk Era, *Middle Eastern Studies*, Vol. 34, No. 4, pp. 44-66.

Browning, J. 1985 *Atatürk's Legacy to the Women of Turkey*, Durham: Centre for Middle Eastern and Islamic Studies.

Buğra, A. 1994 *State and Business in Modern Turkey: A Comparative Study*, Albany: State University of New York.

Bulut, F. 1995a *Ordu ve Din* (The Army and Religion), Istanbul: tümzamanlaryayıncılık.

1995b *Tarikat Sermayesinin Yükselişi* (The Growth of the Brotherhoods' Capital), Ankara: Öteki Yayınları.

Bumke, P. 1989 'The Kurdish Alevis: boundaries and perceptions' in Andrews, pp. 510-19.

Çakır, R. 1993 (1990) *Ayet ve Slogan: Türkiye'de İslami Oluşumlar* (Verses and Slogans: Islamic Developments in Turkey), 6th edn., Istanbul: Metis Yayınları.

1994 *Ne Şeriat ne Demokrasi: Refah Partisi Anlamak*, (Neither Sheria nor Democracy, Understanding the Welfare Party), Istanbul: Metis Yayınları.

Çamuroğlu, R. 1997 'Some notes on the Contemporary Process of

Restructuring Alevilik in Turkey' in Kehl-Bodrogi, Kellner-Heinkele, Otter-Beaujean (eds.), pp 25-34.

De Jong, F. and Radtke, B. (eds.) 1999 *Islamic Mysticism Contested*, Leiden: Brill.

Delaney, C. 1991 *The Seed and the Soil*, California, California University Press.

Din-Devlet İlişkileri ve Türkiye'de Din Hizmetlerinin Yeniden Yapılanması Uluslararası Sempozyumu (International Symposium on State-Religion Relations and the Restructuring of Religious Services in Turkey), 1998, Istanbul: Cem Vakfı.

Din Eğitim Raporu (Report on Religious Education) 1993, Ankara: Directorate of Religious Affairs, Research, Planning and Co-ordination Department.

Dodd, C.H. 1990 (1983) *The Crisis of Turkish Democracy*, Huntingdon: The Eothen Press.

Doğramacı, E. 1984 *Status of Women in Turkey*, 2nd edn, expanded. Ankara: Meteksan.

Dumont, P. 1991 'Le poids de l'Alevisme dans la Turquie d'aujourd-hui' *Turcica*, volume 21, pp. 155-72.

Dursun, T. 1993 *Tabu Can Cekişiyor: Din Bu 2*, (The Death Throes of Taboo; This is Religion 2) 8th edn. Istanbul: Güney Yayıncılık.

Ekrem, S. 1947 *Turkey Old and New*, New York: Scribner's sons.

Eral, S. 1993 *Çaldıran'dan Çorum'a Anadolu'da Alevi Katliamları* (Alevi Massacres in Anatolia from Çaldıran to Çorum). Istanbul: Yalçın Yayınları.

Erbakan, N. nd. (c. 1994) *Adil Ekonomik Düzen* (The Just Economic Order), Ankara: Refah Partisi.

Erseven, İ. 1990 *Aleviler'de Semah* (Semah among the Alevi) Ankara: Ekin Yayınları.

Evans-Pritchard, E. 1949 *The Sanusi of Cyrenacia*, Oxford: Clarendon Press.

Eyuboğlu, İ. 1991 *Sömürülen Alevilik* (Exploited Alevi-ness), Istanbul:

Fallers, L. 1971 *Turkish Islam*, Chicago: Aldine Publishing Co.

Fiğlalı, E. 1988 *Din Kültürü and Ahlak Bilgisi 3* (Religious Culture and Moral Study 3), 10th printing, Istanbul: Milli Eğitim Basımevi.

Finkel, A. and Hale, W. 1990 'Politics and Procedure in the 1987 Turkish General Election' in Sirman and Finkel (eds.), pp. 103-38.

Frye, R.(ed.) 1957 *Islam and the West*, Gravenhage: Mouton & Co.

'*Geleneksel IV Pir Sultan Abdal Kültür Etkinlikleri*' (The Fourth Traditional Pir Sultan Abdal Activities) in *Pir Sultan Abdal Kültür ve Tanıtma Derneği'nin Yayın Organı* (Publication Organ of the Association for the Culture and Recognition of *Pir Sultan Abdal*) 1993, Vol. 2, No. 7, pp. 46-48.

Gellner, E. 1969 *Saints of the Atlas*, London: Weidenfeld and Nicholson.

1973 *The Legitimation of Belief*, Oxford: Basil Blackwell.

1983 *Muslim Society*, Cambridge: Cambridge University Press.

1984 *Nations and Nationalism*, Oxford: Basil Blackwell.

1995 *Anthropology and Politics*, Oxford: Basil Blackwell.

Gerholm, T. and Lithman, Y. 1988 *The New Islamic Presence in Western Europe*, London: Mansell.

Geyikdağı, Y. 1984 *Political Parties in Turkey: The Role of Islam*, New York: Praeger.

Gilsenan. M. 1973 *Saint and Sufi in Modern Egypt*, Oxford: Clarendon Press.

Gökalp, A. 1980 *Têtes rouges et bouches noires*, Paris: Société d'ethnographie.

1986 'Éspace Rural, Village, Ruralité: a la recherche du paysan Anatolien' in Gökalp A. (ed.), *La Turquie en transition, disparités, identités, pouvoirs*, Paris: Maisonneuve Larose, pp. 49-82.

Gökalp, Z. 1959 *Turkish Nationalism and Western Civilization: selected essays*, translated and edited with an introduction by Niyazi Berkes, New York : Columbia University Press.

Göle, N. 1996 *The Forbidden Modern: civilisation and veiling*, Ann Arbor: University of Michigan Press.

Gözaydın-Tarhanlı, İ. (1995) *Türkiye'de Diyanet* (Worship in Turkey), Ankara: Yeni Yuzyil Kitaplığı.

[Gözaydın-]Tarhanlı 1993 *Müslüman Toplum 'Laik' Devlet: Türkiye'de Diyanet İşleri Başkanlığı* (Islamic Society, Secular State: the Directorate of Religious Affairs in Turkey) Istanbul: AFA Yayınları.

Gül, A. 1996 'An Interview with Abdullah Gül', *Islamic World Report*, Volume 1, No 3, pp. 129-34.

Gülen, F. 1997 *The Essentials of the Islamic Faith*, Izmir: Kaynak.

Gündüz, I. (ed.), 1991 *Türk-İslam Sentezi* (The Turk-Islam Synthesis), Istanbul: Sarmal Yayınevi.

Gürsöy-Tezcan, A. 1991 'Mosque or Health Centre' in Tapper, (ed.), pp. 84-101.

Hale, W. 1972 'Aspects of the Turkish General Election of 1969', *Middle Eastern Studies*, Vol. 8, pp. 393-404.

(ed.) 1976 *Aspects of Modern Turkey*, Durham; Centre for Middle Eastern Studies.

1994 *Turkish Politics and the Military*, London: Routledge.

Hann, C. 1990 *Tea and the Domestication of the Turkish State*, Huntingdon: Eothen Press.

(ed.) 1994 *When History Accelerates: Essays on Rapid Social Change, Complexity and Creativity*, London: Athlone Press.

Hann, C. and Dunn, E. (eds.) 1996 *Civil Society: Challenging Western Models*, London: Routledge.

Hasluck, F. 1929 *Christianity and Islam among the Sultans*, edited by Margaret Hasluck, 2 volumes, Oxford: Clarendon.

Heper, M. 1994 *Historical Dictionary of Turkey*, Metuchen (N.J.) & London: The Scarecrow Press.

Heper, M and Israeli, R. (eds.) 1984 *Islam and Politics in the Modern Middle East*, London: Croom Helm.

Heper, M and Evin, A. (eds.) 1988 *State, Democracy and the Military in Turkey in the 1980s*, New York: Walter de Gruyter.

Heper, M. and Landau, J. (eds.) 1991 *Political Parties and Democracy in Turkey*, London: I.B. Tauris.

Heper, M., Öncü, A., and Kramer, H., (eds.) 1993 *Turkey and the West: Changing Political and Cultural Identities*, London; I.B. Tauris.

Heron-Allen. E. 1899 *Edward Fitzgerald's Rubaiyat of Omar Khayyam with their Persian Sources*, London: Quaritch.

Karpat, K. 1959 *Turkey's Politics: the Transition to a Multi-Party System*, Princeton: University Press.

Kaygusuz, İ. 1991, *Son Görgü Cemi*, (The Last *Görgü Cem*) Istanbul: Alev Yayınları

Kazamias, A. 1966 *Education and the Quest for Modernity in Turkey*, London: George Allen & Unwin Ltd.

Kedourie, S. (ed.) 1998 *Turkey: Identity, Democracy, Politics*, London: Frank Cass.

Kehl-Bodrogi, K. 1988 *Die Kızılbaş-Alevitum. Untersuchungen über eine esoterische Glaubensgemeinschaft in Anatolien*, Berlin: Schwarz.

Kehl-Bodrogi, K., Kellner-Heinkele, B., Otter-Beaujean, A. (eds.) 1997 *Syncretistic Religious Communities in the Near East*, Leiden: Brill.

Keşkioğlu, O. nd. [c. 1990] *İslamda Eğitim ve Öğretim* (Education and Teaching in Islam), Ankara: Directorate of Religious Affairs publication no. 249.

Kirgizistan Ülke Raporu (Kyrgyzstan Country Report), 1995, Ankara: Türk İşbirliği ve Kalkınma Ajansı (*TİKA*).

Kocahanoğlu, O. 1995 *Dernerkler Kanunu ve Mevzuatı*, (Association Law and Regulations), Istanbul: Çevik Matbaası.

Lerner, D. 1958 *The Passing of Traditional Society*, Glencoe: Free Press.

Levonian, L. 1932 *The Turkish Press; selections from the Turkish Press Showing Events and Opinions 1925-1932*, translated and arranged under the direction of Lutfy Levonian. Athens: School of Religion.

Lewis, B. 1961 *The Emergence of Modern Turkey*, London: Royal Institute of International Affairs.

1988 *Islam et Laicité*, Paris: Fayard.

1997 *The Future of the Middle East*, London.

Lewis, G. 1965 *Turkey*, 3rd edition. London: Ernest Benn.

1976 'Political Change in Turkey since 1960' in Hale (ed.), pp. 15-20.

Lewis, I. 1961 *Pastoral Democracy*, Oxford: Clarendon.

Lifchez, R. (ed.) 1992 *The Dervish Lodge*, California: University of California Press.

Linke, L. 1937 *Allah Dethroned: A Journey Through Modern Turkey*, London: Constable.

Makal, M. 1954 *A Village in Anatolia*, translated by Sir Wyndham Deedes, edited by Paul Stirling. London: Valentine, Mitchell & Co.

Malcolm, N. 1988 *Kosovo: a short history*, London: Macmillan.

Mango, A. 1990 'The Consolations of Religion in Turkey' in Wagstaff (ed), pp. 16-21.

1991 *Turkey Confidential*, No 19 (May issue).

1999 *Atatürk*, London: John Murray.

Mardin, Ş. 1969 'Opposition and Control in Turkey' in *Government and Opposition*, Vol 1, No 3: 375-388.

1989 *Religion and Social Change in Modern Turkey: the Case of Bediuzzaman Said Nursi*, New York: State University of New York.

Meeker, M. 1989 'The New Muslim Intellectuals in the Republic of Turkey' in Tapper (ed.), pp. 223-253.

Mélikoff, I. 1992 *Sur les Traces du Soufisme Turc; recherches sur l'Islam populaire en Anatolie*. Istanbul: Éditions İsis.

Metin, İ. 1994 (1992) *Aleviler'de Halk Mahkemeleri*, (Folk Courts Among the Alevi), 2 Volumes, Istanbul: Alev Yayınları.

Milli Eğitim İstatistikleri: Örgün Eğitim (National Education Statistics: formal education), (1994-) Ankara: Devlet İstatistik Enstitüsü.

Milli Görüş'ün İktidardaki Hizmetleri (1974-1978), (The Achievements of the National Viewpoint Whilst in Power) nd. [*c*. 1994]. Ankara: Refah Partisi.

Moosa, M 1988 *Extremist Shi'ites*, New York: Syracuse University Press.

Morier, J. 1812 *A Journey through Persia, Armenia, and Asia Minor to Constantinople*, London: Longman et al.

Mortimer, E. 1982 *Faith and Power: the Politics of Islam*, London: Faber & Faber.

Müftüler-Baç, M. 1998 'The Never-Ending Story: Turkey and the European Union', *Middle Eastern Studies*, Volume 34, No. 4, pp. 240-58.

Naess, R. 1988 'Being an Alevi in south-western Anatolia and in Norway: the impact of migration on a heterodox Muslim community' in Gerholm and Lithman (eds.), pp. 174-95.

Nicolas, M 1972 *Croyances et pratiques populaires turques concernant les naissances*, Paris: P.O.F.

Norton, A. (ed.) 1996 *Civil Society in the Middle East*, Leiden: Brill.

Norton, J. 1994 'Turkish Sufis, Saints and Subversives' in Wagstaff (ed.), pp. 4-9.

Nurbaki, H. nd. [*c*. 1990] *İslam Dininin İnsan Sağlığına Verdiği Önem* (The Importance which the Islamic Religion gives to People's Health), Ankara: Diyanet Başkanlığı Yayınları No. 256

Nursi, S. 1992 *The Words: on the Nature and Purposes of Man, Life, and All Things*, translated from the *Risale-i Nur* collections by Ş. Vahide. Istanbul: Sözler.

1994 *The Letters: From the Risale-i Nur Collection*, London; Truestar.

Ocak, A. 1989 *La révolte de Baba Resul ou la formation de l'hétérodoxie en Anatolie au xiii'ième siècle*, Ankara: Türk Tarih Kurumu.

1997 'Un aperçu général sur l'hétérodoxie musulmane en Turquie' in Kehl-Bodrogi, Kellner-Heinkele, Otter-Beaujean (eds.), pp. 195-204.

Olsson, T., Özdalga, E. and Raudvere, C. (eds.) 1998 *Alevi Identity*, Istanbul: Swedish Research Institute in Istanbul, *Transactions* Vol. 8.

Orga, I. 1958 *Phoenix Ascendant,* London: Robert Hale.

Otter-Beaujean, A. 1997 'Schriftliche Überlieferung versus mündliche Tradition: Zum Stellenwert der *Buyruk*-Handschriften im Alevitum' in Bodrogi, Kellner-Heinkele and Otter-Beaujean (eds.), pp. 1-24.

Öz, B. 1995 *Aleviliğin Tarihsel Konumu* (The Place of the Alevi in History), Istanbul: Der Yayınları.

1994 *Kurtuluş Savaşında Alevi-Bektaşiler* (The Alevi-Bektashi in the War of Independence), 5th edn. Istanbul: Can Yayınları.

Özbudun, E. and Kazancıgil, A. 1992 (1981) *Atatürk: Founder of a Modern State*, London: Hurst.

Özcan, G. 1995 *Small Medium Enterprises and Local Economic Development in Southern Europe and Turkey,* London: Avebury Press.

Özdalga, E. 1998 *The Veiling Issue: Official Secularism and Popular Islam in Turkey*, London: Curzon.

Pehlivan, B. 1993 *Aleviler ve Diyanet* (The Alevi and Worship), Istanbul: Pencere Yayınları.

Peters, E. 1990 *The Bedouin of Cyrenaica*, edited by Jack Goody and Emanuel Marx, Cambridge: Cambridge University Press.

Petrushevsky, I. 1985 *Islam in Iran*, London: Athlone Press.

Pope, N. and H. 1997 *Turkey Unveiled: Ataturk and After*, London: John Murray.

Poyraz, E. 1998 *MNP'den FP'e; İhanetin Belgeleri* (From the *MNP* to the *FP*: the Documents of Treason), Ankara: MK Yayıncılık.

Ramsay, Sir W. 1890 *The Historical Geography of Asia Minor*, London: Royal Geographical Society, supplementary papers, vol. 4.

Reed, H. 1956 'Turkey's New *Imam-Hatip* Schools', *Die Welt des Islams*, Vol 4, pp. 150-63.

1957 'The Religious Life of Modern Turkish Muslims' in Frye (ed.), 108-48.

Refah Partisi Kapatma Davası (The Court-Case Closing the Welfare Party) 1998 Istanbul: Kaynak Yayınları.

Rice, C. 1964 *The Persian Sufis*, London: George, Allen & Unwin.

Robinson, R. 1963 *The First Turkish Republic*, Cambridge: Harvard University Press.

Roy, O. 1994 *The Failure of Political Islam*, translated by Carol Volk, London: Tauris.

Rustow, D. 1957 'Politics and Islam in Turkey 1920-1955' in Frye, R. (ed.), pp. 69-107.

1991 'Political Parties in Turkey: An Overview' in Heper, M. and Landau, J. (eds.), pp. 10-23.

Sayarı, S. (1995) 'İslam, Laiklik ve Demokrasi' (Islam, Secularism and Democracy) in *Türkiye'de İslamcılık* (Islamism in Turkey), Istanbul: Yeniyüzyıl Kitaplığı, pp. 52-70.

Schick, I. and Tonak, E. (Eds.) 1987 *Turkey in Transition: New Perspectives*, Oxford: Oxford University Press.

Schiffauer, W. 1987 *Das Leben in einem Türkischen Dorf*, Stuttgart: Klett-Cotta.

1991 *Die Migranten aus Subay : Turken in Deutschland : eine Ethnographie*, Stuttgart : Klett-Cotta.

Schimmel, A. 1975 *Mystical Dimensions of Islam*, Chapel Hill: University of North Carolina Press.

Shankland, D. 1992 'Diverse paths of change: Alevi and Sunni in rural Turkey' unpublished PhD dissertation, Department of Anthropology, University of Cambridge.

1993 'Diverse paths of change: Alevi and Sunni in rural Turkey' in Stirling, P. (ed.), pp. 46-64.

1994 'Social Change and Culture: Responses to Modernisation in an Alevi Village in Anatolia' in Hann (ed.), pp. 238-254.

1996a 'The Demise of Republican Turkey's Social Contract'? in *Government and Opposition*, Volume 31, Number 3, pp. 304-321.

1996b 'Changing Gender Relations among Alevi and Sunni in Turkey' in *Turkish Families in Transition* ed. Rasuly-Paleczek, Peter Lang: Frankfurt, pp. 83-97.

1997a 'Nationality, Ethnicity and Religion in the Republic of Turkey' in *The Transition to Modernity*, ed. Tsiberodou, F., Komotini: Université Démocrite de Thrace, pp 91-104.

1997b 'Old Ideas in New Forms: The Mehti in Modern Turkey' in Bowie F. (ed.), pp. 224-237.

1998 'Anthropology and Ethnicity: the place of Ethnography in the new Alevi Movement' in Olsson, T., Ozdalga, E. and Raudvere, C. (eds), pp. 15-23.

1999a 'Integrating the rural: Gellner and the study of Anatolia', *Middle Eastern Studies*, Vol. 35, No. 2, pp. 132-149.

1999b 'An interview with Paul Stirling', forthcoming in Summer issue of *Turkish Studies Association Bulletin*.

1999c (ed.) *The Turkish Republic at Seventy-Five Years, Progress-Development-Change*, Huntingdon: Eothen.

1999d 'Development and the Rural Community' in Shankland, D.(ed.), pp. 51-66.

Shaw, S. and Shaw, E. 1995 (1977) *History of the Ottoman Empire and Modern Turkey, Vol 2*, Cambridge: Cambridge University Press.

Sirman, N. 1988 'Peasants and Family Farms: the Position of Households in Cotton Production in a village of Western Turkey', unpublished PhD thesis, University of London.

1990 'State, Village and Gender in Western Turkey' in Finkel and Sirman (eds.), *Turkish State, Turkish Society*, London: Routledge, pp. 21-51.

1996 'From Economic Integration to Cultural Strategies of Power: The Study of Rural Change in Turkey' , *New Perspectives on Turkey*, Vol 14, pp. 115-25.

Sirman, N. and Finkel, A. (eds.) 1990 *Turkish State: Turkish Society*, London: Routledge.

Sivas, 2 Temmuz (Sivas, 2 July), 1994 Istanbul: Dergi Ortak Platformu.

Soymen, M. 1979 *Concise Islamic Catechism*, translated by İhsan Ekmeleddin, Ankara: Publications of the Directorate of Reliigous Affairs.

Starr, J. 1992 *Law as Metaphor*, New York: State University of New York Press.

Stirling, P. 1958 'Religious change in Republican Turkey', *Middle East Journal*, Vol. 12, pp. 395-408.

1960 'Death and a Youth Club: Feuding in a Turkish Village', *Anthropological Quarterly*, Washington.

1965 *Turkish Village*, London: Weidenfeld and Nicholson.

1974 'Cause, Knowledge and Change: Turkish Village Revisited' in David, J. (ed.) *Choice and Change: Essays in Honour of Lucy Mair*, London: Athlone, pp. 191-229.

1982 'Social Change and Social Control in Republican Turkey' in *Papers and Discussions: Türkiye İş Bankası International*

226 *Islam and society in Turkey*

Symposium on Atatürk, Ankara: Cultural Publications, Turkiye: İş Bankası, pp. 565-600.
1988 'Labour Migration and Changes in Anatolia'. Edited version of paper delivered to the Conference on Mediterranean Migrations held at Al Hacaima, 11-14th July 1988', For publication.

Stirling, P. (ed.) 1993 *Culture and Society: Changes in Turkish Villages*, Huntingdon: The Eothen Press.

Stokes, M. 1992 *The Arabesk Debate: Music and Musicians*, Oxford: Clarendon Press.

1993 'Hazelnuts and Lutes: processes of change in a Black Sea valley' in Stirling (ed.), pp. 27-45.

Şahiner, N. (Ed.) 1976 *Said Nursi ve Nurculuk Hakkında Aydınlar Konuşuyor* (Intellectuals Discuss Said Nursi and the Nursi Movement), 2nd edn. Istanbul: Yeni Asya Yayınları.

Şener, C. 1982 *Alevilik Olayı* (The Alevi Phenomenon), Istanbul: Yön Yayıncılık.

1991 *Atatürk ve Aleviler* (Atatürk and the Alevi), Istanbul: Ant Yayınları.

1993 *Yaşayan Alevilik* (Living Aleviness]), Istanbul: Ant Yayınları.

1994 *Alevi Sorunu Üstüne Düşünceler* (Thoughts on the Alevi Question), Istanbul: Ant Yayınları

Tapper, N. 1985 'Changing Wedding Rituals in a Turkish Town', *Journal of Turkish Studies*, Vol 9, pp.

Tapper, N. and Tapper R. 1987 'Thank God We're Secular! Aspects of Fundamentalism in a Turkish Town' in Caplan, L. (ed.) *Aspects of Religious Fundamentalism*, London:

Tapper, R. (ed.) 1991 *Islam in Modern Turkey*, London: Tauris.

Tapper, R. and Tapper, N. 1991 'Religion, Education and Continuity in a Provincial Town' in Tapper, R. (ed.), pp. 56-83.

Tekeli, Ş. (Ed.) 1995 *Women in modern Turkish society : a reader*, London: Zed Books.

TEŞHİS, Türkiye'nin Gerçek Durumu Sebepleri (DIAGNOSIS, The Reasons Behind Turkey's True Situation), nd. [c. 1994] Ankara: Refah Partisi.

Toprak, B. 1981 *Islam and Political Development in Turkey*, Leiden: Brill.

1984 'Politicisation of Islam in a Secular State: The National Salvation

Party in Turkey' in Arjomand (ed.), pp. 119-35.

1987a *Islamic Intellectuals of the 1980s in Turkey*, Istanbul: Redhouse.

1987b 'The Religious Right' in Schick and Tonak (eds.), pp. 218-35.

1988 'The State, Politics, and Religion in Turkey' in Heper and Evin (eds.), pp. 119-36.

1993 ''Islamicist Intellectuals; Revolt against Industry and Technology' in Heper, M *et al* (eds.), pp. 237-57.

1996 'Civil Society in Turkey' in Norton, A. (ed.), pp. 87-118.

Trimingham, J. 1971 *The Sufi Orders in Islam*, Oxford: Clarendon Press.

Tuğ, A. 1975 *Village Administration in Turkey*, Ankara: State Planning Organization.

Tunaya, T. 1962 *İslamcılık Cereyanı* (The Islamist Tendency), Istanbul: Baha Maatbası.

Turan, S. 1994 *Din Tacirleri: Bir Siyasinin Negatif Yüzü* (Merchants of Religion: The Negative Side of a Politician), Istanbul: Utku Yayınları.

Turkey Unveiled, nd. [c. 1997], anonymous *samizdat*, 23pp.

Türkdoğan, O. 1995 'Alevi Kimliği' (Alevi Identity) *Türk Kültürü*, (Monthly magazine of the Institute of Research into Turkish Culture) Year 33, No. 383, pp. 68-77.

Uysal, A. (1989) *Yaşayan Türk Halk Hikayelerinden Seçmeler* (Selections from Living Turkish Folk Tales), Ankara: Atatürk Kültür Merkezi.

Vahide, Ş. 1992 *Bediuzzaman Said Nursi*, Istanbul: Sözler publications.

Van Bruinessen, M. 1992 *Agha, Shaikh, and State*, London: Zed books.

1997 '"Aslını inkar eden haramzadedir!" The Debate on the Ethnic Identity of the Kurdish Alevis' in Kehl-Bodrogi, Kellner-Heinkele and Otter-Beaujean (eds.), pp. 1-24.

Wagstaff, M. 1989 *The Role of the Government in the Industrialisation of Turkey, 1938-1980*. London: SOAS, Centre of Near & Middle Eastern Studies.

Wagstaff, M. (ed.) 1990 *Aspects of Islam in Secular Turkey*, Durham: Centre for Middle Eastern Studies.

Walker, W. and Uysal, A. 1966 *Tales Alive in Turkey*, Harvard: Harvard University Press.

Warkworth, Lord. 1898 *Notes from a Diary in Asiatic Turkey*, London: Arnold.

White, J. 1994 *Money Makes us Relatives: Women's Labor in Urban Turkey*, Austin: University of Texas Press.
1996 'Civic culture and Islam in urban Turkey' in Hann and Dunn (eds.) pp. 143-54.
Women in Anatolia: 9000 Years of the Anatolian Woman, 1993. Ministry of Culture, Istanbul/Ankara.
Yalçın, S. 1994 *Hangi Erbakan* (Which Erbakan?), Ankara: Basık Yayınları.
Yalman, N. 1969 'Islamic reform and the Mystic Tradition in Eastern Turkey', *Archives européennes de sociologie*, Volume 10, pp. 41-60.
Yavuz, M 1993 'The Return of Islam?' in *Islamic World Report*, Vol 1, No. 3, pp. 77-86.
Yurtdışı Din Hizmetleri Raporu (Report on Religious Services Abroad) 1993 Ankara: Diyanet İşleri Başkanlığı.
Yücekök, A. 1971 *Türkiye'de Örgütlenmiş Dinin Sosyo-Ekonomik Tabanı* (The Socio-Economic Foundations of Organised Religion in Turkey), Ankara: Siyasal Bilgiler, Yayın 323.
Yorukan, T. 1993 (1957) *Müslümanlık ve Kuran-i Kerim'den Ayetlerle İslam Esasları* (The Muslim Faith and The Essence of Islam according to the verses of the *Kuran*), Ankara: Döğüş Matbaacılık.
Zürcher, E. 1991 *Opposition in the Early Turkish Republic, The Progressive Republican Party*, Leiden: Brill.
1994 *Turkey, A Modern History*, London: Tauris.

Index

The English form for any term has been chosen when there is a comfortable translation, otherwise the Turkish has been used (thus *tekke* has been preferred to monastery because of the latters existing connotations in English). Bold type indicates a main entry, n a footnote.